Sex, Needs and Queer Culture

# About the Author

David Alderson is senior lecturer in modern literature at the University of Manchester and visiting professor at Shanghai Jiao Tong University. He is co-organizer, with Laura Doan, of the Centre for the Study of Sexuality and Culture at Manchester.

# Sex, Needs and Queer Culture

## From liberation to the postgay

DAVID ALDERSON

**ZED**
Zed Books
London

*Sex, Needs and Queer Culture: From liberation to the postgay*
was first published in 2016 by Zed Books Ltd, The Foundry, 17 Oval
Way, London SE11 5RR, UK.

www.zedbooks.co.uk

Typeset in Scala by Swales & Willis Ltd, Exeter, Devon
Index: Ed Emery
Cover design: Michael Oswell

A catalogue record for this book is available from the British Library.

ISBN 978-1-78360-513-2 hb
ISBN 978-1-78360-512-5 pb
ISBN 978-1-78360-514-9 pdf
ISBN 978-1-78360-515-6 epub
ISBN 978-1-78360-516-3 mobi

Printed and bound by CPI Group (UK) Ltd, Croydon, CR0 4YY

# Contents

# Acknowledgements

Writing a book inevitably renders one indebted to others, but in the best possible ways.

I am fortunate to work in the kind of department in which I can count all my colleagues as friends, but some deserve particular mention here. Laura Doan has been a collaborator for well over a decade now. No one could have been more encouraging and generously supportive than she has been at times when my own enthusiasm for this project (and others) was at a low ebb. Jackie Stacey, too, has provided moral support, but has also been resourceful and imaginative in creating spaces for the kinds of intellectual exchange that have both allowed me to try out ideas and challenged me to think afresh. Howard Booth has often reassuringly confirmed my prejudices because his is a judgement I trust (his taste for Kipling and Busoni notwithstanding). Jeremy Tambling has been an irrepressible, but sociable, spur to thought and hard work. Patricia Duncker always raises spirits and offers sound advice.

Beyond the ranks of my Manchester colleagues, I have benefited from numerous conversations with David Halperin on matters related to this book in the different parts of the world we have found ourselves in. Weekends at Benita Parry's house have been an inspiring mixture of uncompromising talk, proper fun and good whisky.

I have discussed the issues explored in this book with David Wilkinson over the years so extensively that it seems fair to say that we have evolved a shared perspective on them. He has also generously offered feedback on more extensive portions of the book than anyone else, and often at short notice. Others who have read earlier drafts of individual chapters and offered valuable suggestions include Iain Bailey, Daniela Caselli, Doug Field, Ben Harker, Graham MacPhee, Stephen Maddison, Benita Parry, Eithne Quinn, Robert Spencer and Jeremy Tambling. Of course, I am solely responsible for the book's shortcomings.

In recent years, I have spent a lot of time in China as a visiting professor at Shanghai Jiao Tong University. In various ways, this has enabled me to focus on this and related projects, but it has also been a fascinating and enjoyable experience. I am thankful to Wang Jie for the invitation, for his remarkable energy in organizing seminars and conferences, and for his splendid hospitality. I am also grateful to my friends in Shanghai, Wang Bin, Chen Jing, Ningjia Zhu and Yin Qinghong, for making my trips there so convivial.

Colleagues in the Raymond Williams Society of Japan invited me to give a version of chapter two of this book as a lecture in Tokyo in 2015. The incisive response from Shintaro Kono and wonderful discussion that followed made this a memorable event for me. I am grateful not only to Shintaro, but also to Fuhito Endo, Masashi Hoshino, Yasuo Kawabata, Asako Nakai and Ryota Nishi for organizing it, and for their thoughtfulness and hospitality.

Lengthy visits to China have made my trips to Spain sadly much rarer in recent years, and I very much regret the consequent loss of contact with friends and collaborators at the Universität Autónoma de Barcelona – namely Sara Martín Alegre, Meri Torras and Diego Falconi Travez – that I enjoyed in the early stages of writing the book. I hope to return soon now that it is finished.

In a more general sense, the Didsbury Discussion Group has kept me informed and on my toes for a long time. In ways they may not be aware of, its hosts, Pat Devine and Elena Lieven, have helped consolidate the political instincts and sensibilities that are evident in the book, as have the annual fellow pilgrims to Hellsgarth.

Jessie, Ian and Heather Alderson have tolerated my absences and anxieties in recent years, and each remains an inspiration to me.

I am delighted that this book is being published by the Zed Books collective. Kim Walker has been an enthusiastic and patient editor. What better qualities could an author hope for?

More formally, I would like to thank the editors of *new formations, Theoretical Studies in Literature and Art* and *Textual Practice* for allowing me to reproduce here material published in those journals in different forms.

The book is dedicated to someone whose example and wisdom impress me more as the years go by: Alan Sinfield.

# Introduction

I began work on the project that has turned into this book many years ago. It was then envisaged as a work on postgay culture. That was not my term, but rather one that had been advanced by others with quite diverse, even opposing, purposes. On the one hand, it was used to highlight the potential for assimilation that now exists (rendering a supposedly strident gay identity and politics obsolete); on the other, it was associated with a perspective that viewed 'gay' as the very sign of assimilation, and demanded new forms of radicalism in its place. In other words, the term seemed instructively contradictory, and I was more interested in those contradictions and what they might produce than in any homogeneous shift supposed to be taking place. The current book retains some of that earlier impulse, but has become a more expansive set of reflections on culture, theory and political economy of the period since the 1960s in their relations with the category of sexuality.

At a certain point in thinking about the book, then, I decided to resist the normally very good advice that one should maintain a precise focus, and instead followed my intuitions in allowing it to become the project it seemed to be straining towards. If the postgay related in some sense to assimilation and its discontents, what kind of order was it that people were now able to assimilate to, and how had this become possible? How had the system changed, and what did it demand of us; or, to put that in other words, what reality principle now obtained? How had systemic change impacted on the politics of sexuality, and to what extent were they still governed by received wisdoms? Why might resistance still be desirable given what was now possible, and what might it entail? What were the implications of assimilation for the category of subculture? But how, in any case, did we understand that latter category and both its limitations and potential?

The processes that guided me towards these kinds of question were neither mystical, nor governed by abstract logic. Intuitions are always conditioned, not only by the convictions of various sorts we have already arrived at, but also by our socio-cultural positioning. That is one way of saying that there is something personal about this book, not in the sense that it emerged out of merely private or idiosyncratic concerns, but that its preoccupations were determined by a particular experience of and disposition towards the historical and theoretical developments of the very decades it treats.

For that reason, I want to risk introducing this project by adopting a loosely autobiographical approach that will help to explain how I came to adopt the peculiar range of theoretical interests that govern my approach to these questions. In doing so, I shall discuss material that will be familiar to many academic readers, and for which I therefore ask their forbearance, but, since my hope is that this book will be read widely beyond the academy in spite of the complexity of much of what follows, I do not wish to presume an acquaintance with that material from the outset. In what follows I seek both to clarify, as well as to begin articulating a position with regard to, some of the formative debates from the decades with which this book is concerned.

I grew up in a working-class family just outside Burnley in the north of England between the late sixties and mid-eighties. In my early years, Burnley was still a predominantly industrial town of cotton mills, engineering works and a few coalmines. As I grew up, it went through various stages of deindustrialization, though the aerospace industry has maintained a presence in the town down to the present day. Productive labour of the sort that thrived in Burnley was not disappearing altogether, of course, but was shifting to other parts of the world, where it was cheaper, because less organized, less regulated and more readily exploitable. Like many other such places, Burnley has never fully recovered from this process. In 2011, it was ranked eleventh most deprived town in the country,[1] though officially there is hope: in 2013, it won a government award for the most enterprising place in Britain.[2]

Burnley was not 'diverse' in the cosy sense often suggested by that term now. There was, and is, a very substantial Asian community, for instance, but it has been a beleaguered one, in spite of the efforts of local anti-racist campaigners on the left. Riots between white and Asian youths broke out in 2001, and were notoriously followed by a degree of electoral success for the British National Party, though the latter is now largely defeated and discredited.[3]

---

1 'Burnley Drops 10 Places in Deprivation Table', *The Burnley Express*, 3 April 2011, http://www.burnleyexpress.net/news/business/local-business/burnley-drops-10-places-in-deprivation-table-1-3246288 (accessed 12 June 2015).
2 See https://www.gov.uk/government/news/burnley-named-most-enterprising-place-in-britain (accessed 12 June 2015).
3 For an account and analysis of these events, see Daniel Trilling, *Bloody Nasty People: The Rise of Britain's Far Right*, London: Verso, 2012, pp. 103–126.

Burnley wasn't very queer either; few places were then. In the early seventies, a brave and imaginative plan by the Committee for Homosexual Equality to establish a non-profit-making gay members' club as part of a projected chain was defeated by a conservative coalition of Christians, local councillors and doctors. Ordinary local people, however, are said not to have been generally hostile to the activists who descended on the town to campaign in support of the club. At a public meeting organized to debate the proposals, one Anglican priest professing concern for the town's youth suggested that 'if a club were formed we would see what we have seen in London'.[4] If there had been a gay club, perhaps fewer people would have felt compelled to leave the town for places like London over the years, and it might have contributed in some small way to a perception of same-sex passion as commonplace and unthreatening, rather than an aspect of cosmopolitan decadence.

I want to resist giving the impression of Burnley as the grim northern place of southern English stereotype, though. My experiences of growing up were probably as mixed as most people's. I mingled with people of diverse convictions, among whom wit and lack of pretention were cardinal virtues, and each of my adult neighbours was known as uncle or auntie, though they were not blood relations. There were good teachers and bad in my school and sixth-form college, and I developed a love of reading and an interest in ideas as the result of an education that was not dominated by tests, narrowly utilitarian or geared principally to employment, but which has clearly shaped my career. I joined a church choir to earn extra pocket money, but discovered a love of classical

---

4   See the account by Alan Horsfall, 'Esquire Clubs – The Burnley Meeting', *Gay Monitor*, http://www.gaymonitor.co.uk/esquire3.htm (accessed 12 June 2015). Jeffrey Weeks gives a brief account of the initiative in context in *Coming Out: Homosexual Politics in Britain*, London: Quartet Books, 1977, p. 210.

music – a term I hate, but what other is there? – that has remained with me. I also took up the trumpet, and played the cornet in brass bands among some exceptionally talented musicians who had been trained by previous generations of bandsmen and women, and often in the army. Though a farmer's grandson, I became a vegan and started hanging out with animal rights activists in nearby Todmorden, which had a reputation for 'hippie' activity.

There is no reason why readers of this book should be interested in any of that. I mention it to stress a point that will become relevant to this introduction: that subjective formation is complex, and draws on a diversity of experience that can only reductively be described in terms of interpellation. Institutions of the sort that were formative for me are likely to be contradictory in one way or another. Brass bands, for instance, have provided musical educations to generations of working-class musicians, some of whom have gone on to become celebrated professionals; they have contributed to the emotional richness of working-class life, and have promoted its dignity and consciousness. They led striking miners back to work in 1985. But they have also been sponsored by employers in order to encourage identification with work, and have been intimately connected to military traditions; for much of their history, they were predominantly male institutions.

I left Burnley in 1985, not for London, but for Newcastle upon Tyne, to become the first member of my immediate family to go to university, where I studied English Literature. Left activism was still a prominent feature of university life, and I was involved in much of it. This could be complemented by a focus on the politics of the discipline of Literature. I never joined a party, not as a matter of principle – actually, I wanted to – but because of a lack of attractive options: the Labour Party under Neil Kinnock was shifting to the right; the Communist Party was fragmenting, and its theoretical journal, *Marxism Today*, appeared by this time to be watering down socialist principles by claiming to adapt to 'new times'[5]; the Trotskyist parties were undemocratic, and I was rarely wholly convinced by their analyses and strategies. I recall moving in circles in which many people had similar feelings.

Though I considered myself a socialist and was attracted to Marxism, then, my sense of what that tradition stood for was frankly clouded by debates that were then taking place about its continuing relevance, especially in its relationships with the so-called 'new social movements'. One of the things one heard in defence of revisionist currents was that the very principles of historical materialism demanded that its assumptions be revisited; they must be historicized. Another was that the greater sophistication of more recent 'theory' was better suited to the needs of a diverse left.

In the same year that I went to university, for instance, Ernesto Laclau and Chantal Mouffe advocated a *post*marxism – the prefix was already becoming ubiquitous – that would abandon illusions about the chimera of unified working-class agency in its struggle against capital, and seek instead to hegemonize the diverse social movements that had emerged since the sixties by 'articulating' their concerns in an anti-capitalist direction. This last possibility still sounds attractive today, but the arguments of Laclau and Mouffe left a great deal unclear, and not only for stylistic reasons: they failed to explain who comprised this left, as apparently distinct from the social movements it sought to articulate, or what form the left's hegemonizing institutions would take, and why – owing,

---

5   See the somewhat diverse contributions to Stuart Hall and Martin Jacques, eds, *New Times: The Changing Face of Politics in the 1990s*, London: Lawrence & Wishart, 1989.

that is, to what perspective or set of interests if not those of class – it should privilege anti-capitalism specifically. This last point was especially moot given that Laclau and Mouffe acknowledged that consumer capitalism had played a significant part in the pluralization of struggle they welcomed.[6] Indeed, their arguments were divisive on the left they sought to marshal, because many were rather less disenchanted with the Marxist tradition virtually in its entirety. In a scathing review that took them to task for parodying that tradition, Norman Geras dismissed the work as 'ex-Marxism' in the pages of *New Left Review*.[7]

If the eighties were confusing for the left, this is because they were also a politically defining period to an extent some were beginning to sense, but no one could have fully anticipated. The confusion was bound up with the emergence and increasing dominance of neoliberalism, both in Britain, through Thatcherism, and globally. This comprised various initiatives: the promotion of a supply-side, or entrepreneurial, economy, especially through tax cuts; tight control of the money supply (monetarism), but deregulation of currency controls; the very purposeful defeat of leftist opposition; cutting back welfare provision; the privatization of nationalized industries; and the active transformation and deregulation of state and

---

6  For instance: 'This "democratic consumer culture" has undoubtedly stimulated the emergence of new struggles which have played an important part in the rejection of old forms of subordination, as was the case in the United States with the struggle of the black movement for civil rights' (Ernesto Laclau and Chantal Mouffe, *Hegemony and Socialist Strategy: Towards a Radical Democratic Politics*, London: Verso, 1985, p. 164).

7  Norman Geras, 'Postmarxism?' *New Left Review* I, 163, May–June 1987, pp. 40–82. Laclau and Mouffe responded in 'Postmarxism Without Apologies', *New Left Review* I, 166, November–December 1987, pp. 79–106, prompting a further retort from Geras in 'Ex-Marxism Without Substance: Being a Real Reply to Laclau and Mouffe', *New Left Review* I, 169, May–June 1988, pp. 34–61.

non-state institutions, such as the stock exchange. Thatcherism specifically, however, was also socially illiberal and nationalistic in ways that were obviously in conflict with much of its economic policy. This apparent traditionalism assisted in deflecting attention from one of its main consequences: a massive redistribution of wealth and power upwards, a process that has continued in more attenuated forms under successive governments.

This way of putting things, though, is one that has only really become academically fashionable retrospectively. There was certainly an obsession on the left with Thatcherism in the eighties, and a substantial amount of writing about it, but by the mid to late eighties many were instead increasingly talking about something called postmodernism. This was variously defined, but in most of those definitions called Marxism's legitimacy into question. Perry Anderson, in carefully tracing the genealogy of the term, has concluded that it is 'in one way or another an appanage of the right ... There could be nothing but capitalism. The postmodern was a sentence on alternative illusions.'[8] At the time, however, postmodernism was frequently presented by its advocates as progressive precisely because it delivered us from those illusions insofar as they were governed by 'metanarratives'.

The latter category was coined by Jean-François Lyotard in his account of *The Postmodern Condition* (first published in French in 1979, and translated into English in 1984). I cannot do full justice to Lyotard's argument here, but some account will be helpful. The book's focus was on science, but its emphases were clearly intended for extrapolation to other spheres. Lyotard claimed that the postmodern condition was characterized by 'scepticism

---

8  Perry Anderson, *The Origins of Postmodernity*, London: Verso, 1998, pp. 45–46.

towards metanarratives'[9] of progress that had paradoxically legitimated science as the basis of that progress since the Enlightenment. 'Paradoxically', because the kinds of proof science sought, Lyotard claimed, spurned narrative as a primitive form 'belonging to a different mentality: savage, primitive, underdeveloped, backward, alienated, composed of opinions, customs, authority, prejudice, ignorance, ideology'.[10] For reasons attributed by Lyotard to capitalist technological development, however, the legitimating metanarrative fell into desuetude in the postwar world, because of a profusion of more localized, relativized and incommensurable scientific 'language games' (Wittgenstein's term) only accountable to the capitalist principle of *performance*, of getting the job done. The overarching, Enlightenment justification for scientific practice had fragmented as a result of this process. This sounds like a dismal situation, but Lyotard saw positive potential in the unintended consequences of the new science's sheer creativity, plurality and *dissensus*. The latter term is especially important: according to that eminent defender of the project of modernity, Jürgen Habermas, the aim of what he calls communicative reason exercised is *consensus*. To a postmodern thinker such as Lyotard, however, consensus is sinisterly associated with closure and restriction, even authoritarianism.

The point of this summary is to highlight a number of aspects of the argument that have tended to characterize a range of work that is often also described as postmodern. I should note, however, that the term and its usage are problematic and contentious, especially as used to cover something called poststructuralism (itself an anglophone coinage for a range of continental thought).

---

9  Jean-François Lyotard, *The Postmodern Condition: A Report on Knowledge*, Manchester: Manchester University Press, 1984, p. xxiv.
10  Ibid., p. 27.

Geoffrey Bennington is particularly scathing about the expansive use of the category of the postmodern, since he considers 'the general aim of such conflation is to lump a lot of things together the better to get rid of them without having to think very hard'.[11] I do recognize that tendency, but the point itself is an instance of one of the most familiar gestures of postmodern thought, the claim that universal identity ('the postmodern') represses the particularity and difference that apparently encourage hard thinking.

If Lyotard is describing a general condition, then, it seems legitimate to extrapolate from his specific account to other work that is philosophically or otherwise sceptical towards metanarratives, and for not dissimilar reasons. Common emphases to be found in such work include the sense that the commitment to truth and progress is actually both culturally western and bound to the west's historic imperialist projects, as Lyotard suggests in his claim about the Enlightenment denigration of narrative, and that its pursuit of truth is irreconcilable with a more desirable, and apparently subversive, heterogeneity. Moreover, and again as we have seen in Lyotard, the subversion that is validated in postmodern thought tends to be immanent to the system in the specific sense, not only of emerging out of it, but being thereby qualitatively so conditioned as to be incapable of outright opposition. If that is the case, the assumption goes, there can be no decisive victory over power, no transcendence of the system to another kind altogether.

Michel Foucault advances such arguments in a work that has been profoundly influential, not only on the field with which this book is mostly concerned, but also more generally, *The History of Sexuality*, vol. 1. The notion that we possess a sexuality that might

---

11   Geoffrey Bennington, 'The Rationality of Postmodern Relativity', in *Legislations: The Politics of Deconstruction*, London: Verso, 1994, p. 172.

be liberated from repression, Foucault argues, is itself an effect of power – specifically, that is, of the discourse of sexuality that produced new forms of subjectivity from the later nineteenth century on through the taxonomy of individuals on the basis of their desires, and the internalization of those taxonomical categories by the individuals themselves. This was the 'perverse implantation'.[12] However, the arguments on power that Foucault develops in that work are ultimately abstracted from the particular history he sketches, such that a work that begins by tracing the emergence of a discursive field of sexuality specifically becomes a theorization of power in general: 'where there is power, there is resistance', Foucault influentially writes,

> and yet, or rather consequently, this resistance is never in a position of exteriority in relation to power ... there is no single locus of Great Refusal, no soul of revolt, source of all rebellions, or pure law of the revolutionary. Instead there is a plurality of resistances, each of them a special case.[13]

In this formulation, the claim about resistance's non-exteriority to power seems also to necessitate recognition of its multiplicity, but there is a telling ambiguity in the phrasing: it is not clear whether the mere fact of there being special cases requires our endorsement of each one, or whether, in describing things in this way, he is refusing the authority implicit in the act of endorsing struggles in the first place. It seems to me that the carefully neutral tone may be a strategic way of keeping both possibilities open: a claim about the nature of resistance in general merges with an

---

12   Michel Foucault, *The History of Sexuality*, vol. 1, trans. Robert Hurley, London: Allen Lane, 1979, pp. 36–49.
13   Ibid., pp. 95–96.

ethical rejection of judgement, and each serves to reinforce by obscuring the other. Thus, diversity is both fact *and* value, and anyone who 'fails' either to recognize or advocate a plurality of resistances must therefore come across as authoritarian. This is a characteristic move in a range of postmodern thought, especially of the sort that is directly engaged with questions of social power.

Foucault's repudiation of the view that power and resistance exist in oppositional form is analogous to the emphasis on plurality in Lyotard, because both have at least substantially in mind the Hegelian Marxist tradition to which Herbert Marcuse belongs ('Great Refusal' is his term). That tradition sees history as generated out of the dialectical conflict between opposing classes and principles; under capitalism, those of capital and labour. That contradiction generates the potential for the emergence of an appropriately revolutionary consciousness on the part of workers that would ideally lead to the establishment of communism, a system that is fully democratic, because in it property is held in common. Put in such crude terms, which no doubt invite incredulity, this is its metanarrative. Postmodern political thought stresses instead that there are diverse forms of resistance relating to diverse features of human life, and that the Marxist narrative is reductively authoritarian either in its reluctance to recognize them, or possibly in its determination somehow to integrate them into the same cause of opposing a capitalism that supposedly determines every aspect of existence.

'The narrative function is losing its great functors, its great hero, its great dangers, its great voyages, its great goal,' wrote Lyotard.[14] It seems fairly clear that the 'lost hero' of Marxism by the time

---

14    Lyotard, *Postmodern Condition*, p. xxiv.

he wrote that was the working class. The reason such agency had been privileged by Marxists was because the systemic, rather than merely narrative, function of the working class – not exclusively, but most directly, and with fewest compensations – was to be exploited. A more sympathetic way of putting the Marxist case than the one that speaks of narratives would suggest that, since capitalism requires the exploitation of labour, labour requires the termination of capitalism: the dynamism of the system, history itself, is generated out of that conflict in complex, mediated ways that mean that we mostly do not experience it directly in such terms; hence, the need for theory.

Nonetheless, the perception that the working class was a lost hero was not specific to postmodern, or postmarxist, thought. Nor was it wholly a consequence of the deindustrialization I described earlier, and its theorization by commentators of various political hues as bringing about the emergence of postindustrial societies.[15] The plausibility of the working class as an agent of transformation had been called into question for some decades prior to the eighties in the west, even by those who claimed some kind of affiliation to the Marxist tradition.

At the start of the sixties, for instance, C. Wright Mills had influentially spoken of 'the labour metaphysic' as 'a legacy from Victorian Marxism that is now quite unrealistic'.[16] In arguments often influenced by Mills, Herbert Marcuse wrote in 1964 of one-dimensional man, a term that referred to the pervasive absence

---

15   The term was used on left and right. On the right, it was influentially advanced by Daniel Bell in *The Coming of Post-Industrial Society*, New York: Harper Colophon, 1974. On the left, there was André Gorz's *Farewell to the Working Class: An Essay on Post-Industrial Socialism*, London: Pluto, 1980.
16   C. Wright Mills, 'Letter to the New Left', in Priscilla Long, ed., *The New Left: A Collection of Essays*, Boston: Horizons Books, 1969, p. 22.

of contradiction in the organization and popular consciousness of contemporary life, even though that life remained unfree. He was writing of societies in the west that have been variously described, often as Keynesian or Fordist, in order to highlight their regulation through techniques that, it was hoped, would match production with consumption, and thereby avoid the kinds of crises to which capitalism was prone. Integration, or assimilation, became especially sinister words on the left during this period. Marcuse wrote in respect of the working class that

> it is precisely ... new consciousness, the 'space within', the space for transcending historical practice, which is being barred by a society in which subjects as well as objects constitute instrumentalities in a whole that has its *raison d'être* in the accomplishments of its overpowering productivity. Its supreme promise is an ever-more-comfortable life for an ever-growing number of people who, in a strict sense, cannot imagine a qualitatively different universe of discourse and action.[17]

The erosion of that 'space within' – that is, the subjection of individual autonomy to powerful pressure from socially heteronomous forces, to put it in the Kantian language of the Frankfurt School – is a process to which Marcuse gave the more general term 'deprivatization'.[18] In other respects, too, postwar societies were one-dimensional, he argued: ordinary language

---

17 Herbert Marcuse, *One-Dimensional Man: Studies in the Ideology of Advanced Industrial Society*, London: Routledge, 1991, p. 26.

18 See the reference to 'the deprivatization of free time' in 'Freedom and Freud's Theory of Instincts', in *Five Lectures*, ed. trans. Jeremy J. Shapiro and Shierry M. Weber, London: Allen Lane, 1970, p. 3. Marcuse first used the term in his critique of Nazism: see the 1934 essay 'The Struggle Against Liberalism in the Totalitarian Use of the State' in *Negations*, p. 39.

philosophy, for instance, represented a form of empiricism that attached even intellectuals to reality as it was currently known; art dealt with, or was integrated into, everyday life on terms prescribed by the latter, thereby undermining its potential for uncompromising critique; and so on.

The problem increasingly alleged of working-class agency, though, related also to what we might call the quantitative and qualitative dimensions of it: in other words, how many it seemed relevant to, and what ends it appeared to serve. In addition to the postmodern claim that Marxism was complicit in the imperialist, universalistic project of the Enlightenment,[19] it also appeared masculine because concerned principally with a working class that was largely male and presumptively heterosexual, owing to historic divisions of labour.

The increasing theoretical displacement of Marxism I have been discussing here bore increasingly on my own experience in a particular sense. I came out, to no one's great surprise, in my final year at university, and got involved in lesbian and gay politics, as they were called then, at the time of the campaign against Clause 28 of the Local Government Bill. This aspired to prevent local government from 'intentionally promot[ing] homosexuality or publish[ing] material with the intention of promoting homosexuality', or from 'promot[ing] the teaching in any maintained school of the acceptability of homosexuality as a pretended family relationship'. The framing of the Bill reflected the fact that lesbian and gay politics in Britain at that time were

---

19  Important challenges to such claims include those of Aijaz Ahmad, 'Marx on India: A Clarification', in *In Theory: Classes, Nations, Literatures*, London: Verso, 1992, pp. 221–242, and Kevin Anderson's more extensive, though similar, arguments in *Marx at the Margins: On Nationalism, Ethnicity and Non-Western Societies*, Chicago: University of Chicago Press, 2010.

unambiguously associated with the left, whether liberal, socialist or anarchist, though there was an instructively moribund Conservative Group for Homosexual Equality.[20] Clause 28 was in part designed to embarrass the 'loony left' said by the Tory press to dominate certain Labour-controlled councils.[21] Some of these had helped to fund lesbian and gay centres and supported switchboards, and had promoted positive-image agendas in schools and elsewhere.

In the campaign against Clause 28, the socialist left played a conspicuous part. Its analysis was mostly that lesbian and gay oppression was generated by capitalism's dependence on the family, and that lesbian and gay liberation consequently required the abolition of capitalism. It was a neat argument, and appeared somewhat plausible, but one problem with it was that this thing called capitalism seemed to be doing quite well out of commercial gay venues even then; the entrepreneur, Richard Branson, owned the huge London nightclub, Heaven. Nowadays, commercialized gay areas are, of course, a feature of most reasonably large cities in many parts of the world, same-sex marriage is available in substantial parts of the western world and Latin America, and the family itself has diversified during the very period when markets have increasingly been deregulated.[22] The most widespread Marxist argument about lesbian and gay oppression at that time was questionable then, and has become more so over time.

---

20  See, for instance, Matthew Parris's comments on this marginal phenomenon in *Chance Witness: An Outsider's Life in Politics*, London: Viking, 2002, pp. 300–303.
21  For a detailed poststructuralist analysis of the debates about this legislation, see Anna Marie Smith, *New Right Discourses on Race and Sexuality*, Cambridge: Cambridge University Press, 1994, pp. 183–243.
22  Jeffrey Weeks celebrates and summarizes many of these developments in *The World We Have Won: The Remaking of Erotic and Intimate Life*, London: Routledge, 2007.

On leaving Newcastle in 1990, I went to study as a postgraduate at the University of Sussex on the MA programme in Critical Theory. Being taught by people such as Jonathan Dollimore and Alan Sinfield made me more conscious of the tradition of cultural materialism, but it also introduced me to the emergent fields of queer studies/theory with which both were critically engaged. Others had bravely pioneered lesbian and gay studies, of course, but queer was different, and often polemically argued its case as such. Substantially inspired by Foucault, queer was anti-essentialist and supposedly anti-identitarian. It privileged the non-normative, and refused accommodation with dominant values, not least through its symbolic appropriation of an insult. Nonetheless, it is worth recalling that the term was not universally welcomed at the time, and there are still those who will *discreetly* express their dislike for it. Ironically, this very discretion is a symptom of the normative status 'queer' has achieved in the academy.

From the start, I found myself deeply ambivalent about queer theory, though not because of its disdain for those considered insufficiently radical to embrace its avant-gardism. Queer's historicist emphases were appealing because they opened up the essentialist category of the homosexual, among others, to necessary scrutiny, and thereby rendered plausible possibilities for change. But it also appeared to close them down in other respects: I found its preoccupation with the minutiae of the subject's determination by power uncongenial. Too often queer theory seemed to me another way of returning 'political' conversation to the (now complexly decentred) *individual,* in spite of – but also through – its antihumanist emphasis on her 'subjectification'.

Partly, my resistance to all of this was a matter of disposition. I have never felt either proud or ashamed to be gay; 'unapologetic' would describe my stance best, though I have been militantly so at times. Actually, I have never particularly liked the term much, but tend to use both it and queer because they are in general use. I take no great pleasure in being different, and discern in that some of the values of my upbringing, which instilled in me the virtue anathematized in queer theory of being normal. While I am not at all oblivious to the conformism that may be promoted by that category, or the conditions it often places on who might aspire to be normal in the first place, there was another, more valuable dimension to it: normal people didn't think themselves very special, and certainly not *superior*. This perception highlights one of the problems with which this book is pervasively concerned in one way or another: the difficulties of valuing difference in conditions of inequality, and of being able to distinguish differences from distinctions, in Bourdieu's sense of the latter as those finely grained tastes and preferences generated by class and status as a means of reinforcing them through what he calls symbolic capital.[23] To anticipate one aspect of my discussion in chapter two, I have no doubts that my intuitive dislike of the word gay has to do with its historic class resonances.

Queer theory is arguably a kind of postmodern thought; certainly it is poststructuralist and anti-humanist, and for that reason I retained another reservation about it throughout my postgraduate years, though it was one I tended to internalize as too commonsensical. This was a humanist conviction that the subject is not merely discursively produced, but a substantial entity in its own right, a figure whose powers and potentialities may go fulfilled or unfulfilled. Over the years, I have come to believe with greater force that a theory that failed to take account of this was

---

23   Pierre Bourdieu, *Distinction: A Social Critique of the Judgement of Taste*, London: Routledge and Kegan Paul, 1984.

inevitably impoverished and inadequate. After all, if the subject is only ever construed as subjectified, why should the particular arrangements under which she was so 'produced' be of concern to anyone? Peter Dews long ago registered an objection to the Foucaultian theorization of power along these lines:

> If the concept of power is to have any critical import, there must be some principle, force, or entity which power 'crushes' or 'subdues', and whose release from this repression is considered desirable. A purely positive account of power would no longer be an account of power at all, but simply of the constitutive operations of social systems. At many points, Foucault appears to believe it possible to adopt such a neutral stance – indeed this may be described as his fall-back position – while at others he continues to use the concept of power in a critical sense.[24]

Kate Soper makes a similar point when she suggests that 'anti-humanist positions are themselves quite ready to employ a rhetoric of "loss", "lack", "subjection" and "repression" suspiciously akin to that of traditional humanism'.[25] I find the same constitutive ambiguity time and again in queer theory and other poststructuralist work. The result is that the humanism it tacitly harbours goes unexamined, and when it does emerge it consequently sounds sentimental.

Nonetheless, no one concerned with sexuality could have overlooked the force of Foucault's work. For a very long time, under the influence of his rejection of 'Freudo-Marxism', I was

---

24  Peter Dews, *Logics of Disintegration: Poststructuralist Thought and the Claims of Critical Theory*, London: Verso, 1987, p. 162.
25  Kate Soper, *Humanism and Antihumanism*, London: Hutchinson, 1986, p. 123.

reluctant to read the work of Herbert Marcuse when there were so many other claims on my time, especially after I embarked on an academic career in 1993 at a time of increasing casualization of employment, burgeoning bureaucratization and increasing surveillance of the work we did. Though I did read Marcuse's most famous work, *One-Dimensional Man*, in the nineties, some of it appeared dated, some was opaque (because I had not read *Eros and Civilization*), and much seemed like a version of ideas one could get from Adorno in any case. Having been one of the most celebrated radical thinkers of the sixties, Marcuse was now rarely cited, and almost always in negative terms when he was. In an influential survey of thinking about sexuality, Jeffrey Weeks followed Foucault's lead in dismissing, by lumping together, the quite divergent, and even mutually antagonistic, 'Freudo-Marxists', claiming that this group 'depends ... on a theory of sexuality which, because of its rigid biologism, is ahistorical to a degree which Freud's actually is not'.[26]

I had no particular reasons other than curiosity and a desire to remedy an embarrassing deficiency for belatedly reading *Eros and Civilization* in (I think) 2008. When I did so, I found it extraordinarily compelling, in spite of my resistance to its insufficiently critical acceptance of some key Freudian terms. I began to see how it might provide a framework and terminology for thinking about the relations between capitalism and sexuality that were absent from queer theory, which was quite simply not constituted for that purpose. Moreover, Marcuse's emphases were not exactly incompatible with Foucault's. For the latter, there could be no sexual liberation, since power worked through the very

---

26 Jeffrey Weeks, *Sexuality and its Discontents: Meanings, Myths and Modern Sexualities*, London: Routledge & Kegan Paul, 1985, p. 168.

hypothesis that we are repressed, but he nonetheless concludes *The History of Sexuality* with a notoriously vague, unsatisfactory advocacy of 'the claims of pleasures, bodies, and knowledges, in their multiplicity and the possibility of resistance'.[27] For Marcuse, there could be no sexual liberation either, because our investment in sexual pleasure specifically, and the intensity we derive from it, results from a historical narrowing of more general sensuous experience into this kind of satisfaction. It sounds rather like he is also advocating pleasures and bodies – not to mention a transformation of reason away from its constitutive dismissal of the body – as an alternative to the regime of sexuality.

Marcuse's utopian critique of the Freudian account of subjective development, but also of the western philosophical tradition, generates a framework and set of terms that have become indispensable to me. Reading *Eros* and the rest of Marcuse's output, moreover, persuaded me that the project about postgay culture I thought I was embarked on would benefit from a return to the period of gay liberation itself; not necessarily the specific phenomenon, but rather the more general counterculture out of which it emerged. Marcuse was treated as something of a guru in the sixties, but he did not necessarily welcome that treatment, and was sometimes sharply critical of the movements that adopted his slogans. His approach is one that encourages us to view sexuality, the erotic and the labour required to reproduce our societies as systemically determined; that is, as the mutually defining qualitative elements of a totality. It is this totality, capitalism, that socialists aim to transform in order to establish democratic control (not mere regulation) of the principal area of life in which it is denied to us under the private ownership of the

---

27 Foucault, *The History of Sexuality*, p. 157.

means of production, or what is described in reified terms as 'the economy', that alien, implacable, capricious, irrational, malignant and incomprehensible – and hence, for some people, exciting and seductive – entity that is nonetheless generated out of ordinary human labour.

Foucaultian thought has encouraged us to think in terms of productive, rather than repressive, power, but such ways of putting things are frequently misleading; insofar as they are intended to call Marxism's value into account, very obviously so, since Marx's work focuses critically on production, growth, the extraordinary dynamism of the system and the exploitation that makes it possible. If Marxism has also stressed negative power in the form of *state* repression (and rightly so), that is because it views the state as the means of enforcing capitalist social relations. In contemporary conditions, however, the state does so largely through non-coercive means, by preference; through the achievement of what the Italian Marxist, Gramsci, influentially called 'hegemony'. Nonetheless, the state will still resort to repressive ones when necessary. In recent years, students in Britain protesting against the undemocratically achieved tripling of university tuition fees – facilitated by a report compiled by the former CEO of British Petroleum, Lord Browne – have experienced this 'necessity'.

It is not only the state that secures hegemony, though. Many institutions of civil society contribute to the stabilization of hegemonic power, not least through what Marcuse identified as 'repressive tolerance'[28] – that is to say, the deployment of a rhetoric, not only of tolerance, but liberty, to defend the way things are. The 'free press', for instance, is free in the sense that it is

---

28  Herbert Marcuse, 'Repressive Tolerance', in Robert Wolff, Barrington Moore, Jr., and Herbert Marcuse, eds, *A Critique of Repressive Tolerance*, Boston: Beacon Books, 1969, pp. 81–123.

formally independent of the state, but it is mostly owned by private interests who use their considerable influence to serve their own purposes, as well as those of business more generally. The free press, in other words, does not serve democracy, truth or justice (all concepts desperately in need of defence as critical terms); in fact, it mostly opposes them in the guise of supporting – indeed, embodying – them. Another specific, and striking, recent instance of repressive tolerance is the US Supreme Court's decision in 2010 to lift all restrictions on corporate funding of electoral campaigns on the grounds that corporations should enjoy the benefits of free speech accorded individual citizens.[29]

Gramsci's importance as a thinker only came to be appreciated outside Italy in the late sixties and early seventies, long after his death, as part of the revival of Marxist theory that formed the project of the New Left, though his influence was mostly felt in Europe. In the US, Michael Denning describes Gramsci as 'a minor presence'[30] – a significant fact from the perspective of this book. He was of particular importance to Raymond Williams, whose elaboration of a cultural materialism was in part motivated by a desire to avoid the reductivism of Althusserian structuralist Marxism, with its emphasis on subjectification by an undifferentiated 'ideological state apparatus' (though Althusser also invoked Gramsci as an influence, his most important theoretical influences came from elsewhere). In the essay of that name, schools, churches, trades unions, political parties and other institutions are all conceived as shaping acceptance of the system, not least through the very

---

29  See Wendy Brown's analysis of this as an 'economization' of the law in *Undoing the Demos: Neoliberalism's Stealth Revolution*, New York: Zone Books, 2015, chapter five, pp. 151–173.
30  Michael Denning, *Culture in the Age of Three Worlds*, London: Verso, 2004, p. 156.

'misrecognition' they generate that subjects are individuals at all.[31] Thus, his theory of ideology was also, and inseparably, a theory of the subject, who appears in it as strikingly insubstantial.

Williams's resistance to Althusserian thought did not mean he underestimated the scope of hegemony. Like Althusser – and in a way that seems to me to have been influenced by him – Williams understood it as achieved not merely through the dissemination of ideas, but also through the material organization of everyday life. The hegemonic project, he wrote, is one that aspires to establish a kind of common sense 'that saturates society to such an extent ... that it corresponds to the reality of social experience'.[32] This kind of thinking, once thought sophisticated and academic, is now a commonplace among politicians. Strategists in the current British Tory government, for instance, speak about their desire to 'make the facts on the ground more Tory'.[33] Reality is not neutral; Wendy Brown speaks intriguingly, but without elaboration, of 'the reality principle' of neoliberalism.[34]

Nonetheless, Williams argues that there are elements of social life that are not expressions of the *dominant* – his alternative word for hegemonic.[35] These are either inoffensive, and thus

31  Louis Althusser, 'Ideology and Ideological State Apparatuses', in *Essays on Ideology*, London: Verso, 1976, pp. 1–60.
32  Raymond Williams, 'Base and Superstructure in Marxist Cultural Theory', *New Left Review I*, 82, November–December 1973, p. 8.
33  Anonymous senior Conservative, quoted in Andrew Rawnsley, 'As Labour Tries to Resolve its Past, the Tories are Mapping Out the Future', *The Observer*, 7 June 2015, p. 31.
34  Wendy Brown, *Undoing the Demos: Neoliberalism's Stealth Revolution*, New York: Zone Books, 2015, p. 35.
35  Actually, this usage contradicts that of Gramsci, who counterposed direction, or leadership, through consent with domination by force. See, for instance, Martin Jay, *Marxism and Totality: The Adventures of a Concept from Lukács to Habermas*, Cambridge: Polity Press, 1984, p. 165.

merely alternative, or cause problems for it, and are therefore oppositional, in which case they need to be suppressed, assimilated or possibly transformed through some combination of the two. Such elements might, in turn, be bound to the *residual* – which is to say, remnants of older modes of life that persist (the Anglican Church in Britain, for instance, which isn't always concerned to be 'modern', and occasionally criticizes governments) – or they might be *emergent* social movements of one sort or another. The recent Occupy movement might be an example of the latter, though Williams seems to have had in mind more durable phenomena. Williams's emphasis on implicitly diverse movements clearly held the potential to expand the traditional concerns of Marxism with working-class agency, narrowly conceived, while still relating them back to a system of class dominance and capitalist relations.

Williams suggests that cultural production of various kinds may take place in relation to these dominant, residual or emergent forces. For reasons I come to in chapter one, however, it is important to note that the forces themselves are not conceived in cultural terms. Feminism, for instance, may inspire forms of cultural production – the plays of Caryl Churchill, let us say – but culture is only one dimension of its project. Moreover, culture is not simply a complex manifestation of the consciousness determined by the economic forces and relations of production, as a cruder Marxist base/superstructure model suggests, but is governed by specific institutional pressures. Neither movements nor institutions are wholly autonomous, but take place within the totality of relations that define them as dominant, residual, emergent, alternative or oppositional.

By way of a further example, let me return again to higher education, since this will serve to explain why I find Williams a crucial supplement to the book's emphasis in other respects on

Marcuse. We might view cultural criticism of the sort I pursue here as itself a form of production, taking place within institutions, mostly universities, that will determine the qualitative elements of that production, including the demand that it engage in scholarly fashion with the work of others to which it is indebted, or from which it must differentiate itself. Such scholarship reflects the status of universities as somewhat autonomous from the rest of society, according to the old value of disinterestedness. This, however, has in turn been despised by elements of that society for its remoteness and presumed superiority – in other words, for evincing an 'ivory tower' detachment from 'the real world'. As the universities are increasingly, and quite self-consciously, integrated into the reality principle of business and capital accumulation, however, that insult has been internalized by them. It is now effectively levelled by managers at those academics who remain resistant to prioritizing markets and growth. Thus, relative autonomy is being progressively eroded, and the universities' residual independence has been very substantially undermined. This is undoubtedly a further instance of the tendency described by Marcuse as 'one-dimensionality'. Note the difference from Lyotard in this respect: from a Marcusean perspective, the emphasis placed on knowledge as performance is intolerable, and should be resisted as part of a progressive agenda.[36]

The erosion of academia's independence is serious and substantial, and is being pursued with determination. Even now, though, universities provide spaces in which critical, dissenting work may be produced, and the value of cultural materialism is that it encourages us to reflect on what kind of dissent that

---

36  I shall simply note here that Marcuse uses the term 'performance' in a different, but not wholly unrelated, sense. I discuss it further in chapter one.

space makes possible. The problem with the category of one-dimensionality is that it encourages the view that either there must be revolutionary opposition, or nothing is possible. Cultural materialism is able to register nuance and complexity in a way that offers an alternative to disabling pessimism,[37] but it is nonetheless a variant of Marxism and entails a commitment to some form of programmatically socialist politics.

I now live and work in Manchester, not very far from where I was born. A new train line has just been constructed between the two places in the hope that some of Manchester's relative prosperity will be channelled Burnley's way in a spatial exemplification of trickle-down economics. Manchester is familiar to me from my youth, but it has also been transformed. It now has an airport with good connections to the rest of the world, and an extensive gay village where I sometimes drink. It feels quite cosmopolitan, as those who shaped its development intended it should, but every time I visit London I am struck by the far greater concentration of national and international wealth in evidence. My life here is a comfortable one, in spite of the erosion of academic pay and conditions that has taken place over the decades, but I am very conscious that I lead a fairly privileged existence in a society in which austerity now bears down most heavily on those who can least tolerate it. The homeless are more in evidence on the streets.

Marcuse was born in 1898 and died in 1979. Williams was born in 1921 and died in 1988. Foucault was born in 1926 and died in

---

37   Actually, one of his last and best works, *Counterrevolution and Revolt*, saw him developing a more strategic position through his endorsement of Rudi Dutschke's proposal for a 'long march through the institutions' (see *Counterrevolution*, Boston: Beacon Press, 1972, pp. 55–56). This might be regarded as his most Gramscian text.

1984. Of the three, however, it is Foucault whose work feels most contemporary, but that is surely because it is most frequently and reverentially returned to in order to insist on its contemporaneity. There is much to admire in that work and its ambitious attempt to theorize the institutions, discourses and governmentality of modernity. But its relevance also benefits from a narrative of theoretical advance and supersession in the anglophone academy that tends to suggest that the British cultural studies tradition was displaced by a more rigorous, but ultimately untenable, structuralist Marxism (Althusser's), and that this necessarily gave way to the *post*structuralism and postmodernism still dominant in one form or another. That narrative is in my experience deeply embedded in the university curriculum in the Humanities; I would even say it is taught as truth.[38] I obviously dissent from it in ways that I have begun to indicate in this introduction and develop further in the rest of this book.

Nonetheless, the book's principal concern is with other matters that this biographical sketch has helped me to introduce: the political economic changes that have taken place in the period since the sixties, and their consequences for the politics of sexuality that emerged in that decade, and have contributed to the remarkable transformation of many societies across the world. Such transformation has not on the whole been what was anticipated or hoped for back in the sixties. As Lisa Henderson succinctly puts it, in recent decades "'gay" and "queer" ... have taken form

---

38   One instance of this narrative with which I have substantial political sympathies, as well as disagreements, is Jeremy Gilbert's *Anticapitalism and Culture: Radical Theory and Popular Politics*, Oxford: Berg, 2008. Gilbert is influenced by Laclau and Mouffe, as well as Deleuze. An alternative, cultural materialist vision of the future of cultural studies is offered by Andrew Milner, *Reimagining Cultural Studies: The Promise of Cultural Materialism*, London: Sage, 2002.

amid socially and politically crippling economic conditions and a national culture of hyper-accumulation'[39] (she is speaking of the US, but her comments are more generally relevant). In returning time and again to these years and our modes of understanding of what has taken place, this book also attempts to provide alternative ways of grasping the category of sexuality that connects it back to a capitalist totality I would like to see superseded for reasons that cannot be articulated through the focus on sexuality alone. Those reasons have to do with the more general category of needs highlighted in the title. This should be understood as referring, not merely to those of the individual, but those of the collective from which the individual is rigorously, but ideologically, distinguished in essentially bourgeois traditions of thought. That explains why the chapters of this book, like this introduction, are far from exclusively focused on sexuality – indeed, they often ignore sexuality altogether for lengthy stretches – but are concerned instead with more general theoretical frameworks, especially as these relate to our understanding of historical processes.

In chapter one, I consider two competing ways of understanding the period since the sixties as a form of transition. One of these ways has been tacitly superseded by having become unfashionable, without having been adequately critiqued, except by those who never accepted it in the first place. This is the claim that we moved from modernity into postmodernity. In order to examine it, I focus both on Fredric Jameson's classic statement of the case, as well as a less well-known one to which I am very much indebted, though mostly because it has forced me to think carefully about my disagreements with it. This is Marianne DeKoven's *Utopia Limited*

---

39   Lisa Henderson, 'Queers and Class: Toward a Cultural Politics of Friendship', in David Alderson, ed., *Queerwords: Sexuality and the Politics of Culture*, special issue of *Key Words*, 13, 2015, p. 21.

(2004), which argues through detailed discussion of a wide range of cultural production and theory from the sixties, described by her as 'late modernist', that postmodern emphases are discernible in it and that it therefore anticipated the (apparently definitive) evolution that was about to take place.

There are a number of reasons for choosing the work of Jameson and DeKoven. Jameson's is an explicit influence on DeKoven's, though hers exemplifies the scepticism towards (Marxist) metanarrativizing highlighted by Lyotard. The claims of both are also crucially informed by the work of both Marcuse and Williams, but I seek to show that the use they make of Williams's categories of dominant, residual and emergent to chart postmodernity's emergence is problematic, and that if we return to his elaboration of these terms as outlined above they provide us with a valuable means of apprehending the transition that the modernity–postmodernity narrative occludes: the transition to neoliberal capitalism and flexible accumulation. This, I suggest, has generated the conditions that have made possible what I call the diversified dominant, which has been the means through which sexually dissident subcultures have been assimilated. While the chapter is highly critical of a more or less tacit dependence on Marcuse's analysis of one-dimensionality in arguments about postmodernity, I nonetheless seek to establish what I find most valuable in his work, and especially what may be retrieved from it in order better to understand the neoliberal present.

The concern of chapter two is sufficiently evident, I hope, in its title. Given the Marxist affiliations I am happy to acknowledge, it might be thought obvious what my answer to its question will be, but in fact those affiliations are what make a decisive – which is to say, undialectical – response difficult. Ultimately, it seems to me, we must interrogate the very category of progress, and consider its qualitative dimensions in ways that 'scientific' Marxism of various sorts has sadly neglected. Once again, Marcuse permits us to do precisely this, and crucial to my argument is a defence of his category of 'false needs' as well as a revision of his account of 'repressive desublimation' as 'repressive incitement'.

These first, very broadly contextualizing and theoretical, chapters then give way to a more typically cultural materialist preoccupation with the very category of culture. In them, I distinguish between two terms that are sometimes treated as almost synonymous, counterculture and subculture. The emergence of the former is the obvious context for any consideration of the lesbian and gay liberation movements at the end of the sixties, after the Stonewall riots. The category of counterculture tends to be used very loosely, but I return to its specific coinage as a defence of the forms US radicalism had taken on by contrast with that of Europe. The suggestion here is that the historical pressures that gave rise to New Left and countercultural protest, in addition to the subsequent fate of the counterculture, have shaped the emergence of queer theory quite as much as any theoretical innovations coming from France (and, yes, this entails some endorsement of arguments about American exceptionalism). Still, countercultural influences travelled rapidly and held the potential both to critique and fuse with other left traditions. In the final section of this chapter I attempt to recover Mañuel Puig's remarkable novel, *The Kiss of the Spider Woman*, from those accounts that see it as postmodern in one way or another.

Countercultural politics have powerfully conditioned the very possibility that there might be a specifically sexual radicalism. Nonetheless, there were queers before Stonewall who organized and socialized, and John d'Emilio has demonstrated that the events of 1969 were not some spontaneous outburst, but rather emerged out of forms of consciousness that subcultures were generating for years beforehand.[40] That account does a great deal to reinforce Alan Sinfield's explicitly cultural materialist theorization of subcultures, and it is to this that I turn in chapter four in order to attempt an evaluation of its continuing relevance. According to it, LGBTQ subculture is a mixed, rather than necessarily radical, space, and the value Sinfield places on it takes account of that fact. Sinfield's work resists avant-gardism, whether queer or Marxist, while remaining principled in its socialist engagements. Subcultures are persistent in this account of them, but the chapter is concerned with their qualitative development and integrity under conditions dictated by the diversified dominant.

Concluding a book of this sort has presented significant difficulties. I can offer no grounds for great optimism for socialists, or for the potential in current circumstances of a politics of sexuality to converge with their aspirations. We live in times of crisis that offer renewed potential for critique, because that crisis is not an accident of the system, but part of the way it works. Nonetheless, there is no inevitably progressive way out of these times, and they have already damaged millions of people's lives. For those who simply want sex, capitalism can deliver the goods in superabundance; their 'sex needs' can be amply satisfied. Or, at least, this is the impression that is given in relation to those who have a reasonable income and live in the right parts of the world, as many who read this book will do. As I shall argue, though, that superabundance is part of the problem in a variety of senses, and the paths to some form of liberation lie rather in resisting it, without falling prey to puritanism.

---

40  John d'Emilio, *Sexual Politics, Sexual Communities: The Making of a Homosexual Minority in the United States*, Chicago: University of Chicago Press, 1983.

Finally, though, I must acknowledge a limitation to the account I provide here with which I have consciously struggled throughout. The book is overwhelmingly, if not exclusively, concerned with gay male contexts. What could be more *un*queer than that? Gay men are frequently enough held up as the quintessential 'homonormative' subjects these days on account of the potential they hold for assimilation by virtue of being men, and especially if they are white and even relatively prosperous (as I must acknowledge I am). In anticipation of that criticism, I can only say a number of things: I think that gay male experience *is* distinctive for better and worse, and in any case for very specific historical reasons explored in chapter two especially; that either blurring this distinctiveness with the general ferment of queer, or simply repudiating it, may be a means of avoiding necessary scrutiny of it; and that, for precisely these reasons, gay male experience is a legitimate focus. I do not believe that some gay men's social privileges in certain respects make them necessarily reactionary individually, but I doubt anyone will accuse the book of being uncritical or self-congratulatory. It may be thought that the very act of focusing on gay male experience perpetuates the very distinctiveness I highlight, but that is a problem I have found insuperable in relation to the present project without extending its scope yet further.

I

## Transitions

### Postmodernity, neoliberalism, hegemony

In 1984, Fredric Jameson published his essay, 'Postmodernism, or the Cultural Logic of Late Capitalism', claiming we had entered 'the purest form of capital yet to have emerged',[1] and one which was for that reason qualitatively distinctive. As I remarked in the introduction, the category he used to describe this stage has since substantially fallen out of fashion, though it is one that he has consistently defended.[2] Jameson's essay may well be less familiar to readers today than it was to those of my generation, among whom it was ubiquitous, so I shall rehearse some of its key arguments here. In doing so, however, I want to focus on certain influences on Jameson's highly eclectic presentation of his case that are not normally accorded such prominence. These are ideas associated with Williams and Marcuse, some of which I have already outlined

---

1  Fredric Jameson, *Postmodernism, or the Cultural Logic of Late Capitalism*, London: Verso, 1991, p. 36. The original essay, reproduced largely unchanged in this book-length account, was published in *New Left Review I*, 146, July–August 1984, pp. 53–92.
2  Most recently, by focusing on the category of singularity, as well as the displacement of temporal by spatial consciousness, in 'The Cosmonaut's Report' (*New Left Review*, 92, March–April 2015, pp. 101–132).

in the introduction. My reasons for focusing on them have to do with a dissatisfaction with the ways that he and others theorize the period with which this book is concerned, and especially the kind of qualitative transition in capitalism that most would agree has taken place.

I focus largely on Jameson's first essay on the topic rather than later accounts by him, both because of its general influence, and because it is necessary to an understanding of a less well-known adaptation by Marianne DeKoven in her book, *Utopia Limited* (2004), of many of the ideas expressed there. DeKoven presents arguments about politics that draw on, but are not consistent with, Jameson's purposes. Whereas Jameson professes a certain moral neutrality with regard to postmodernity on the grounds that it is an established fact there is no point in lamenting,[3] DeKoven is instead a positive enthusiast for the phenomenon. She views it as an advance in all sorts of ways over modernity, in spite of a certain nostalgia she feels for the latter, and especially for the idealism of the movements of the sixties. Her position is therefore more characteristic of the postmodern left than Jameson's, and there is no question in her case about the appropriateness of that label; it is one she embraces.

The late capitalism of Jameson's title is an allusion to a book whose argument underpins his. Ernest Mandel describes a three-stage development from freely competitive to monopoly capitalism, and thence to a late capitalism that first emerges in the 1940s. This last stage is characterized by multinational corporations, increasingly global markets, and intensified consumerism, though Mandel also presciently places great importance on the mobility of the finance capital that has since taken on an even more

---

3 Jameson, *Postmodernism*, pp. 46–47.

extravagant life of its own. Jameson claims that the three stages Mandel outlines have successively determined aesthetic realism, modernism and postmodernism.[4] The defining features of this last stage consist in two kinds of 'prodigious expansion' whose intimacy seems to prompt this identical phrasing about them, even though the precise nature of their relationship is left unclear.

The first of these expansions is that of capital itself 'into hitherto uncommodified areas'[5] that most strikingly include the formerly pre-capitalist third world in consequence of the 'green revolution' in agriculture,[6] and the subjective unconscious through the influence of the media and advertising. These two 'spaces' have generated distinctive kinds of resistance in the past. The second expansion Jameson points to is of a formerly semi-autonomous culture that has now become disseminated

throughout the social realm, to the point at which everything in our social life – from economic value and state power to practices and to the very psyche itself – can be said to be 'cultural' in some original and yet untheorized sense.[7]

This expansion is a curious one, since it is predicated on a supposed prior restriction of modernist culture, whose limited circulation among a self-conscious aesthetic elite facilitated its preservation of a certain utopian promise through the artwork's distance from, critical relation to and transfiguration of reality.

---

4   Ibid., pp. 35–36.
5   Ibid., p. 36.
6   To be clear, this term refers to the dramatic postwar increases in agricultural productivity that are actually contributory factors to the ecological crisis we face.
7   Jameson, *Postmodernism*, p. 48.

Under postmodernism, by contrast, culture has apparently expanded, not merely through the culture industry as identified by the Frankfurt School, but also through the proliferation of images and other modes of signification attendant on developments in the field of communication technology to the point of having become absolutely ubiquitous. Of course, since this essay was written, all the developments said to have determined the emergence of postmodernism have intensified (think of smartphones, for instance, and the even more rapid circulation they facilitate). If Jameson was right back in 1984, we must be more securely postmodern now than ever. Marianne DeKoven even cites this as the reason for the term's demise: the postmodern condition is so ubiquitous as to have 'become invisible'.[8]

The cultural effects of capital's expansion, however, are made evident to us in Jameson's account through readings of novels, poetry, art photography, architecture, painting and so on. These works may have an ideological character, he suggests, in their playfully diverting qualities, but they also manifest a certain realism. This is not because they are generically realist – they do not aspire to recreate a plausible, recognizable world for us – but because they effectively convey traits that are associated with contemporary sensibilities. These include: the resort to blank pastiche and affectlessness, rather than parody; a displacement of temporal awareness by spatial consciousness; random heterogeneity, fragmentation and incoherence. The purpose in highlighting these characteristic works may be evinced from Jameson's concluding point that a

8  Marianne DeKoven, *Utopia Limited: The Sixties and the Emergence of the Postmodern*, Durham, NC: Duke University Press, 2004, p. 9.

new political art (if it is possible) will have to hold to the truth of postmodernism, that is to say, to its fundamental object – the world space of multinational capital – at the same time at which it achieves a breakthrough to some as yet unimaginable new mode of representing this last, in which we may again begin to grasp our positioning as individual and collective subjects and regain a capacity to act and struggle which is at present neutralized by our spatial as well as our social confusion.[9]

In considering Jameson's argument in more detail, though, I shall not be concerned with his specific readings of artworks; in relation to these, I shall simply say that his tendency to divorce the ideological from the realistic properties of those works, without taking into account questions of cultural production – institutions and ideologies of art, that is, that mediate their relations with reality – is one that is abrupt and obviously problematic. However, I am more concerned with his characterization of the kind of world that generates the consciousness said to be evinced by these works.

When Jameson speaks of the cultural dominance of modernism and postmodernism, he clearly means two quite distinct things. Whereas artistic modernism is held to have been dominant because it was the most advanced, most self-consciously uncompromising and experimental form of cultural production of its time, culture under postmodernism is dominant in the sense that it is everywhere. Modernism occupied a peculiar status in a distinct cultural sphere, but postmodernism saturates society with a culture that takes on uncritical, because integrated, commodified forms. At various points, Jameson qualifies this claim by allowing for 'the presence and coexistence of a range of very different, yet

---

9 Jameson, *Postmodernism*, p. 54.

subordinate, features',[10] but appears to be contradicting himself.[11] Jameson's formulation proposes that culture as he understands it here is coextensive with capitalist totality as such ('everything in our social life'). This accounts for his initial 'failure' to distinguish between postmodernism (a style) and postmodernity (a historical period)[12]: the latter is defined by the other's utter pervasiveness, so that the two are inseparably merged.

The most significant influence on Jameson in this essay is that of the Hegelian Marxist tradition, though not in the form of the most obvious candidate, Georg Lukács, about whom Jameson has written extensively and sympathetically, and often against the grain of Marxist theorizing.[13] The account of modernist culture's critical relationship to capitalist society draws instead on the arguments of Marcuse in his famous essay on 'affirmative culture',[14] but I would go so far as to say that Marcuse is plausibly the dominant

---

10    Ibid., p. 4.
11    Perry Anderson offers a compelling defence of Jameson, but he is too confident that Jameson is describing 'a dominant ... and no more' (*The Origins of Postmodernism*, London: Verso, 1998, p. 64). Steve Best does an excellent job of defending Jameson from the charges of postmodern thinkers that his insistence on totality negates difference in 'Jameson, Totality, and the Poststructuralist Critique', in Douglas Kellner, ed., *Postmodernism/Jameson/Critique*, Washington, DC: Maisonneuve Press, 1989, pp. 333–368. Elsewhere, indeed, Jameson has acknowledged that his account of postmodernity is a totalizing one: 'Marxism and Postmodernism', in Kellner, ed., *Postmodernism/Jameson/Critique*, pp. 369–387.
12    Mike Davis points out this failure, 'Urban Renaissance and the Spirit of Postmodernism', *New Left Review I*, 151, May–June 1985, p. 107, and Jameson corrects himself in 'The Cosmonaut's Report', p. 104, but in a way that does not adequately address the problem.
13    Jameson wrote in powerful defence of Lukács in the early seventies in *Marxism and Form: Twentieth Century Dialectical Theories of Literature*, Princeton: Princeton University Press, 1974, pp. 160–205.
14    Herbert Marcuse, 'The Affirmative Character of Culture', in *Negations*, London: Allen Lane, 1968, pp. 88–133.

influence on Jameson's whole essay, since it effectively describes a state of one-dimensionality that is even more entrenched than that proclaimed by Marcuse in the sixties. Not only did Marcuse there first draw attention to the integration of art into consumer society, but he also spoke of repressive desublimation, or the commodified sexualization of everyday life. The main distinction between the world Marcuse describes and the one we encounter in Jameson relates to the third world, whose often militant resistance to western imperialism in the postwar world had apparently been exhausted by the early eighties. Today, under conditions often described as 'globalized', the very category of third world is redundant,[15] though continuing disparities of wealth and divisions of labour are indicated by reference instead to the global south. Jameson is arguing that postmodernism represents the globalization of one-dimensionality.[16]

While basing her account on Jameson's, DeKoven presents a compressed, somewhat different version of this shift. She gives an abstract and schematic discussion of the distinctive properties of modernity and postmodernity that goes beyond the economic and cultural foci of Jameson's essay to allude to political movements. Modernity, she claims, was dominated by ideals of freedom that were nonetheless contradicted by their hegemonic form. Hence, 'the white, bourgeois western man [was] the Self of modernity ... defined in opposition to its oppressed, suppressed Others of race, gender, class, nation, and location.'[17] Modernism, however, as

---

15  For reflections on the transition I am alluding to here, see Michael Denning, *Culture in the Age of Three Worlds*, London: Verso, 2004.

16  He has, indeed, spoken casually of 'one-dimensional societies like our own' (Fredric Jameson, 'The Antinomies of Postmodernity', *The Cultural Turn: Selected Writings on the Postmodern, 1993–1998*, London: Verso, 1998, p. 56).

17  DeKoven, *Utopia Limited*, p. 13.

the dominant aesthetic movement of the early twentieth century, was bound to various crises in which 'modernity's hegemonies'[18] came to be contested by those 'Others'. Modernity is therefore characterized by dialectical forms of contestation and conflict.

Postmodernity, by contrast, results in a displacement of such clashing forces through the emergence of a dominant, globalized capitalism characterized by pervasive commodification, dramatic technological innovation and spectacular cultural forms, bringing with it inequality and environmental destruction. Although these conditions appear to sponsor unwelcome resistant fundamental-isms DeKoven notes but does not consider, they have also gener-ated diverse, particularistic and localized movements that do not presume to challenge the system as such, but are to be welcomed for this very reason.[19] This indicates her postmodern affiliations: such movements are simultaneously more democratic and less utopian than those that typified modernism. 'The democratic proj-ect of modernity', she suggests, 'has become in postmodernity at once (in its historical link with capitalism) a project of capitalist globalization, and also, at the same time, a project of egalitarian populism.'[20]

Indeed, DeKoven's case might be put more strongly: contem-porary movements are more democratic precisely because they are not utopian. The reason for this is that so-called master, or meta-, narratives now seem to her not only implausibly ambitious, but actually 'oppressive',[21] as they entail a privileging of certain

---

18   Ibid., p. 14.
19   DeKoven draws on 'The Antinomies of Postmodernity', in which Jameson speaks of postmodernity in terms of the (apparent) erosion of any sense of productive contradiction (*The Cultural Turn*, pp. 50–72).
20   DeKoven, *Utopia Limited*, p. 15.
21   Ibid., p. 16.

political struggles over others. While claiming to be attracted in some respects by the idealism of the past, then, Dekoven engages in the kind of extended critique of the supposedly modernist left that has animated and preoccupied postmodern thought in general far more consistently than any disagreements it has with the political right.

I find DeKoven's account unclear on key points it seems relevant to mention, though these are not the issues I wish to focus on especially. For instance, metanarratives seem to legitimate what she calls 'modernist hegemonies', and also to be the framework within which oppositional movements work. Thus, at one level, she seems to be suggesting a certain equivalence between the dominant and those who opposed it on the basis of their common formal, 'narrative' justifications, but without clarifying what the significance for her of that equivalence is. In other words, these movements seem somehow appropriate to the forms of hegemony to which they responded, and yet to reproduce the oppressive, because exclusive, features of those hegemonies. Furthermore, modernity was characterized by diverse oppositional movements, even on DeKoven's account, but they were also frequently solidaristic, so it is not wholly clear why they are also convicted of consistently privileging one cause over another. One can easily think of instances where this was the case, of course – and even of ones where the labour movement reproduced racism, or anti-colonialism reproduced sexism – but it is surely a reductive history that suggests this was always and everywhere so. Moreover, postmodernity may have generated a proliferation of movements in DeKoven's description of it, but it isn't clear why we should simply welcome their plurality as such without evaluatively considering their particular causes. Nor is it clear why their singularity is a virtue, given that this suggests – or, at least, must surely facilitate

– an absence of solidarity, and may even sponsor a competitive spirit among them. The sense that these movements constitute a desirable diversity attributes to them a kind of unity that is predicated on a perspective left inexplicit.

Moreover – and to move on to a point more pertinent to my overall argument – while DeKoven recognizes, at least in passing, that postmodernity has brought with it greater inequality, she is unclear about what relationship she is proposing between that inequality and the 'egalitarian populism' she welcomes. Alan Sinfield, by contrast, has argued that it is naïve to perceive a more general democratization taking place in the breakdown of high and low cultural forms: 'it is likely,' he writes, 'that the fading of certain kinds of hierarchy is producing the compensatory strengthening of others'.[22] Pop music in Britain, for instance, is now dominated by the privately educated,[23] even while it reproduces the gestural repertoire of revolt against the mature and supposedly conservative in the cause of (mostly sexual) desire. The highly privileged now dominate even the popular cultural sphere as celebrities, because there are lucrative careers to be made there, and money is the great solvent of any principled commitment to 'cultural standards' elite schools might have instilled in the past. This is a far from trivial point, as it highlights the ways in which social relations are mediated in the kind of totality with which we are concerned.

DeKoven's validation of postmodernity also occurs through an explicit revision of Marcuse's arguments about one-dimensionality

22  Alan Sinfield, *Literature, Politics and Culture in Postwar Britain*, third edition, London: Continuum, 2004, p. 334.
23  'Public School Singers Take Over the Pop Charts', *The Daily Mail*, 5 December 2010, http://www.dailymail.co.uk/tvshowbiz/article-1335880/Public-school-singers-pop-charts-60-acts-privately-educated.html (accessed 6 June 2012).

(and, implicitly, of Jameson's tacit reliance on them). She claims that Marcuse's wholly negative account of one-dimensional life evinces a characteristically modernist, revolutionary sensibility that blinds him to postmodern truths and possibilities. What Marcuse regards as one-dimensionality, she suggests, 'also often describes what has come to be positively valued in some postmodern theories as complicitous critique or resistance from within'. Postmodern resistance, by contrast, rejects master narratives

> in favour of broader, more egalitarian, and more realistic notions of everyday tactics [that] involve partial, local refunctioning and subversion, not of a totalized domination but of an incomplete, malleable, shifting, continually redefined, recontested, and reinstituted hegemony.[24]

One-dimensionality is not so stark, after all, and is actually more agreeable than the situation that obtained under modernity.

DeKoven also follows Jameson's mode of thinking about the transition to postmodernity in terms of Williams's categories of dominant, residual and emergent to which I now turn. At stake here is the distinction between the categories of totality and hegemony I have been so far merely alluding to, so let me attempt a brief account of that distinction. Totality is a term that has been invoked in different ways within the Marxist tradition as a means of grasping capitalism as a system.[25] It rejects the empiricist analysis of phenomena as isolated facts, and insists rather on understanding them in their relations with each other

---

24  DeKoven, *Utopia Limited*, p. 30.
25  Martin Jay charts these differences in usage in *Marxism and Totality: The Adventures of a Concept from Lukács to Habermas*, Cambridge: Polity Press, 1984.

in a way that helps us appreciate their determination by the forces and relations of production, the material means by which that society is quite literally made. For the most part, this system has been grasped as contradictory, and therefore productive of crisis and conflict, but Marcuse's one-dimensional totality is defined by its absence of contradiction, an absence that is accentuated still further by Jameson.

Hegemony is distinct from this. As we have already seen, in the most influential version of it elaborated by Gramsci, it relates to class direction, or leadership, of society, and the ways this secures popular consent for that leadership. The exercise of hegemony, in other words, may be said to take place within a complex and contradictory totality as a means of seeking to stabilize it. Admittedly, this distinction is a difficult one to think through, given the intimacy of the two in any society in which hegemony is effective, and especially in Williams's version of it as a dominant that is evident not simply through the dissemination of ideas, but also the structuring of lived experience.

Williams was very clear about this distinction and his reasons for preferring Gramsci over Lukács (who defined the Marxist tradition in terms of its concern with totality):

> the key question to ask about any notion of totality in cultural theory is this: whether the notion of totality includes the notion of intention. For if totality is simply concrete, if it is simply the recognition of a large variety of miscellaneous and contemporaneous practices [as Williams suggests it is in Lukács], then it is essentially empty of any content that could be called Marxist. Intention, the notion of intention, restores the key question, or rather the key emphasis. For while it is true that any society is a complex whole of such practices, it is also true that

any society has a specific organization, a specific structure, and that the principles of this organization and structure can be seen as directly related to certain social intentions, intentions by which we define the society, intentions which in all our experience have been the rule of a particular class.[26]

If we accept for the sake of this discussion, at least, that the category of totality as it was developed by Lukács was indeed devoid of a sense intentionality, that void has been further emphasized in subsequent accounts that have been influential on Jameson. Marcuse's description of postwar, Fordist-Keynesian societies emphasizes a pervasive regulation and uniformity, such that 'control is normally administered by offices in which the controlled are the employers and the employed'.[27] Jameson accepts the Marcusean argument about deprivatization,[28] and may also have been less consciously influenced by the anti-humanist 'sophistication' of structuralist Marxism,[29] but, in any case, when he does speak somewhat vaguely of 'the class origins of postmodernism', he does so only in the context of 'late capitalism', and 'as some "non-human" logic of capital'.[30]

26  Raymond Williams, 'Base and Superstructure in Marxist Cultural Theory', *New Left Review*, 82, November–December 1973, p. 7.
27  Herbert Marcuse, *Eros and Civilization: A Philosophical Inquiry Into Freud*, London: Routledge, 1987, p. 98. This comes in a section that anticipates that in *One-Dimensional Man*.
28  Jameson, *Postmodernism*, pp. 14–15.
29  Althusser and Etienne Balibar famously highlight a term used by Marx when they write that 'the structure of the relations determines the functions occupied and adopted by the agents of production, who are never anything more than the occupants of these places, insofar as they are "supports" (*Träger*) of these functions' (*Reading Capital, Reading Capital*, trans. Ben Brewster, London: Verso, 1970, p. 198).
30  Fredric Jameson, 'Marxism/Postmodernism', in Kellner (ed.), *Postmodernism*, pp. 382–383.

Williams's focus on intention contrasts with this, and I shall return to it in a moment.

Both Jameson and DeKoven adopt and adapt Williams's categories to convey the transition to postmodernity as, in Steven Best's words, an '*ab utero* shift within the general conditions of capitalism'.[31] Perhaps this is best registered by DeKoven's phrasing of the case: 'the modern,' she writes, 'was dominant in the sixties, then became residual; the postmodern was emergent in the sixties, then became dominant'. She claims to use these terms as 'markers of the specific dynamics of historical change, without the implications of progress from capitalism to socialism (or of any teleology) that inhere in Williams's Marxist development of these terms.'[32] She nonetheless suggests an all-too-obvious teleology based on her summary of Jameson's clearly totalizing case: postmodernism represents 'the cultural dominant of a triumphant consumer capitalism'.[33]

In fact, Williams's categories are not obviously teleological. The sense of a periodizing transition that both DeKoven and Jameson convey through them represents a problematic revision of his purposes.[34] Talk of aesthetic modernism, Williams once claimed, entails the retrospective imposition of a selective tradition that fetishizes exceptional, cosmopolitan perspectives with all of their sense of linguistic and cultural dislocation. From the perspective of modernism, Williams suggests, 'all that is left to us is to become

---

31  This is Steven Best's phrasing about Jameson ('Jameson, Totality', p. 357).
32  DeKoven, *Utopia Limited*, p. 18.
33  Ibid., p. 10.
34  It may be that these terms lend themselves to this usage because they arguably retain an organicist dimension from his early work. On this, see Terry Eagleton, *Criticism and Ideology: A Study in Marxist Literary Theory*, London: Verso, 1976, pp. 32–42.

postmoderns'.[35] The important point to stress, again, is that the categories of dominant, residual and emergent are *not* primarily cultural categories. They are invoked to establish in the present a simultaneity of different, though temporally determined, social forms and values that may be productive of conflict. The nature of any such conflict is not specified, and the outcome is not taken for granted.

I am aware that all of this may sound merely technical, or academic in the pejorative sense, but actually the restoration of Williams's original emphases may permit us to appreciate more clearly transitions in capitalism that are effectively masked by what is presented as a smooth, if consequential, shift from modernity to postmodernity. After all, in his own introduction to the revised edition of *Late Capitalism* in 1975, Ernest Mandel notes that 'belief in the permanence of the "mixed economy" has proved a myth'.[36] Mike Davis has pointed out that it was Mandel's purpose in *Late Capitalism* to understand the postwar boom that was bound up with such mixed economies, and which he understood to have ended by the mid-seventies.[37] The narrow emphasis in both Jameson's and DeKoven's work on commodification/consumption, along with the postulation that *these* are 'dominant', facilitates the cultural-theoretical elision of that profoundly dramatic historical shift. It can be grasped in two somewhat distinct, but related, ways. I shall rely on the versions of both offered by David Harvey.

The first is of a transition to neoliberalism, and my reasons

35   Raymond Williams, *The Politics of Modernism: Against the New Conformists*, London: Verso, 1989, p. 32.
36   Ernest Mandel, *Late Capitalism*, London: New Left Books, 1975, p. 8.
37   Davis, 'Urban Renaissance and the Spirit of Postmodernism', pp. 107–108.

for coming to it first are bound up with Williams's focus on intention. Harvey's case is that neoliberalism emerged out of the economic crises of the seventies through the spreading influence of the ideas promoted by Friedrich Hayek, Milton Friedman, the Mont Pelerin Society and the Chicago School of Economics more generally, but also through other think tanks and institutions that proliferated as a result of the breakdown of the Keynesian consensus. Subsequent accounts have tended to provide more detailed confirmation of the one found in Harvey, even if they sometimes suggest questionable limitations to Harvey's characterization of what this entailed.[38]

These versions, moreover, are more satisfactory than the one we get in the influential account given by Foucault in 1979, but only recently published and translated, which overemphasizes the role of the German 'ordoliberal' traditions and the example of the postwar Federal Republic of Germany that had, by then, 'become the programme of most governments in capitalist countries'.[39] However, the lectures themselves were given in the year of Thatcher's accession to power in Britain, and one year before Reagan's in the US. Daniel Stedman Jones's account , by contrast, emphasizes the importance of a 'transatlantic alliance'

---

38  Jones, for instance, claims that neoliberalism was not merely dominated by neoclassical economics, or the Chicago School, but was 'a cocktail, united not just by a belief in the superiority of markets – or, more reductively, corporations – but also by a distrust of state authority, intervention, and bureaucracy'. He also emphasizes 'new bridges between the academy and politics' (*Masters of the Universe*, p. 14). The traits he appears to suggest are not registered by Harvey – or by others, such as Andrew Glyn – seem to me apparent in Harvey's account, even if it is less detailed than Jones's own.

39  Michel Foucault, *The Birth of Biopolitics: Lectures at the Collège de France, 1978–79*, ed. Michel Senellart and trans. Graham Burchell, London: Picador, 2008, p. 149.

in which ordoliberal influence figured, but was not especially prominent.[40]

Harvey's account is distinct from others that broadly confirm it, however, in drawing on the work of Gérard Duménil and Dominique Lévy[41] to suggest that neoliberalism was a project aimed at re-establishing class power, even if it did so ultimately through the reconfiguration of that power. That it has been informed, or justified, by a certain utopianism of its own about market freedom being the indispensable basis of individual freedom is clear, but Harvey pointedly demonstrates that, while 'neoliberalization has not been very effective in revitalizing global capital accumulation ... it has succeeded remarkably well in restoring, or in some instances (as in Russia and China) creating, the power of an economic elite'.[42] To return to the argument I am pursuing, then, we might recapitulate the objection Williams makes about Lukács: whereas Jameson's and DeKoven's accounts of postmodernity may be concrete, and in this sense materialist, others restore a properly Gramscian emphasis on intention by speaking of neoliberal hegemony.

The account Harvey gives us is of an ultimately global dominant that has resulted from a confluence of often quite disparate forces,

---

40  Daniel Stedman Jones, *Masters of the Universe: Hayek, Friedman, and the Birth of Neoliberal Politics*, Princeton: Princeton University Press, 2012, pp. 85–133. Broadly speaking, this is confirmed by Jamie Peck in *Constructions of Neoliberal Reason*, Oxford: Oxford University Press, 2010, pp. 39–81.
41  Harvey's account is deeply indebted to that of Gérard Duménil and Dominique Lévy in *Capital Resurgent: Roots of the Neoliberal Revolution*, Cambridge, Mass.: Harvard University Press, 2004. See also their summary of this case in 'The Neoliberal (Counter-)Revolution', in *Neoliberalism: A Critical Reader*, Alfredo Saad-Filho and Deborah Johnston, eds, London: Pluto, 2005, pp. 9–19.
42  David Harvey, *A Brief History of Neoliberalism*, Oxford: Oxford University Press, 2005, p. 19.

not always consciously acting in concert, but nonetheless under specific conditions and to obvious purposes. This accords with the popular rhetoric that sees the world now configured in the interests of the 1%. While this is clearly a symbolic figure, since those who comprise it have not been the only beneficiaries, it is nonetheless a telling one: a recent Oxfam report indicates that that proportion of the world's population will own over 50% of its wealth by 2016.[43] There are actually quite widely publicized means of grasping global capitalism as a totality dominated by certain interests.

A further factor that may have facilitated Jameson's and DeKoven's discussion of the postmodern is that the shift to neoliberalism has surely been more apparent *outside* the US, since capitalism there in the postwar period was relatively speaking less pure, to use Jameson's term.[44] The 'welfare capitalism' that Sinfield describes as having been installed in Britain after the war, for instance, is so called to stress its character as a compromise formation intended to protect against more radical, possibly even revolutionary, demands,[45] but it has commonly been seen in the US as socialism itself. Indeed, the emergence of neoliberal hegemony is plausibly regarded as Americanization.[46]

---

43 The report can be found at http://policy-practice.oxfam.org.uk/publications/wealth-having-it-all-and-wanting-more-338125 (accessed 19 January 2015).
44 A good summary of the continuities, as well as shifts, in the US is offered by Al Campbell, 'The Birth of Neoliberalism in the United States: A Reorganization of Capitalism', in Saad-Filho, *Neoliberalism*, pp. 187–198.
45 Sinfield, *Postwar Britain*, p. 19.
46 The most extensive elaboration of such a view is offered by Leo Panich and Sam Gindin in *The Making of Global Capitalism: The Political Economy of American Empire*, London: Verso, 2013, the implications of which I regret not to have had the opportunity to incorporate fully into this book. Actually, Americanization is how Jameson accounts for postmodernity (Jameson, *Postmodernism*, p. 5).

While the Reagan agenda included punitive cutbacks to what was a more limited welfare state, as well as attacks on unions, the transition to neoliberalism in most of the world outside the US has been more disruptive of postwar norms because politics were always less 'consensual' in the US. The New Deal regime never enjoyed wholehearted support, and the genealogy of Reaganism takes us back to Barry Goldwater's unsuccessful campaign for the presidency – to which Milton Friedman gave advice[47] – in the sixties. Elsewhere, therefore, neoliberalism has been accompanied by more intense, often violent and deeply traumatic forms of politicized conflict that have left lasting marks socially and culturally. In Britain, for instance, the extraordinary year-long miners' strike of 1984–1985 was a watershed in the very purposeful defeat of the left.[48] This was but one example of the peculiar rapacity of a neoliberal capitalism that Harvey argues has been determined by its renewed dependence on crude accumulation by dispossession, rather than merely accumulation through expansion; that is, through land and resource grabs, evident in the continuing privatization of state industries and public services, as well as the 'new imperialism' of the war for oil in Iraq.[49] Meanwhile, Naomi Klein speaks convincingly of neoliberalism as having been advanced substantially through deployment of the shock doctrine: the inducement or exploitation of crises in order to impose free-market

47  See Jones, *Masters of the Universe*, pp. 197–201.
48  See, for instance, my account of the strike and lingering sympathy for the miners in relation to the film *Billy Elliot*: 'Making Electricity: Narrating Gender, Sexuality, and the Neoliberal Transition in *Billy Elliot*', *Camera Obscura*, 25(3), 2011, pp. 1–27.
49  David Harvey, *The New Imperialism*, Oxford: Oxford University Press, 2003, pp. 137–182.

'solutions',[50] a tactic still evident today in attempts to impose austerity as the appropriate response to the system's own most devastating and persistent financial crisis to date.

I am not, of course, arguing that either Jameson or DeKoven is unaware of neoliberalism as either dogma or practice, or indeed of other features of contemporary capitalism that I shall come to in a moment: the point is rather that they do not recognize its distinctiveness on the basis of its historical emergence through intensified class conflict.[51] Their account of the emergence of postmodernity, indeed, encourages us to overlook it.[52]

To speak of neoliberal, rather than postmodern, hegemony is therefore to emphasize a very determined kind of right-wing agency as pursued through, and transformative of, institutions: the purposeful dissemination of ideas and the establishment of a kind of common sense that aspires to saturate society 'to such an extent ... that it corresponds to the reality of social experience'.[53] Wendy Brown recognizes precisely this when she claims that neoliberalism

> must be conceived of as more than a set of free market economic policies that dismantle welfare states and privatize

---

50  Naomi Klein, *The Shock Doctrine: The Rise of Disaster Capitalism,* London: Allen Lane, 2007.

51  Unsurprisingly, perhaps, this is not wholly true of Jameson. In an essay published the same year as the 'Postmodernism' one, 'Periodizing the Sixties', he acknowledges – again via Mandel – the global economic crisis that brought that decade to an end (Sohnya Sayres, Anders Stephanson, Stanley Aronowitz, and Fredric Jameson, eds, *The Sixties Without Apology,* Minneapolis: University of Minnesota Press, 1984, pp. 204–209).

52  This, indeed, was the thrust of Davis's response to Jameson's essay in his alternative account of postmodern architecture's relations to finance capital, and the redevelopment of Los Angeles ('Urban Renaissance and the Spirit of Postmodernism', pp. 108–110).

53  Williams, 'Base', p. 8.

public service in the North, make wreckage of efforts at democratic sovereignty or economic self-direction in the South and
intensify income disparities everywhere [...] it also involves a
specific and consequential organization of the social, the subject and the state.[54]

There are nonetheless a number of criticisms that might be
made of Williams's categories. The first is that, although there
can be no doubt on the basis of his work as a whole that he was
committed to the achievement of a *socialist* hegemony, his model
suggests few terms for grasping it as a possibility. Rather, the
implication is that the dominant is forced to assimilate residual or
emergent forces that challenge it. Hence the charge levelled at him
of gradualism. More significant for the context I am concerned
with, though, is that this account failed – understandably, no
doubt – to anticipate the possibility that the political *right* might
itself generate emergent forces that would carry an inherent
potential for achieving hegemony in appropriate conditions,
since they went in many respects with the grain.[55] Stuart Hall
was right to characterize Thatcherism as a transformation within
the hegemonic bloc,[56] and we must acknowledge along with this

---

54 Wendy Brown, 'American Nightmare: Neoliberalism, Neoconservatism,
and DeDemocratization', *Political Theory*, 34(6), 2006, p. 693. My focus
on hegemony, however, contrasts with Brown's Foucaultian one on a more
abstract political rationality in *Undoing the Demos*.

55 Something like this was subsequently recognized by Williams in
his abstract, but compelling, account in 1983 of 'Plan X' as a future-
oriented, rather than conservative, politics that was nonetheless 'a willed
and deliberate unknown, in which the only deciding factor is advantage'
(*Towards 2000*, London: Hogarth Press, 1983, p. 244).

56 This is how Stuart Hall theorizes Thatcherism: see 'The Great Moving
Right Show', in *The Hard Road to Renewal: Thatcherism and the Crisis of the
Left*, London: Verso, 1988, pp. 39–53.

its sequestration of terms such as freedom, modernization and progress, though recent crises may have begun to dislodge some of these ideological appropriations.

In coming to the second transition I want to emphasize, I have to acknowledge a certain sleight of hand on my part in the argument so far by having contrasted DeKoven's and Jameson's writings on the postmodern with Harvey's on neoliberalism specifically. That is to say, I might more appropriately have invoked the latter's own earlier work, *The Condition of Postmodernity* (1989). My defence is that I wanted to highlight more acutely the contrast between the categories of hegemony and totality. In his book on postmodernity, the transition with which Harvey is concerned is that from Fordism to post-Fordism, and the world he describes is more consistent with the one we find in Jameson. In the specifics he provides, however, Harvey provides a further challenge to the adequacy of the latter's account.

His case is that the characteristic elements of a postmodern sensibility have been determined by an uneven, but manifest, shift away from Fordist regimes of accumulation to globalized non- or post-Fordist forms of flexible accumulation, necessitated, like the shift to neoliberalism, by the overaccumulation crises of the late sixties and seventies. I phrase this very carefully, as Harvey only tentatively accepts the language and thinking of the regulation school of economists on which he draws for the Fordism/ post-Fordism distinction. The pervasiveness of the material transformations he describes of corporate restructuring and outsourcing of production, along with an increasing deregulation of work, extraordinary levels of technological innovation – not least in forms of communication – and greater efficiencies in production and distribution (e.g. just-in-time delivery), cannot be doubted. They have generated a remarkable diversification and turnover of products. Crucially, all of this has been accompanied and facilitated by an exponential growth in and deregulation of the financial sector. The result of these pressures has been an extraordinary intensification of what Harvey calls the time–space compression of modernity – the experience, that is, of a shrinking and faster world – with characteristically disorienting effects. In cultural terms, he suggests, 'the relatively stable aesthetic of Fordist modernism has given way to all the ferment, instability, and fleeting qualities of a postmodernist aesthetic that celebrates difference, ephemerality, spectacle, fashion, and the commodification of cultural forms'.[57]

I have so far distinguished between two kinds of transition, from Keynesianism to neoliberalism, and from Fordism to post-Fordism, but these two may actually be regarded as one, since the terminology of post-Fordism not only relates to shifts in the forces and relations of production, but also the modes of economic (de)regulation that have accompanied and galvanized them. Nonetheless, neoliberalism deserves special acknowledgement in consequence of its peculiar and prominent militancy. If I were to summarize the argument so far, then, I would stress that, instead of speaking of postmodernity, it would be better to speak of neoliberalism as hegemonic within prevailing post-Fordist conditions. However, there are debates about the legitimacy of the terms Fordist and post-Fordist that I do not wish (and am

---

57   David Harvey, *The Condition of Postmodernity: An Enquiry Into the Origins of Cultural Change*, Oxford: Blackwell, 1990, p. 156. John Bellamy Foster and Fred Magdoff emphasize economic stagnation and capital overaccumulation as the spur to financialization in a series of crucial articles collected in *The Great Financial Crisis: Causes and Consequences*, New York: Monthly Review Press, 2009.

not competent) to adjudicate on here.[58] However, I dislike the persistent use of the 'post-' prefix as a means of defining the contemporary in terms of an (incomplete) supersession; it seems to me prone to nostalgia. Moreover, the past encompasses much, and there are traces of all of it in our present. Hence, I prefer to speak of neoliberal capitalism.[59] Where I have cause to, I refer to flexible accumulation, since this at least provides a positive characterization. However, one cannot simply choose one's terms, and 'postmodernism' has been used, often quite self-consciously, to refer to certain styles and sensibilities that are undoubtedly related to the kinds of material developments in capitalism Harvey outlines. I shall have cause from time to time to use that term – though also, at others, to resist it – while not accepting the validity of the further claim that we live in postmodernity.

It is necessary in light of all this to make some very brief and general distinctions – some of which I develop in later chapters – about the kinds of determination implied by the proliferation of commodity production under flexible accumulation, on the one hand, and the exercise of neoliberal hegemony, on the other. If neoliberalism seeks positively to determine a specific outlook, and thereby risks appearing authoritarian, inhuman, coercive or an affront to certain established forms of value or common

---

58 For a summary and critical evaluation of the terms, see Bob Jessop, 'Fordism and Post-Fordism: A Critical Reformulation', in A. J. Scott and M. J. Storper, eds, *Pathways to Industrialism and Regional Development*, London: Routledge, 1993, pp. 43–65. A good selection of papers on post-Fordism is contained in *Post-Fordism: A Reader*, Oxford: Blackwells, 1994, with an excellent introduction by Ash Amin, pp. 1–39.

59 In this respect, I echo the comment of Jordana Rosenberg and Amy Villarejo that 'neoliberalism is a qualifier for the more precise analytic and historical category of neoliberal capitalism', in 'Introduction: Queerness, Norms, Utopia', *GLQ*, 18(1), 2012, p. 3.

sense[60] – sometimes, indeed, as just plain stupid – an intensified commodification may not only fail to appear obviously ideological, but even encourages a sense of 'subversiveness' predicated on the market's circular production and 'satisfaction' of desires. This is not to suggest that dominant intention is absent from the sphere of consumption – after all, we do not merely buy, but *are sold*, things in ways that are seductive, aggressive or duplicitous – but there is at least some sense of needs being addressed. There are, however, areas in which the attempt to inculcate dogma converges with individualism with more mixed results, as when we are encouraged to view ourselves as consumers of, say, education or healthcare: we may or may not like it, but experience is structured in a way that renders resistance practically impossible. Only thus, perhaps, do we 'consent'.

There is, moreover, a further, related contradiction to emphasize here: flexible accumulation may produce ever more stuff, stimulating desire and dissatisfaction in equal measure, but it is predicated on intensified forms of exploitation and greater 'precarity' in work.[61] The problem with the kind of totality that DeKoven and Jameson outline is that it equates culture with consciousness, and sees both as determined (and exhausted) by the fact of an all-pervasive commodification that largely ignores the commodification of labour and its implications in terms of exploitation and alienation. Experience of the latter is pervasive, and is temporally

60 Jeremy Gilbert points out that even a closely argued Gramscian or post-Gramscian account of neoliberalism as hegemonic does not necessarily presume acceptance of, or enthusiasm for, its ideas among populations: 'What Kind of Thing is "Neoliberalism"?' *new formations*, 80–81, winter 2013, pp. 18–19.
61 See, for instance, Guy Standing, *The Precariat: The New Dangerous Class*, London: Bloomsbury, 2011. 'Precarity' is only new by comparison with Fordist-Keynesian regimes; prior to them it was the norm.

absolutely coincidental with capital accumulation: it cannot be described as residual or emergent, though it may give rise to emergent movements.

These latter points prompt me now to turn to a more direct engagement with Marcuse in a way that will allow me both to develop the critique I have been pursuing so far, and also to attempt a recovery of important insights from his earlier work, *Eros and Civilization*. This will – *finally*, the reader might say – allow me to connect that critique up with the category of sexuality.

## The performance principle

In 1970, Alasdair MacIntyre published an influential polemic against Marcuse, accusing him of being a pre-Marxist left-Hegelian who was 'endlessly willing to talk of "man" rather than of men'.[62] This is a somewhat exaggerated claim, though not one wholly without justice (even if it fails to correct the tendency to neglect sexual difference evident in much of Marcuse's work).[63]

---

62  Alasdair MacIntyre, *Marcuse*, London: Collins, 1970, p. 21. MacIntyre's case short-circuits any debate about Marx's indebtedness to Hegel. See W. Mark Cobb on both MacIntyre's and Foucault's critiques of Marcuse in 'Diatribes and Distortions: Marcuse's Academic Reception', in *Herbert Marcuse: A Critical Reader*, John Abromeit and W. Mark Cobb, eds, New York: Routledge, 2004, pp. 163–187. Peter Lind convincingly repudiates the charge, and questions MacIntyre's grasp of Marxism in *Marcuse and Freedom*, London: Croom Helm, 1984, pp. 11–15.

63  Marcuse was highly sympathetic to feminism as it emerged out of the general radicalism of the 1960s. See, for instance, *Counterrevolution and Revolt*, Boston, Mass.: Beacon Press, 1972, pp. 74–78. In *Eros*, though, the analysis inherits a Freudian focus on the male subject, even – and perhaps especially – when Marcuse positively entertains the possibility of a 'castration wish' through identification with the mother (pp. 228–233). Nonetheless, this represents a critique of bourgeois masculinity.

It is especially relevant to Marcusean claims of one-dimensionality, and may consequently also be suggested of those who extend that principle to talk of a pervasive postmodern consciousness.

Alex Callinicos makes the plausible argument that talk about postmodernity results from the experience of the defeat of revolutionary aspirations in the late 1960s among those who were destined for, and enjoyed the increasing benefits of, a middle-class existence that had expanded to absorb more people. During the seventies and eighties, this class enjoyed the benefits of an 'overconsumptionism' sponsored by redistributions of wealth upwards. This sounds crude, and there is no precise correspondence between the historical events and processes, on the one hand, and the emergence of ideas said to be postmodern, on the other, but Callinicos adds an important caveat:

> I do not claim that, say, Foucault's philosophy or Rushdie's fiction is in any very direct sense to be derived from the economic and political developments discussed above. I am rather concerned to explain here the *acceptance* by quite large numbers of people of certain ideas.[64]

Jameson is not an advocate of postmodern thought in this sense, but is rather attempting to theorize the conditions under which we live. Nonetheless, in his focus on the commodity, there is remarkably little attention paid to class differentiation. Lauren Berlant suggests that 'he mistakes the flat affects of a small elite sector of the aesthetic public for the experience of a general population'.[65]

---

64  Alex Callinicos, *Against Postmodernism*, Cambridge: Polity, 1989, p. 168.
65  Lauren Berlant, *Cruel Optimism*, Durham, NC: Duke University Press, 2011, p. 65.

Recently, for instance, Jameson has suggested that Marxist ideological analysis is

> predicated on the presupposition that a space existed outside the system ... This space – the Archimedean point of ideology – could ordinarily be formulated in intellectual terms, as a place or point from which something else could be thought ... yet it was always dependent on a social launch pad of some sort – whether the existence of a radically different national space abroad (the USSR, Cuba, certain third world countries) or the existence of certain classes, underclasses, concrete groups, and collectivities here which were not completely incorporated into the system.

What Jameson calls postmodernism, however, and *'what began to be more visible since Reagan and Thatcher* – is then indeed the definitive incorporation of all these remainders'.[66] The emphasis here is mine and intended to register a frustration with this kind of reiteration of Jameson's position, for reasons that have already been touched on in the foregoing discussion. What has become more visible since Reagan and Thatcher depends on where you look. An entrancement by forms of commodification that takes little account of whether people seek their commodities amid other people's rubbish, in Lidl, Walmart, Waitrose or Harrods, or whether they get on a bus or fly to New York to do their shopping, is an odd kind of socialist perspective, however it may be legitimated by various western Marxist traditions. Are all those now 'internal' to capitalism really as *completely* and *definitively* assimilated or incorporated into it, as Jameson alleges?

---

66  Fredric Jameson, 'Ideological Analysis: A Handbook', in *Valences of the Dialectic*, London: Verso, 2010, p. 357.

There are surely different ways of thinking about both Marxism and the present situation under capitalism. First, the Marxist tradition has traditionally seen the potential of the working class as bound to its location at the heart of the system, rather than 'outside' it, through the exploitation of that class in the production of capital. Second, some of the most compelling work of recent years has expanded on Marx's grasp of capital generation as contradictory in other respects too. David Harvey has recently written of seventeen kinds of highly consequential contradiction, ranging from that between use and exchange value to the obvious incompatibility between the abstract demand for compound economic growth and ecological principles.[67] The sense that, under postmodernity, a purification has taken place consisting in the expansion into, and consequent annulment of, residual and emergent spaces by the commodity form in order to become omnipresent contrasts with one that would suggest this purification has actually, and necessarily, intensified both exploitation and other forms of contradiction, *especially* since the time of Thatcher and Reagan. Between 1951 and 1973, the period of Bretton Woods, there were no global economic recessions; since 1979, there have been five, the latest being the most devastating and sustained to date.[68]

Jameson's focus on commodification leads him, nonetheless, to critique those apologists for postmodernity who emphasize

67  David Harvey, *Seventeen Contradictions and the End of Capitalism*, London: Profile Books, 2014. In a similar spirit, see also Wolfgang Streeck, 'How Will Capitalism End?' *New Left Review II*, 88, July–August 2014, pp. 35–64.
68  Robert Skidelsky, *Keynes: The Return of the Master*, London: Allen Lane, 2009, pp. 116–117.

its valorization of social difference or identities of various kinds, given that this process is so closely linked to 'the celebration of consumer goods, free enterprise, and the eternal wonder and excitement of the market itself'.[69] DeKoven is plausibly regarded as one of these apologists. Her valuation of difference, moreover, carries the danger of reifying that which it claims to recognize, one evident above all in her resignification of the conventional language of the left when she invokes both a humanistic language of oppression and a discourse of equality – but in relation to causes rather than persons. Thus, *narratives* are said to be 'oppressive', and egalitarianism resides in a greater plurality of *movements*. Whereas, in the context of so-called master narratives, identities seemed to serve some future form of liberation in which they might become obsolete, the importance attached to them by DeKoven becomes circular: the point of recognizing difference is the recognition of difference as such, and in this way ends are collapsed into means and promoted as 'democracy', conceived not in terms of popular *control*, but representation.

I have been suggesting that the arguments advanced in *One-Dimensional Man* help to obscure our understanding of the present as they are recycled through Jameson's influential account of postmodernity, in part because they were a way of accounting for a specifically Fordist capitalism that has now been superseded. This is not to suggest that Marcuse's arguments were adequate to their own times. Malcolm Miles notes that figures on the European left were bemused and frustrated by Marcuse's position on

---

69  Fredric Jameson, '*History and Class Consciousness* as an Unfinished Project', in *Valences of the Dialectic*, p. 213.

working-class incorporation.[70] Even in the US, moreover, things were not clear cut: the late sixties saw the most pervasive labour disputes for decades,[71] many of them focused on the very automation that Marcuse suggested had facilitated workers' integration into the workplace through its rhythms, lessening fatigue and alienation, and complementing corporatist industrial relations.[72] One trade unionist of the time, Charles Denby, by contrast, described on the basis of personal experience how 'all workers who battle against automation know its life-and-death meaning – its speedup, its inhuman way of work, its death by overwork, its unemployment, its permanently depressed areas, its ghost towns'.[73] Moreover, there are good grounds for arguing that *One-Dimensional Man* is not only guilty of overstatement, but that its pessimism was bound to its historical moment prior to the upsurge in radicalism of various sorts in the later sixties, many of whose causes Marcuse critically

---

70  Miles highlights Lefebvre's response to meeting Marcuse in 1968: *Herbert Marcuse: An Aesthetics of Resistance*, London: Pluto, 2012, p. 123. Marcuse did recognize the differences between US and European working-class movements, but worried about Americanization: see Herbert Marcuse, 'The Problem of Violence and the Radical Opposition', *Five Lectures*, pp. 99–100.

71  Barbara Ehrenreich, *Fear of Falling: The Inner Life of the Middle Class*, New York: HarperCollins, 1989, p. 121.

72  Marcuse, *One-Dimensional Man*, pp. 26–37.

73  Charles Denby, 'Workers Battle Automation', in Long (ed.), *New Left*, p. 151. Some of these features are acknowledged by Marcuse (p. 33). Paul Mattick rigorously and presciently contests the economic claims made by Marcuse about the stability generated by automation and 'organized capitalism' from an orthodox Marxist perspective, though he acknowledges a certain legitimacy to the category of 'one-dimensionality', and admires Marcuse's analyses of ideological tendencies: *Critique of Marcuse: One-Dimensional Man in Class Society*, London: Merlin Press, 1972.

supported.[74] Indeed, the book's year of publication, 1964, has been described as a turning point in the New Left's decisive rejection of New Deal-type liberalism in the US.[75]

While *One-Dimensional Man* secured unprecedented fame for Marcuse, having sold 100,000 copies in the US and been translated into sixteen different languages within five years of its publication,[76] it might plausibly be regarded as an exceptional work. In any case, more important for my purposes is his earlier, more abstract theoretical contribution, *Eros and Civilization* (1956). This is often viewed as more straightforwardly optimistic than *One-Dimensional Man*. José Esteban Muñoz, for instance, has recently described it as 'almost a blueprint for sexual liberation'.[77] There are problems with that perception, though, since Marcuse does anticipate the later book's emphasis on individual subjection to social heteronomy by arguing that contemporary life has witnessed a flattening out of the radical tensions an earlier form of bourgeois society had generated in the subject between id, ego and superego. Social control was now exerted through commodification and the satisfaction of pleasurable, notably sexual, urges, as well as the increasing displacement of the mediating figure of the paterfamilias by more direct institutional and cultural forms of authority.[78] Indeed, Marcuse brilliantly acknowledges the fetishization of *youth*

---

74  For his falling out with Adorno over the student movement, see their 'Correspondence on the German Student Movement', trans. Esther Lesley, *New Left Review*, 233, January–February, 1999, pp. 123–136.
75  See, for instance, Todd Gitlin, *The Sixties: Years of Hope, Days of Rage*, New York: Bantam, 1987, pp. 162–166.
76  Barry Kätz, *Herbert Marcuse and the Art of Liberation*, London: Verso, p. 168.
77  José Esteban Muñoz, *Cruising Utopia: The Then and There of Queer Futurity*, New York: New York University Press, 2009, p. 133.
78  Herbert Marcuse, *Eros and Civilization: A Philosophical Inquiry Into Freud*, Abingdon: Routledge, 1998, pp. 94–105.

in postwar societies: 'In the struggle between the generations, the sides seem to be shifted: the son knows better; he represents the mature reality principle against its obsolescent forms.'[79]

The often quite abrupt shifts in Marcuse's work between an 'optimism' that registers two-dimensionality and a 'pessimism' focused on one-dimensionality,[80] even in the same text, are evidence of a certain kind of dialectical temperament and desire to search out revolutionary potential. DeKoven is not wrong to highlight this, but she presumes that Marcuse's limitations in this respect are characteristic of totalizing, modernist Marxist and socialist traditions as such. Others might be more inclined to see something of the messier reality she acknowledges, though not in the forms she does, or as the basis for accepting that capitalism's triumph is either desirable or permanent. Marcuse's earlier work offers critical terms that might inform counter-hegemonic, anti-capitalist projects.

Reference to a contemporary reality principle in the quotation from Marcuse above requires explanation. This is the Freudian term he finds it necessary to revise, and it is through this revision that he generates a complex understanding of what liberation might mean. Marcuse begins *Eros* by accepting Freud's proposition in *Civilization and its Discontents* that repression is a necessary feature of any kind of human society. Socialization entails an acceptance on the part of the child that gratification must be deferred in order to achieve accommodation with the reality principle, because fundamental to any order is the work that goes into its reproduction. However, Marcuse points out that Freud's insight is problematically abstract in its talk about civilization in the singular: actually, different societies have required different levels of repression, and others are possible. Hence, it is wrong to speak of only one reality principle, one degree of necessary repression, and recognition of this opens up the possibility of a critical relation to the given social order and the specific demands it makes on us.

Under capitalism, Marcuse points out, we are subject to the insatiable, abstract demand for a growth that is predicated on exploitative social relations. Subjection to such an order generates *surplus* repression. The tacit allusion here is to Marx's claim that capital is generated by the extraction of surplus value through the euphemistically labelled 'efficiencies' constantly sought from the labour process itself.[81] Consequently, Marcuse suggests, the specific reality principle of capitalism should rather be known as the performance principle.[82] His description of this is worth quoting at length:

The performance principle, which is that of an acquisitive and antagonistic society in the process of constant expansion,

---

81  Marcuse and other members of the Frankfurt School in exile had to be highly circumspect about their Marxism, as Douglas Kellner has pointed out: *Herbert Marcuse and the Crisis of Marxism*, London: Macmillan, 1984, p. 115. During the McCarthyite years, when *Eros* was written, this was presumably especially necessary. There is no mention of Marxism in the book, nor are there any positive references to socialism or communism, though there are negative references to Stalinism.
82  Elsewhere in the text, Marcuse suggests that the performance principle describes any society – pre-capitalist as well as capitalist – in which the extraction of surpluses takes place. Nonetheless, the dynamism he associates with the performance principle seems characteristic of capitalism specifically. Where I refer to the performance principle in this book I am referring specifically to the reality principle of capitalism.

presupposes a long development during which domination has been increasingly rationalized: control over social labour now reproduces society on an enlarged scale and under improving conditions. For a long way, the interests of domination and the interests of the whole coincide: the profitable utilization of the productive apparatus fulfils the needs and faculties of the individuals. For the vast majority of the population, the scope and mode of satisfaction are determined by their own labour; but their labour is work for an apparatus which they do not control, which operates as an independent power to which individuals must submit if they want to live. And it becomes the more alien the more specialized the division of labour becomes. Men do not live their own lives but perform pre-established functions. While they work, they do not fulfil their own needs and faculties but work in *alienation*.[83]

This is a richly dialectical account of capitalism's development of the productive forces, stressing both their potential to enhance the satisfaction of general needs, but also their reliance on rationalization (divisions of labour that reduce people to functions) and alienation in the Marxist sense (the fact of working for others in such conditions, and of the products of our labour consequently seeming independent of, and hostile to, us). Since the interests of those who control the means of production are served by the persistent pressure on workers for greater productivity in return for less remuneration, the result is the expansion of production through antagonism. Moreover, the performance principle fuels the growth in consumption that serves as its justification, since 'the definition of the standard of living in terms of automobiles,

---

83  Marcuse, *Eros and Civilization*, p. 45.

television sets, airplanes, and tractors is that of the performance principle itself'.[84] We might update and expand this list, of course, by adding any amount of contemporary gadgetry, all of it more or less obsolete as soon as it is released, and conditioning our sense of civilizational progress as an effect of such obsolescence. Its complement is that endlessly, irrationally fetishized priority in contemporary life, 'innovation'.

DeKoven's privileging of *One-Dimensional Man* in her argument about postmodernity means that she overlooks Marcuse's account of the performance principle, since the term is absent from that later analysis, possibly because Marcuse believed its demands had relaxed as a result of automation. This was an unjustified assumption at the time, but, under conditions of flexible accumulation, privatization and deregulation, it is plausible to suggest that the performance principle has become more, not less, pervasive, and more demanding. We should acknowledge, however, an aspect of it underplayed by Marcuse in his focus on alienation (again, he appears principally to have in mind Fordist conditions): its exploitative intensification of work for less remuneration.

Few are exempt. In her investigation into the conditions of the low-paid in Britain, for instance, Polly Toynbee highlights the ways in which public-sector jobs have been outsourced to private companies that have lowered pay and reduced staffing, resulting in tougher work regimes. Writing of dinner ladies with whom she worked at a state school, she claims they hated their employers and 'said the work was impossible, unbearable, grossly undertimed and underpaid [but they] liked the school, the staff, the head and one another. More than that, it was as if the very harshness of the work bound them together in a daily challenge

---

84  Ibid., p. 153.

to keep going.'[85] Toynbee tellingly suggests that these attitudes are comparable with those she witnessed among coal miners thirty years before.[86] These attitudes are an instance of what Gramsci regarded as contradictory consciousness, or 'the co-existence of two conceptions of the world, one affirmed in words and the other displayed in effective action'.[87]

The category of the performance principle therefore offers a valuable way of grasping present conditions. Through the ways it connects production with consumption, it describes capitalist totality far more satisfactorily than the Jamesonian emphasis on commodification's saturation of it, and it complements the kind of base–superstructure spatialization Harvey derives from Marx in his description of postmodernity by conveying capitalism's qualitatively relentless, acquisitive, dispiriting and enervating dynamism. But, as the instance of the dinner ladies illustrates, the performance principle no longer merely applies to industrial production; it is pervasive. Marcuse's brilliance was to establish this principle as the basis for thinking about the relations between labour, the sexual and the aesthetic in ways we need to interrogate further.

At the heart of the bourgeois social order as analysed by Freud, rather than Marx, was the family, the institution primarily responsible for the individual's socialization, discipline and accommodation with the reality principle through assent to the socially pervasive work ethic. The bourgeois familial ideal was

---

85  Polly Toynbee, *Hard Work: Life in Low-Pay Britain*, London: Bloomsbury, 2003, p. 109.

86  Ibid., p. 111.

87  Antonio Gramsci, *Selections from the Prison Notebooks*, ed. and trans. Quintin Hoare and Geoffrey Nowell Smith, London: Lawrence & Wishart, 1971, pp. 326–327.

therefore one in whose name erotic pleasure was repressed or sublimated. As we have already seen, Marcuse noted that the integrity of this ideal was breaking down; he was to speak of the obsolescence of the Freudian model of subjectivity.[88] Nonetheless, his description of bourgeois marital relations is important. He argues that they were the consequence of a historically 'long and cruel process of domestication' founded on a certain contradiction, namely that

> while, outside the privacy of the family, men's existence was chiefly determined by the exchange value of their products and performances, their life in the home and bed was to be permeated with the spirit of divine and moral law ... The full force of civilized morality was mobilized against the use of the body as mere object, means, instrument of pleasure; such reification was tabooed and remained the ill-reputed privilege of whores, degenerates and perverts. Precisely in his gratification, and especially his sexual gratification, man was to be a higher being, committed to the higher values; sexuality was to be dignified by love.[89]

Here and throughout this book, I shall call the familial principle as outlined here 'heterosacramentalism'.[90] This is the view that sexual pleasure stands in need of redemption, whether conceived in religious or humanistic terms, and that this endows the sacramental relationship with a qualitative moral and emotional superiority over all others. Marcuse's point here is that erotic

---

88 Marcuse, *Five Lectures*, pp. 44–61.

89 Marcuse, *Eros and Civilization*, p. 201.

90 Jeffrey Weeks speaks in somewhat similar terms of 'the sacramental family' in relation to nineteenth-century ideals in *Sex, Politics, and Society: The Regulation of Sexuality Since 1800*, Harlow: Longman, 1981, pp. 38–56.

pleasure should be its own justification, and it is a mark of the general condition of (surplus) repression in a society that it should be thought otherwise. He also, at least implicitly, suggests that the privatization and domestication of human relations through marriage sanction and help to perpetuate the instrumentality of those beyond it.

While heterosacramentalism in the strict form articulated by Marcuse here may well seem archaic,[91] the ideal nonetheless survives institutionally and ideologically to the extent that marriage continues to thrive and is romantically, symbolically and financially invested in. The achievement of lesbian and gay marriage in much of the west, parts of Latin America and probably in the not too distant future Taiwan, testify to that continuing dominance. Couched in egalitarian terms, this represents the extension of the principle under liberalized conditions: sacramentalism for all.

If Marcuse developed a productive critique of Freud in this respect, his indebtedness also entailed the acceptance of ideas that are more difficult to endorse. In particular, I am thinking of hydraulic Freudian drive theory,[92] of energies blocked, channelled or released, and of Eros's complex relations with Thanatos. There are reasons for indulging him, since the way Marcuse develops compelling arguments through an engagement with Freud's

---

91 Kevin Floyd suggests that it was archaic even at the time of *Eros*'s publication (*The Reification of Desire: Toward a Queer Marxism*, Minneapolis: Minnesota University Press, 2009, p. 134), but, as I show above, Marcuse was conscious of this.

92 This is the way John H. Gagnon and William Simon critique psychoanalysis in *Sexual Conduct: The Social Sources of Human Sexuality*, Chicago: Aldine, 1973, pp. 9–19. One result of it, however, is that conduct almost entirely displaces desire as a mode of accounting for human behaviour.

categories and narratives also sometimes indicates that he sees in them a certain symbolic value.[93] Moreover, he is keen to integrate them into a larger discussion of the history of western philosophy and that tradition's definitive separation of reason and the body from Plato on. The value of the category of the aesthetic for Marcuse, for instance, resides in its mediation of these terms, and its anticipation of a possible future reality principle predicated on their integration.

There is a sense throughout the 'philosophical inquiry' of the book, then, that the specific categories and systems of thought invoked are not so much to be defended on their own terms as regarded as expressions of a desire for an alternative order that only materialist thought suggests is a realizable possibility on the basis of specific historical conditions. In principle, then, such philosophical discourse can only be heuristic, never wholly adequate to the task. Nonetheless, following Freud, this desire is presented by Marcuse as the memory of a former ontogenetic and phylogenetic wholeness that acts as a negating force in relation to repressive civilization. Thus, as Jay Bernstein notes, Marcuse's 'exhortation to remember an "imaginary *temps perdu*" allowed him to smuggle an a priori philosophical anthropology into Critical Theory'.[94]

The proposal that future utopian existence may be governed by a logic of return, that regression constitutes progress, may be appealing in one sense – that of being able to strip away the

---

93  This is how Marcuse redeems Freud's frequently critiqued anthropological speculations (*Eros and Civilization*, p. 60).

94  Jay Bernstein, *Marxism and Totality*, p. 236. Jay develops his case on the basis of observations made by Fredric Jameson in *Marxism and Form: Twentieth Century Dialectical Theories of Literature*, Princeton: Princeton University Press, 1971, pp. 112–116.

disciplinary mechanisms of civilization – but Marcuse perhaps provokes most scepticism, most resistance, in us when he speculates about the features of a future non-repressive society. I would not want to underestimate the extent to which such scepticism is itself one consequence of our conditioning by the performance principle, but he surely tries too hard to persuade us that the lion really can lie down with the lamb. After all, even according to the Freudian theory he deploys, any civilization must be predicated on repression (the deferral of gratification), and Marcuse is clear that disagreeable work will not simply go away. Moreover, the myth of wholeness risks introducing a degree of normativity about which we should be cautious.

Marcuse inherits the problem from Hegel, not Freud, of course: it is the end-of-history thesis, the belief that the subject–object dialectic will be resolved, that we can finally rest or at least be active in harmony with each other and our environment. But, as that other Hegelian Marxist, Georg Lukács, came to recognize in his autocritique of *History and Class Consciousness*,

> objectification is ... a phenomenon that cannot be eliminated from human life in society. If we bear in mind that every externalization of an object in practice (and hence, too, in work) is an objectification, that every human expression including speech objectifies human thoughts and feelings, then it is clear that we are dealing with a universal mode of commerce between men.[95]

Thus, the political and historical struggle is over the conditions of

---

95  Georg Lukács, 'Preface to the New Edition' (1967) of *History and Class Consciousness: Studies in Marxist Dialectics*, trans. Rodney Livingstone, London: Merlin, 1971, p. xxiv.

objectification, including – as Lukács intriguingly suggests here in his reference to speech – the production of culture.

In spite of this, Marcuse's utopian commitment to the principle that a different order of things is demanded by the kind of beings humans are is, in my view, indispensable: without it, the left – any left, even of a pragmatic sort – cannot survive, and probably doesn't deserve to. To what other principle would we render society accountable? The problem is that such a necessarily normative argument carries with it the potential to perpetuate oppressive convictions, heteronormative ones among them.

Hence the appeal for me of the particular defence of the category of human nature by Norman Geras. By contrast with conservative accounts, he argues that this resides in the dialectical relation between certain clearly generalizable needs – for food, shelter, some kind of sociality, for instance – and the distinctively human creative potential to satisfy them through such things as the use of tools or symbolic forms of interaction. It follows from this that the immense variety of human societies and cultures is proof of, rather than against, human nature. Moreover, this argument is relevant to historical materialism because it

> highlights that specific nexus of universal needs and capacities which explains the human production process and man's organized transformation of the material environment; which process and transformation it treats in turn as the basis both of the social order and of historical change.[96]

---

96 Norman Geras, *Marx and Human Nature: Refutation of a Legend*, London: Verso, 1983, p. 108. Geras' self-conscious preference for the category 'man' to designate the universal is regrettable, but I do not think it invalidates his argument.

There is one implication of this argument I think it necessary to draw out further, though. When Geras points out that the claim for the existence of human nature is an abstraction, but a valid one,[97] this should lead us to conclude not only that it must remain an abstraction in any conceivable historical conditions, but that any argument that human nature might be wholly realized within them is itself the mark of oppressively normative reason.

In this way, it is surely possible to cut through a whole range of unhelpful and obscurantist debates around essentialism, anti-essentialism and strategic essentialism predicated on the assumption that nature and culture are, or have been imagined to be, binary opposites.[98] Sexual needs, for instance, may be posited abstractly, but it is difficult to conceive of them in any way separately from the social prioritization of them and the various cultural means we have developed to inhibit or satisfy them – means that may become a kind of second nature of their own, as is the case when we speak of 'having' a sexuality. It therefore does make sense to speak of the denial of sexual needs, and in this limited sense of their repression, but this does not necessarily imply that some elemental or quantitative force is being contained that must find expression directly or indirectly, as some of the movements for sexual liberation, following Freud, have assumed.

I see no problem therefore in speaking of the performance principle as alienating and exploitative in relation to a humanity that is constitutively capable of experiencing alienation and exploitation. To regard human beings as passively 'socially constructed' by

---

97 Ibid., p. 115.
98 Diana Fuss presents a good account of the problems associated with these various positions in *Essentially Speaking: Feminism, Nature, and Difference*, London: Routledge, 1989, though she remains within a poststructuralist framework that I would suggest is productive of them.

an order that simply pre-exists them is to collude with the power that controls social production and reproduction through its failure to recognize that human beings are also, always and simultaneously, socially construct*ing*, making history not in circumstances of their own choosing through their capacities in order to satisfy needs in diverse ways. Through this process, indeed, needs expand. 'Social construction' should be grasped as a *relation* (of the active and passive; that which we do and which is done to us), not a mere process of 'interpellation'.[99] My emphasis on intention earlier in this chapter is predicated on that view. Hence, political economic struggle might be directed not towards constructing a society that is at one with our nature, but towards a society that is not inimical to that nature.

When Marcuse speaks of a non-repressive reality principle he is referring to the possible end to 'surplus repression necessitated by the interests of domination': in '"ideal" conditions of mature industrial civilization, alienation would be completed [sic] by general automatization of labour, reduction of labour time to a minimum, and exchangeability of functions'.[100] At the same time, he understood that labour itself might become more fulfilling and continuous with the rest of life – more erotically satisfying, indeed, in his expansive sense of that term to refer to the sensuous more generally. It is not necessary to accept the Freudian concept of the libido in order to find plausible the claim that the conditions he describes might sponsor a more general reduction in the antagonistic relations between work and pleasure, morality and satisfaction, and that this would plausibly bring about a profound

---

99  Kate Soper examines pertinent issues in this respect with her usual clarity in '*Constructa Ergo Sum*', in *Troubled Pleasures: Essays on Gender, Politics and Hedonism*, London: Verso, 1990, pp. 146–161.
100  Marcuse, *Eros and Civilization*, p. 152.

transformation in sensibilities.[101] I accept Marcuse's fundamental proposition that for the left this should be the context for thinking about sexuality. Nonetheless, it is necessary to adapt Marcuse's arguments still further, and in ways that acknowledge MacIntyre's critique of his tendency to speak of 'man', if we are fully to realize their relevance to contemporary life.

I wrote earlier of sacramentalism as a persistent ideal. Of course, though, it is both pervasively demystified in everyday contemporary existence, and adhered to contradictorily and hypocritically, because sexual temptation assaults us from all sides through its commodification in one form or another. Sex as ultimate satisfaction is ironically a remnant, or reinflection, of sacramentalism, but under the performance principle its intensity is not predicated on scarcity: rather, we are encouraged to believe we can, and even should, have more and better sex. The investment in sex as ultimate satisfaction, moreover, means that it serves as the perfect metaphor for the potential of commodities, but it is also frequently enough invoked as the experience that consumption will facilitate. Donald M. Lowe argues that 'the characteristics designed into the commodity as a package destabilize and reconstitute the use value of a commodity in late capitalism ... The "use value" ... is the promise advertising makes to the buyer's sexual fantasy.'[102] The pervasiveness of this technique, and of individuals' sense of themselves becoming the image of the thing they buy, means that

---

101  Douglas Kellner makes a similar point in 'Marcuse and the Quest for Radical Subjectivity', in *Herbert Marcuse: A Critical Reader*, John Abromeit and W. Mark Cobb, eds, New York: Routledge, 2004, pp. 86–89.

102  Donald M. Lowe, *The Body in Late-Capitalist USA*, Durham, NC: Duke University Press, 1995, p. 134. There are echoes here of the analysis in Wolfgang Fritz Haug's *Critique of Commodity Aesthetics*, trans. Robert Bock, Cambridge: Polity Press, 1983. Nonetheless, Lowe problematically assumes that the consumerist gaze is male.

existence is now suffused with the consciousness of and sensitivity to sexual appeal in oneself and others.

Life these days is sexy, then; the term may be applied to just about anything from computers to cars and probably even certain sorts of wellington boots in order to highlight their desirability. It is related to, and overlaps with, that other prevalent popular aesthetic category of 'cool', which has received significant attention from cultural critics. The first to highlight its importance was Thomas Frank in *The Conquest of Cool* (1997), in which he demonstrated how a desire to overturn moribund business practices in the fifties and sixties paralleled, drew on and ultimately encouraged the countercultural rejection of obsolescent tradition. Over time, business explicitly enlisted the 'symbolic and musical language' of the counterculture in order to feed cycles of consumption to the extent that such language has become

> a permanent fixture on the American scene, impervious to the angriest assaults of cultural and political conservatives, because it so conveniently and efficiently transforms the myriad petty tyrannies of economic life – all the complaints about conformity, oppression, bureaucracy, meaninglessness, and the disappearance of individualism that became virtually a national obsession during the 1950s – into rationales for consuming.[103]

Jim McGuigan has explored the implications of this argument in greater detail. He illustrates that cool – as a style, an ethic and a disposition associated with creativity and innovation – functions as a mode of symbolic capital, thereby reinforcing class hierarchies

---

103  Thomas Frank, *The Conquest of Cool: Business Culture, Counterculture, and the Rise of Hip Consumerism*, Chicago: University of Chicago Press, 1997, p. 31.

through the mediation of taste, and even assists in structuring the social relations of production.[104]

Just as cool hints at its countercultural emergence,[105] so sexy discloses its origins in the repressive desublimation of postwar life. Through it, sexuality began to lose its dangerous, even oppositional, quality to the extent that taboos were relaxed, and bound people instead to the system through the particular mode of sensuality it promoted. When Marcuse wrote that 'sexual morality has been greatly liberalized; moreover, sexuality is operative as commercial stimulus, business asset, status symbol',[106] he clearly hinted at, but did not dwell on, the way in which the desirable commodity not only served capital, but also mediated class differences. 'Sexy', then, represents a 'desublimated' form of symbolic capital. Along with cool, and a host of other popular aesthetic categories, it assists in determining the abjection of others according to stylistic norms and modes of sensibility that render them *un*desirable. In *Revolting Subjects*, for instance, Imogen Tyler highlights what she describes as the social abjection of asylum seekers, travellers and 'chavs', among others.[107]

Nonetheless, the concept of desublimation as an aspect of that more general process Marcuse described as deprivatization, is

104 Jim McGuigan, *Cool Capitalism*, London: Pluto, 2009.

105 McGuigan provides a more specific and detailed genealogy of cool (*Cool Capitalism*, pp. 1–8); by 'emergence', I refer to its popular adoption in the form that has more clearly transmuted into current usage.

106 Herbert Marcuse, 'The Obsolescence of the Freudian Concept of Man', in *Five Lectures: Psychoanalysis, Politics, and Utopia*, trans. Jeremy J. Shapiro and Shierry M. Weber, London: Allen Lane, 1970, p. 57. The category of 'repressive desublimation' is first articulated in 1964 in *One-Dimensional Man*, London: Routledge, 1991, pp. 59–86. It is nonetheless a problematic way of thinking that I return to consider below.

107 Imogen Tyler, *Revolting Subjects: Social Abjection and Resistance in Neoliberal Britain*, London: Zed Books, 2013.

problematic. These two terms suggest a form of developmentally acquired selfhood or autonomy (sublimation/privatization) that is subsequently hollowed out. For Marcuse, deprivatization under capitalism can only be repressive, though it is not immediately experienced as such. The logic of Marcuse's argument is that it should be resisted: 'the need to "relax" in the entertainments furnished by the culture industry is itself repressive', he suggests, 'and its repression is a step toward freedom'. The problem with the argument advanced by Marcuse here is that it may lead to demands for a kind of left puritanism in the face of the pleasures afforded us by consumerism. I focus on this at various points in the book.

Let me now turn to the production of one aspect of the kind of culture that Jameson claims is dominant by reference to a particular instance relevant to this book's preoccupations. The majority of the world's sex toys – something like 70% – are produced in China's notorious Special Economic Zones. According to the *Taipei Times*, workers at the Shaki Adult Factory on the People's Love Technology Park in Shenzhen in 2005 earned the equivalent of between $80 and $100 a month, performing dull, repetitive production-line work in near silence for eight hours a day making blow-up dolls, bondage gear and vibrators. One female employee is quoted as saying that 'for the first few days this job felt a bit strange. But after that you forget what you're holding. It becomes just another object.'[108] The category of alienation is unfashionable in contemporary theory, but this worker expresses it in classic form: her work, producing use values for the wealthier elsewhere, ceases to be culturally 'strange', only to become absolutely meaningless

---

108 'Sex Toys are China's Latest Booming Industry', *Taipei Times*, 26 June 2005, p. 4.

to her, except through the pay she takes home. The very term 'love technology', moreover, draws our attention to the qualitative dimension of such production: its euphemistic, fake propriety only serves to highlight the fact that sexual stimulation is regulated, not by idealization, but an instrumental reason that regards 'the sexual organs' as parts to be serviced. A truly critical perspective should not uphold the 'love' that is being traduced here, but rather recognize that typically modern forms of pleasure are not 'private' acts to be vindicated outside of larger social relations and values. Meanwhile, Chinese workers such as the ones at Shenzhen mostly retain a 'conservative' commitment to the principle of the family, and an investment in it – however adequately fulfilled – as the primary alternative to their dehumanizing labour. These are the kinds of globalized contradictions a libertarian left must grapple with.

This instance should also further undermine any tendency to speak of 'man'. It forces us to acknowledge rather that the performance principle distributes privileges, pleasures and sufferings unequally and contradictorily. It does not determine general levels either of repression or satisfaction, even if, formally at least, all kinds of commodities are available (it doesn't mean just anyone can afford them). I do not accept that Marcuse's account of Fordist conditions as one-dimensional was adequate, but any extrapolation from it to contemporary conditions must entail a further, and more serious, falsification, this time of life under neoliberal capitalism. Hence, there is a difference between speaking of one-dimensionality as a powerful pressure within contemporary life, and speaking of it as an accomplished fact, determining either pervasive uncritical acquiescence or a pluralized, but always reincorporated, postmodern politics under an abstract hegemony of 'commodification'. If, as Williams argued, hegemony is a category distinguished by its recognition of social intention, that intention has been thoroughly at work in recent decades deregulating the performance principle.

## The diversified dominant

The rather casual, but instructively misleading, appropriation of Williams's terms is symptomatic of a more general theoretical eclecticism in Jameson's and DeKoven's accounts (and not only there, one might add). Thus, when DeKoven describes postmodernity in terms of 'an unevenly, porously hegemonic global consumer capitalism in antinomy with ... a diffuse, multidirectional, fluid, oscillating proliferation of power and resistance throughout society and culture',[109] the specific sequence of metaphors she deploys facilitates the conflation of a Gramscian discourse of hegemony with a Lukácsian one of totality, supplemented for good measure by Foucaultian and Deleuzian – her references – abstractions about power and resistance. All of this is nonetheless the precise theoretical, or at least rhetorical, correlative of her specific project's drive to reconcile the radical impulses of the sixties with a pragmatism supposedly appropriate to contemporary conditions.

This is not all, however, because one further consequence of viewing things in the way DeKoven does is an unfortunate tendency to suggest that the left's development can be evaluated through an aggregation of its causes, such that retreats in one respect may be offset by advances in another, as if by way of compensation. Hence the rhetoric of diffusion, porosity and multidirectionality. However, it might be better to acknowledge that the left's causes

---

109  DeKoven, *Utopia Limited*, p. 15.

as they emerged in and from the sixties have fared very differently, and for specific, rather than abstract, reasons. If we are speaking of the labour–capital relation, no one can doubt that the latter has consistently, relentlessly gained in power. In this respect, these have decidedly not been decades of give and take. In other respects, however, the situation has been very much more mixed, precisely because libertarian advances of specific qualitative kinds have been made through the market, to the extent that the assumption that they are specifically leftist causes has been put seriously in question. This is undoubtedly the case with the sexual freedoms I focus on in this book, since, as David T. Evans has argued, the amoral market has played a crucial role in determining gay – and, we might add, other forms of queer – citizenship in the years following decriminalization.[110] Thus, we have to confront the more troubling possibility that left disunity has resulted from diverse, and even opposing, fortunes as these have been determined by neoliberal capitalism.

Recognition of this also contrasts with that tendency I noted in the introduction in certain forms of Marxism to argue that capitalism is the root of all evil, whether the specific evil be racism, sexism or heterosexism. Nicola Field provides one instance when she claims that 'homophobia is part of a huge economic, political, social and ideological system of mass oppression'.[111] If, however, capitalism is understood as a truly complex totality, such an implausible claim might be avoided. It would be more convincing to suggest that there is a relative autonomy of oppressions and resistances within the structuring whole of capitalism, and also

110 David T. Evans, *Sexual Citizenship: The Material Construction of Sexualities*, London: Routledge, 1993, pp. 89–113.
111 Nicola Field, *Over the Rainbow: Money, Class, and Homophobia*, London: Pluto, 1995, p. 58.

that there are different *modalities* of power, about whose dynamics it is important to be precise.

Nancy Fraser, for instance, distinguishes between forms of justice relating to distribution, on the one hand, and recognition on the other, while nonetheless appreciating that 'economic injustice and cultural injustice are usually interimbricated so as to reinforce each other dialectically'.[112] I have reservations about Fraser's precise articulation of this case,[113] but part of her point is surely that injustices of recognition will not necessarily come to an end in an economically more just, possibly socialist, future, and that they therefore demand of us specific, active forms of engagement. Hoping that 'the revolution' will bring about universal justice in the twinkling of an eye, as it were, is a delusion of religious provenance.

Speaking of a relative autonomy of modes of power, moreover, should entail neither a belief that they are not themselves pervasive, or even systemic, nor that there is a hierarchy of oppressions that requires that the left must prioritize anti-capitalist struggle in all circumstances. Indeed, the recognition of different modalities of power may compel quite different priorities. For instance, class power is dynamic because it is exercised through the production of history

---

112 Nancy Fraser, 'From Redistribution to Recognition: Dilemmas of Justice in a Postsocialist Age', in *Justice Interruptus: Critical Reflections on the 'Postsocialist' Condition*, New York: Routledge, 1997, p. 15. She develops and pursues her arguments in dialogue with Axel Honneth in *Redistribution or Recognition: A Political Philosophical Exchange*, London: Verso, 2003. Her original argument provoked a debate with Judith Butler that has been widely commented on: see Butler, 'Merely Cultural', *New Left Review*, 227, January–February 1998, pp. 33–44, and Fraser, 'Heterosexism, Misrecognition, and Capitalism: A Reply to Judith Butler', *New Left Review*, 228, March–April 1998, pp. 140–149.

113 These are well summarized by Rosemary Hennessy, *Profit and Pleasure: Sexual Identities in Late Capitalism*, New York: Routledge, 2000, pp. 221–224. Fraser's model suggests to me the need for a Solomon-like rationality at the level of the state in order to address inequalities.

(understood in materialist terms). Other modalities, by contrast, are frequently predicated on the denial of either the desirability or the possibility of historical change – thus, racial inferiority is said to be permanent, women to be naturally submissive, and same-sex desire unnatural (or sinful) – and are often all the more peremptory, demeaning and absolute for that. Of course, such conservatisms must also be exercised in history and have themselves determined oppressive social divisions of labour still not wholly obsolete (through slavery and the confinement of women, for instance). But if the challenge to conservatism must inevitably be made on the basis of an appeal to history – to change or progress, that is – then we must acknowledge that anti-conservative political struggle in a neoliberal world takes place within, and will be conditioned substantially by, capitalism. Indeed, the very dynamism of capitalism and its 'denaturalizing' pressures is precisely what generates its potential appeal in this respect. Failure to recognize this means either denying that we can, or should, speak in any meaningful sense about capitalism as a totality, as some have proposed,[114] or accepting that capitalism must be a given in the pursuit of particular political ends, which is explicitly DeKoven's position.[115]

---

114    In an influential work that claims to be both feminist and queer theoretical, J. K. Gibson-Graham argues that talk of capitalism as a totality constructs reality in ways that are debilitating for the left, whereas more nuanced discursive constructions of reality might facilitate more hopeful possibilities for activism. See *The End of Capitalism (As We Knew It): A Feminist Critique of Political Economy*, Oxford: Blackwell, 1996. The strong social constructionism of this account is implausible, and the way the case is handled is contradictory, for reasons I do not have the space to elaborate on here.
115    Cf. Andrew Ross: 'our imaginary of Capital still belongs for the most part to a demonology of the Other. This is a demonology that inhibits understanding and action as much as it artificially keeps alive older forms of *ressentiment* that have little or no purchase on a postmodern consumer society' ('Introduction' to *Universal Abandon? The Politics of Postmodernism*, Minneapolis: University of Minnesota Press, 1988, pp. xiv–xv).

Nonetheless, there may be some historical justification for the belief that the left's causes were indeed once bound up with each other. When Williams spoke in 1973 of the dominant in terms of class hegemony specifically, he nonetheless remarked that oppositional emergent and residual formations will not necessarily be class-based.[116] In saying this, he probably had in mind diverse New Left and countercultural causes, and this impression is reinforced by his statement ten years later that

> all significant social *movements* of the last thirty years have started outside the organized class interests and institutions. The peace movement, the ecology movement, the women's movement, solidarity with the third world, human rights agencies, campaigns against poverty and homelessness, campaigns against cultural poverty and distortion: all have this character, that they sprang from needs and perceptions which the interest-based organizations had no room or time for, or which they had simply failed to notice.

He could still assert, though, that 'there is not one of these issues which, followed through, fails to lead us into the central systems of the industrial-capitalist mode of production and among others into its system of classes'.[117] Today, such a claim seems less plausible, in part because at least some of these movements have substantially assimilated through their marketization. In relation to feminism, for instance, Janet Newman points out that the enterprise culture of the 1980s opened up possibilities for individual women to become successful, highlighting the ways in which 'the articulation

---

116  Williams, 'Base and Superstructure', p. 12.
117  Raymond Williams, *Towards 2000*, London: Chatto & Windus, 1984, pp. 172–173.

of women's collective interests has become more problematic with the co-option of a progressive vocabulary and feminist demands' by the system.[118] That case can in principle be extrapolated to others in the context of pervasive demands for equality of opportunity. Indeed, it has become clearer that the kind of class domination consolidated by neoliberalism is not incompatible with social liberalism, possibly of a very radical kind.

Taking a long-term perspective, Philip Bobbitt has argued that we increasingly live in market, rather than nation, states:

> whereas the nation-state justified itself as an instrument to serve the welfare of the people (the nation), the market-state exists to maximize the opportunities enjoyed by all members of society ... the market-state is classless and indifferent to race and ethnicity and gender.[119]

This cannot be endorsed without strong qualifications: Bobbitt is self-consciously speaking of tendencies, and acknowledges that the distinction is not that clear-cut in practice; when he speaks of classlessness, he is evidently speaking of a meritocracy that he overestimates, because widening inequality both militates against any such actuality and compounds other modes of injustice; and when he speaks of market states, it would be better to speak of neoliberal ones in order to recognize that they are contradictory in ways that go beyond any residual tensions between their historical

---

118   Janet Newman, 'Enterprising Women: Images of Success', in Sarah Franklin, Jackie Stacey and Celia Lury, eds, *Off-Centre: Feminism and Cultural Studies*, London: Harper Collins, 1991, p. 257.
119   Philip Bobbitt, *The Shield of Achilles: War, Peace and the Course of History*, London: Allen Lane, 2002, pp. 229–230.

'national' and contemporary 'market' features.[120] What Bobbitt recognizes here is a greater equality of identities considered in the abstract, and there is no reason in principle to exclude sexual ones from this list.

A further objection to Bobbitt's argument is that he speaks as if market states have spontaneously generated these conditions, whereas it would be more appropriate to acknowledge that the integrity of once globally dominant, white western bourgeois societies – central to which was the traditional family, its morality and its sexual divisions of labour – has been subject to persistent pressure and challenge in consequence of the very exercise of power, as DeKoven acknowledges, but also through globalization.[121] Under neoliberal capitalism, then, that dominance has fragmented as a result of various forces listed here in no particular order of priority: first, there has been the continuing pressure from the social movements that emerged out of the sixties, with their specific emphases, as well as their often substantial accommodation and transformation through the market's individualization of freedoms, and in many cases their global expansion beyond the west; second, there has been the greater mobility of people bound up with the material dynamics of time–space compression, placing considerable pressure on cultural 'integrity', not to mention the planet's habitability; and third, there has been the neoliberal development of once subordinate states to become formidable capitalist powers self-conscious of themselves as challenging

---

120 Harvey insists on these contradictory qualities: *A Brief History of Neoliberalism*, pp. 64–86.
121 Colin Leys offers an account of deregulation and marketization of state institutions that emphasizes the pressures of globalization in *Market-Driven Politics: Neoliberal Democracy and the Public Interest*, London: Verso, 2001, esp. pp. 8–79.

western hegemony, in part – though not in all cases – because of their formerly colonial status (Brazil, Russia, India and China are only the most obvious examples; attention has more recently been focused on the so-called MINTs – Mexico, Indonesia, Nigeria and Turkey – and no doubt there will be other acronymized achievers for us to cheer or bet on in future).

Thus, it may now be possible to speak legitimately of a *diversified dominant* under neoliberalism, not in order to highlight an established and stable fact, since very little about this world is stable, but rather to indicate a general, sometimes contested, tendency for hegemonic legitimation to be achieved through such diversification as one indication of its sponsorship of an expanded freedom.[122] I am barely able to assert such a thing, however, without immediately acknowledging it as problematic, with many local variations in terms of particular states and regions. I am also very well aware of populist conservative resistance to this dominant, as exemplified, for instance, by state-sponsored homophobia in Russia, or the increasing anti-immigrant nationalism of much of Europe. However, even this resistance is ironically frequently framed in terms of home-grown, or otherwise particular, cultural specificities that demand their proper recognition on an equal basis with all the others. The liberal assumption that diversification and tolerance go spontaneously together, because differences are private and neutral, remains a manifest delusion, and the postmodern assumption that difference and dissensus are necessarily somehow healthily innovative is surely an ideological extension of

122  The argument here differs from Jodi Melamed's suggestion that a neoliberal multiculturalism provides a veneer for the way that US power and capital sustain racially inferiorized groups ('The Spirit of Neoliberalism: From Racial Liberalism to Neoliberal Multiculturalism', *Social Text* 89, 24(4), 2006, pp. 13–20).

it. Still, pressure can be exerted on cultural integrity and conservatism through the diversified dominant. On his 2015 visit to Kenya to promote the interests of US capital in competition with that of China, the first black President of the US prominently raised the issues of women's and gay rights. Referring to the latter, President Kenyatta responded that 'there are some things we must admit we don't share'.[123]

Another word for diversified dominance might be cosmopolitanism, but that is a contested term. It references a Kantian, Enlightenment ideal of peaceful global integration and egalitarianism, but also simultaneously registers the problematic realization of it amid widening global inequalities of class (if not nations). Its most appropriate synecdoche might well be the cocktail to which it gives its name, since it is mostly a cultural reality linked to style. Daniele Archibugi's hopes for the achievement of what he calls cosmopolitical democracy – forms and institutions of global justice – have met with considerable scepticism on the left, given the record of suprastate organizations of various kinds being pressed into the service of dominant, mostly US, interests, or alternatively sidelined by those interests. Nations, by contrast, have occasionally been, and may be in future, important spaces of resistance to global neoliberal governance and further enforced deregulation.[124] Thus, to speak of diversified dominance is to highlight the extent to which a pluralism that might well be considered desirable in the abstract is nonetheless caught up in, and even determined by,

---

123   'Barack Obama Tells African States to Abandon Anti-Gay Discrimination', *The Guardian*, 25 July 2015, http://www.theguardian.com/us-news/2015/jul/25/barack-obama-african-states-abandon-anti-gay-discrimination (accessed 25 July 2015).
124   See the contributions to Daniele Archibugi, ed., *Debating Cosmopolitanism*, London: Verso, 2003.

vectors of class power and distinction.[125] 'Resistance' to it may take the *ugly* form of racism and *ressentiment*, and I use the aesthetic category here advisedly in order to highlight a contrast with the coolness and sexiness of cosmopolitan style. Those of us on the left who can be satisfied with neither diversified dominance, nor the atavistic response to it, often find ourselves wrong-footed by these dynamics.

Given all of this, it seems to me necessary to resist the kind of breezy position adopted by Walter Benn Michaels, who argues that state and institutional initiatives promoting diversity serve above all to distract us from a proper concern with economic inequality.[126] Whatever validity the claim possesses profoundly underestimates forms of resistance to social diversification that are frequently also bound up with resistance to modernity as such from a range of social forces – conservative, religious, even leftist – some of which either aspire to, or do in fact, deploy the resources of the state in order to regulate social norms. There are, after all, very few who believe that our necessary interdependence should be entirely mediated by exchange value. Hence a specific problem that has attended the marketization of freedoms to which we may aspire: through this alignment they frequently appear as a threat to other kinds of value, especially those grounded in the idealized family, and consequently as inhuman.

Thus, in addition to demonstrating a certain complacency, Michaels also neglects crucial questions around the *qualitative*

---

125  Robert Spencer reviews various theories of the cosmopolitan, and calls for 'a *dialectical* understanding of cosmopolitanism' that simultaneously grasps actual and potential modes (*Cosmopolitan Criticism and Postcolonial Literature*, Houndmills: Palgrave Macmillan, 2011, pp. 18–39).

126  Walter Benn Michaels, *The Trouble With Diversity: How We Learned to Love Identity and Ignore Inequality*, New York: Metropolitan/Henry Holt, 2006.

nature of a freedom bound to neoliberal diversification and the ends it serves. It is with such qualitative issues that I am concerned in the next chapter through the interrogation of a claim that is made more frequently in various ways, and by various sources, than one might expect: the claim that capitalism is progressive in relation to sexuality, not least queer sexuality. I address this argument now because there are compelling reasons for taking it seriously, even if my predisposition towards the case has surely been fully anticipated here.

2

---

# Is Capitalism
# Progressive (for Queers)?

In her important article, 'Thinking Sex' (1987), Gayle Rubin made a powerful case for sexuality as a distinct field of study. Her argument was polemical, aiming to 'identify, describe, explain and denounce erotic injustice and sexual oppression'.[1] In doing so, though, she lent support to the expansion of commercial sexual goods and services. As a means of reassuring her presumptively leftist readership that such an argument was one they too should support, she pointed out that 'Marx himself considered the capitalist market a revolutionary, if limited, force. He argued that capitalism was progressive in its dissolution of pre-capitalist superstition, prejudice, and the bonds of traditional modes of life.' Clearly, she anticipated objections from those who were not convinced that sexual freedoms should be underwritten by market ones: 'keeping sex from the positive laws of the market economy hardly makes it socialist,' she suggested.[2]

---

1   Gayle Rubin, 'Thinking Sex: Notes for a Radical Theory of Sexuality', in Carole S. Vance, ed., *Pleasure and Danger: Exploring Female Sexuality*, London: Routledge & Kegan Paul, 1984, p. 275.
2   Ibid., pp. 289–290.

A specific instance of the kind of progressiveness Rubin talks about is offered by Michael Warner and Lauren Berlant in their critique of the normalizing effects of the zoning law of former New York mayor, Rudolph Giuliani, in the nineties, which sought to regulate the location and density of sex-related commerce. Warner and Berlant's complaint was that the law aimed 'to restrict any counterpublic sexual culture by regulating its economic conditions',[3] and thereby threatened to undermine the diverse and substantial culture that had been consolidated on Christopher Street over the years. 'The point here,' they write, 'is not that queer politics needs more free-market ideology but that heteronormative forms, so central to the accumulation and reproduction of capital, also depend on heavy interventions in the regulation of capital.'[4] Berlant and Warner thus appear more anxious than Rubin about advancing the case, but they nonetheless claim that policing heteronormativity distorts the market. The difference between Giuliani, on the one hand, and Berlant and Warner, on the other, maps on to distinctions I explore later in this chapter: whereas Giuliani's was a neoconservative measure, relying on the interventionist power of the state to enforce traditional morality, theirs is ultimately compatible with a neoliberal perspective on the side of non-regulation. This is obviously not to suggest that they (or, indeed, Rubin) *are* neoliberals: many of us who would reject that label are frequently thrown back on such arguments. Effectively, I am concerned here with why this should be the case and with what effects. Ultimately, we must interrogate what it means to be 'progressive' in the first place: is this only ever a question of breaking with traditions and norms, of always needing

---

3   Lauren Berlant and Michael Warner, 'Sex in Public' in Michael Warner, *Publics and Counterpublics*, New York: Zone, 2002, pp. 203–204.
4   Ibid., p. 205.

to be more and yet more 'modern'? Why, ultimately, must progress be conceived and experienced as something that is done to us (by capitalism)?

We might first clarify Marx's perspective. Rubin cites the *Grundrisse* to support her case, but Marx there seeks to demonstrate both that it is the circulation of exchange value (money, the universal form of value) that underwrites bourgeois equality and freedom, and that this is also the basis of a distinctive form of inequality and unfreedom through money's transformation into capital, realized exploitatively in the workplace. Thus, equality and inequality, freedom and unfreedom are identical with each other – they are dialectically inseparable – within bourgeois society.[5] It was Marx's specific contribution – the thing that really did make him 'Marx himself' by distinguishing him from bourgeois economists – to recognize this. Merely to stress capitalism's progressiveness is to overlook the central contradiction that he insisted was constitutive of it, and demanded its supersession.

Moreover, this sense of capitalism as contradictory was bound up with Marx's specific understanding of the temporal logic of progress. Bourgeois society was progressive for him, not in the sense that it represented a gradual improvement on feudal or neofeudal orders, but that it revolutionized them. Similarly, though communism is made possible by the advances in productivity generated by technological developments under capitalism, it would be discontinuous with capitalism, qualitatively quite different in its collectivism. Famously, the untranslatable Hegelian term, *Aufhebung*, which Marx uses in various places, including the *Grundrisse*, signals this dual quality of preservation

---

5  Karl Marx, *Grundrisse: Foundations of a Draft of Political Economy*, trans. Martin Niclaus, London: Penguin, 1993, pp. 248–249.

and annulment, immanence and transcendence, to give definition to the kind of transformation he had in mind.

For Marx, then, progress was not strictly speaking a linear process, as is sometimes misleadingly claimed, or an intensification of existing trends. One result of his thinking in this respect, though, was a tendency in his writing to neglect further consideration of the possibilities for progress within capitalism, as well as to take for granted the improvements that communism would bring. Hence a key problem within Marxist theory: the tendency to disavow utopian speculation and rather to assume that the specific advances of bourgeois society – not only the expansion of the productive forces, but the freedoms it had produced through greater subjective autonomy – would be preserved and extended in a non-capitalist future, at the same time as they would be reconciled with a renewed appreciation of our necessary interdependence and equality.

This possibility, of course, is precisely what those such as Friedrich Hayek would deny: for them, collectivism, at least in the form of state planning, was necessarily the enemy of freedom *and* prosperity because it sought to prescribe individual wants and set limits to aspiration. Hence, the emphasis on historical regression signalled in the title of Hayek's polemic against such planning, *The Road to Serfdom* (1944). Moreover, from the perspective of this chapter at least, it may be considered no mere linguistic accident that among the virtues Hayek praised in the admirably market-loving British were 'non-interference with one's neighbour and tolerance of the different and queer ... a healthy suspicion of power and authority,' qualities he felt were being threatened by the expansion of the state.[6] As if to confirm Hayek's arguments – but

---

6   F. A. Hayek, *The Road to Serfdom*, London: Routledge, 2001, pp. 220–221.

writing from positions on the left – Alan Sinfield demonstrates that postwar welfare capitalism in Britain suppressed and discriminated against various marginal groups even as it claimed to be inclusive,[7] and a recent account of this period by Richard Hornsey celebrates the queer possibilities opened up by the popular and commercial by contrast with the heteronormativity sponsored by the state.[8]

There is greater agreement between Marx and Hayek, however, on one aspect of the progressiveness of capitalism. As Terry Lovell observes, 'there is no suggestion to be found in Marx's writings that commodities are ... second-rate goods, nor that the wants which they satisfy are not "real" wants. For Marx there is no such category, essential to left pessimism, as "false needs".'[9] It was left to the Frankfurt School, then, to argue that capitalist mass production produced a degenerate culture that rendered critical consciousness virtually impossible.

'False needs' is Marcuse's term for

those which are superimposed upon the individual by particular social interests in his repression: the needs which perpetuate toil, aggressiveness, misery, and injustice ... Most of the prevailing needs to relax, to have fun, to love and hate what others love and hate, belong to this category of false needs.[10]

There is no suggestion here that false needs are not actually relaxing or even, in a sense, fun (a category I return to below);

7   Alan Sinfield, *Literature, Politics and Culture in Postwar Britain*, third edition, London: Continuum, 2004, p. 341.

8   Richard Hornsey, *The Spiv and the Architect: Unruly Life in Postwar London*, Minneapolis: University of Minnesota Press, 2010.

9   Terry Lovell, *Pictures of Reality: Aesthetics, Politics, Pleasure*, London: British Film Institute, 1980, p. 59.

10   Herbert Marcuse, *One-Dimensional Man*, London: Routledge, 2002, p. 7.

they are not false in any crudely naturalistic or immediate sense of being merely unnecessary.[11] Marcuse speaks of superimposition, but he isn't only highlighting the fact that my need for a can of Coke, let's say, is the result of the propaganda of the advertisers (a social constructionist argument). It goes beyond this, since 'false' is used here in the teleological, Hegelian sense of inhibiting the realization of that freedom that exists as a potentiality in the present. False needs are prioritized as such by the system: we 'need' them because they satisfy the performance principle by perpetuating and intensifying it. Indeed, it is a relatively trivial point to suggest that that I don't *really* need this can of Coke, that I have been persuaded by the marketing people to believe I need it, and actually a glass of water would probably serve me better. On that level, the unanswerable response is: 'So what? I like Coke.' The far more substantive point is that such a need is false in the larger scheme of things, in which needs are not simply about what would satisfy me in the moment.[12] The category therefore serves to draw attention both to the relation between individual and collective needs, and to the fact that the recognition and pursuit of true needs may entail the suppression of immediate urges prompted by a consumerist society that both relies on 'toil,

---

11   See, for instance, Kate Soper, 'Alternative Hedonism, Cultural Theory and the Role of Aesthetic Revisioning', *Cultural Studies*, 22(5), 2008, p. 574. Nonetheless, I find Soper's work immensely suggestive and important, as will be clear from other sections of this book. Lovell's comments suggest agreement with Soper. Marcuse's differentiation between true and false needs, moreover, distinguishes him from Donald Morton, whose objection to queer theory is that it privileges exchange value and desire over use value and need as conceived by him in naturalistic fashion (see 'Birth of the Cyberqueer', *PMLA*, 110(3), 1995, pp. 369–381).

12   And in this sense, Soper and Marcuse are in agreement: see, for instance, 'A Difference of Needs', in *Troubled Pleasures: Writings on Politics, Gender and Hedonism*, London: Verso, 1990, pp. 71–86.

aggressiveness, misery, and injustice', and – as Marcuse also knew – is ecologically unsustainable.

There is also a qualitative claim being made in Marcuse's account, though, since he suggests that false needs enforce conformity by virtue of having been mass-produced, sinisterly thereby determining what all will love and hate. The obvious rejoinder from neoliberals to Marcuse's critique in this respect would be that, in a socialist society, it would be the collective, or even the state, that directed people's needs. Moreover, the claim about conformity is historically problematized by the fact that flexible accumulation has facilitated an extraordinary diversity of production that contrasts with the Fordist standardization Marcuse clearly had in mind. Now, the range of choices we face is often bewildering, and even self-defeating.

Some, indeed, have discerned in Frankfurt School Marxism a complicity with reactionary and elitist critique through an alleged appeal to non- or pre-industrial modes of life and art. If, as Marcuse accepts, capitalism has generated an expansion in productive capabilities that hold the potential to eliminate scarcity, then it becomes difficult to despise its efficiencies. When he disparages frozen food at one point, for instance, suggesting it as a synecdoche for standardization not only of products but of consciousness,[13] what exactly does he have in mind as an alternative, and how widely available might it be? What sort of social order does he imply, and what level of material transformation would be necessary to bring it about? Is there a tacit romanticism in Frankfurtian perspectives, in spite of their consciousness of this danger? Sinfield pointedly suggests that Adorno shared with the obviously reactionary

---

13  Herbert Marcuse, *Eros and Civilization: A Philosophical Inquiry Into Freud*, Abingdon: Routledge, 1998, 100.

F. R. Leavis a conviction that he could distinguish real art from commercial culture,[14] and regards this kind of assumption on the left as a key mistake for reasons I return to in chapter four.

These questions are relevant to a concern with the supposed progressiveness of the market in relation to sexuality because a different way of expressing the argument that capitalism challenges tradition is to suggest that it profanes the higher values of heterosacramentalism, just as it is said to hollow out aesthetic value (this is merely another way of putting Rubin's argument). Berlant and Warner imply that the family's value to capital resides in its largely unremunerated reproduction of the labour force, but the family's continuing importance cannot simply be explained on grounds of its utility in this respect, otherwise surely no one would fall for it. The family is also the centre of affective life for many, perhaps most, people – those Chinese workers in Shenzhen I noted in the last chapter, for instance – not only because of those profound feelings, for as long as they last, of 'belonging' to another person, but also because reproduction is 'miraculous' and further testifies to, by blessing, that fusion of spirit and matter that distinguishes sacramental love. Moreover, 'having a family' – and precisely because it is unpaid and entails sacrifices – simultaneously evinces the responsibility of the couple, given that societies and communities are conceived as extending across time as well as space, and that the family remains for most the primary unit of socialization, despite pervasive deprivatization.

Thus, the family is both private and public at the same time,[15] though the way in which that distinction is constituted has varied

---

14  Sinfield, *Postwar Britain*, p. 330.
15  Michael Warner notes the ubiquity and contradictoriness of the public/ private distinction in a thorough exposition of its origins and implications in 'Public and Private' (*Publics and Counterpublics*, pp. 21–64).

socially and historically, along with the sense of what it means to belong to a society or a community. People who have been told all their lives not only that they will find fulfilment, but that they are doing the right thing by getting married and having children feel understandably angry when they find it difficult or impossible to sustain their life together because of material hardship, especially when surrounded by images of plenty. They are rightly perplexed or outraged by those who say that their plight is no one else's business, and certainly not the state's.

This is the awkwardness of Margaret Thatcher's notorious claim in 1987 that 'there is no such thing [as society]! There are only individual men and women, and there are families.' She went on in the same speech to make a series of incoherent, yet moralistic, statements about 'lifestyles' in respect of AIDS, claiming that 'a nation of free people will only continue to be a great nation if your family life continues and the structure of that nation is a family structure'.[16] There is no precise sense to be made of all this. Rather, it goes to the heart of the contradictions of Thatcherism itself; the suggestion seems to be that AIDS is a consequence of the failure (but on whose part?) magically to resolve the tension between being a free people (individuals) and a great nation (family).

This places the family, too, in a complex position in relation to our understanding of progress. Lawrence Stone claims that the modern family is one product of what he calls an 'affective individualism' attendant on historical shifts towards a greater

---

16   The transcription of this *Woman's Own* interview of 1987 from which Thatcher is often misquoted can be found at http://www.margaretthatcher. org/document/106689 (accessed 5 September 2012).

sense of personal autonomy,[17] and the sense that family life should be personally fulfilling informed the middle-class principle that marriage be predicated on love, by contrast with the aristocratic one that it was about consolidating connections, wealth and status. Moreover, love is still seen to be winning out today. Prince William's choice of the 'commoner'[18] Kate Middleton for his bride represents a further 'democratization' of the Royal Family after the disastrous (and typically aristocratic) match of Charles and Diana, royal propagandists tell us. More significantly, arranged marriages tend to be viewed as pre-modern and an affront to individuals' human rights.[19] Gay marriage is said finally to confer public recognition on the validity, equality and dignity (implicitly: the potential fidelity) of same-sex passion. Hence, the western, bourgeois ideal of marriage is both advocated as something that might be progressively extended, at the same time as it is defended as a conservative institution by some of those, such as Andrew Sullivan or David Cameron, who have promoted that extension.[20]

All of this, however, must be understood as taking place in the context of a continuing neoliberalization that sees the family and the dependencies it fosters as the appropriate alternative to the

---

17 Lawrence Stone, *The Family, Sex and Marriage in England 1500–1800*, London: Weidenfeld and Nicolson, 1977, pp. 225–238. I have preserved Stone's lack of specificity as regards causation in this formulation.

18 Non-British readers may be surprised to hear that this was in fact the way she was habitually referred to, if not wholly without irony, in British media reports on the engagement.

19 I should clarify this point: 'tend to' here refers obviously enough to a modern, but not necessarily western, perspective.

20 Cameron defended the policy of establishing gay marriage on the grounds that this was a specifically conservative move in his speech at the 2011 Conservative Party Conference. I discuss Sullivan below.

state provision that is being attacked.[21] In addition to being both public and private, then, the family is simultaneously reinforced by marketization and represented as a haven from it, the repository of truly non-commercial values otherwise under threat. Hence, a temporal paradox: the family binds us to a human future distinguished from the progress that is visited on us as an alien, implacable force by the market. It is because the family supposedly underwrites the possibility of an unalienated future, or at least offers relative alleviation from that alienation, that non-normative forms of gender and sexuality are perceived as such powerful threats to it, especially when they appear conspicuously marketized.

In the reflections on these complex dynamics that follow, I shall trace and retrace aspects of the history already touched on in chapter one, where I noted the transition from patriarchal familialism to an uneven, incomplete and even contradictory diversified dominant that has accompanied the shift to neoliberalism and flexible accumulation, since the innovations of the latter have renewed the identification of capitalism with progress as such. First, however, it is necessary to turn to more general historical dynamics, and also to the socialist tradition's entanglement in them in ways that have determined its historic (and often continuing) anti-queer sentiments.

## Freedom and commitment

The tendency for Marx and Engels to see progress in the dialectical terms of both preservation and abolition is evident not least in their various comments on the family, which they see as both

---

21 Cora Kaplan makes this point in relation to Blairism in 'The Death of the Working Class Hero', *new formations* 52 (2004), p. 98.

anticipating 'higher' forms of intimate relations in postrevolutionary circumstances and destined for destruction by the revolution.[22] In the case of the working class, they argued, familial breakdown had already occurred as one consequence of poverty and capitalist industry's reorganization of work.[23] In the case of the bourgeoisie, for whom marriage had by contrast been consolidated, the end of the family would result from the abolition of private property. Both emphases are to be found in Engels' influential *The Origins of the Family, Private Property and the State* (1884). There he claims that the monogamy and seclusion demanded of women in bourgeois marriage was necessary to ensure that the husband's biological children would inherit his wealth. Hence, bourgeois marriage fostered the double standard by licensing the male resort to prostitution necessitated by supposed male sex needs. Far from seeing such commercialization of sex positively, Engels believed its eradication would be a desirable consequence of socialist transformation, and even though he assumed that marriage as an institution would be a casualty of that revolution, he also suggested that the transformation of social conditions would result in a higher form of freely chosen heterosexual monogamy. This would have been prefigured by bourgeois love, but would be unconstrained by the continuing tendency of it to be directed towards members of the same class.

The evolutionary emphasis in Engels's argument determines his sense that the enslavement of women in ancient Greece by

---

22   Richard Weikart provides a helpful survey of Marx and Engels' mostly brief comments on the family, placing them in the context of broader nineteenth-century socialist and anarchist ideas: 'Marx, Engels and the Abolition of the Family', *History of European Ideas*, 18(5), 1994, pp. 657–672.
23   See, for instance, *The Communist Manifesto* in David McLellan, ed., *Karl Marx: Selected Writings*, second edition, Oxford: Oxford University Press, 2000, pp. 259–260.

Athenian men 'was avenged on the men and degraded them also till they fell into the abominable practice of sodomy and degraded their gods and themselves with the myth of Ganymede'.[24] Sodomy here appears as the historical complement to the slavery of women, as if it were the necessary counterpart to a more general imbalance in the natural order of things. Engels therefore tacitly naturalizes both society and history in a way that Marxists have regarded as classically ideological.[25] Moreover, his deployment of Judeo-Christian terminology and morality to judge the Greeks' own mythological justifications for sex between men is indicative of the extent to which he also remained trapped within the religious logic of the time. Naturalization and sanctification, then, are at work in his idealization of cross-sex relations, which are made to function allegorically as reconciling historical dialectics in much the same way as marriage had traditionally been used to symbolize the resolution of social problems in the conventional Victorian novel (and, indeed, in comedic narrative more generally): history would have a happy ending, and spontaneous heterosacramentalism exemplified the unity of freedom with mutuality that the revolution would bring.

Engels's argument on the family was treated as authoritative within much of the Marxist tradition, though the sacramentalism

---

24　Frederick Engels, *The Origin of the Family, Private Property and the State*, Harmondsworth: Penguin, 1985, p. 95. On the homophobia in Marx and Engels' letters, see Hubert Kennedy, 'Johann Baptist von Schweitzer: The Queer Marx Loved to Hate', in Gert Hekma, Harry Oosterhuis and James Steakley, eds, *Gay Men and the Sexual History of the Political Left*, New York: Harrington Park, 1995, pp. 69–96, and Andrew Parker, 'Unthinking Sex: Marx, Engels and the Scene of Writing', in Michael Warner (ed.), *Fear of a Queer Planet: Queer Politics and Social Theory*, Minneapolis: Minnesota University Press, 1993, pp. 19–41.

25　Engels is both aware of this danger and falls for it in *The Dialectics of Nature*, London: Lawrence & Wishart, 1987.

defended by him has in practice tended to underwrite support for, rather than opposition to, the institutionalized family unit.[26] Michèle Barrett and Mary MacIntosh helpfully summarize why it is that the family has persistently functioned as an important symbol of a postcapitalist future: 'Marx's "from each according to his ability, to each according to his needs" is an ideal to which the nearest approximation we can imagine is a caring family where the contribution of each is not subjected to exact calculation.'[27] As this implies, though, to continue to privilege the family as the site of such non-instrumentalized bonds not only colludes with the continuing idealization of an institution in reality associated by many with confinement, misery and abuse, but also marks an obvious failure on the part of socialist thought to imagine a transformation in relations beyond it. Indeed, it is at least arguable that the family continued to function in the supposedly socialist states of the twentieth century as much as in capitalist ones as the justification for their particular kinds of exploitative and alienated relations, determined by authoritarian models of development. In this, as in other respects, such states have served to reinforce perceptions of capitalism's merit in underwriting the freedom of the individual, here in relation to sexuality.

If bourgeois hegemony resulted in the sanctification of marital relations, it would nonetheless be true to say that capitalism in

---

26  Michèle Barrett and Mary MacIntosh, *The Anti-Social Family*, London: Verso, 1982, p. 18. Eli Zaretsky: 'Within the socialist movement Engels' book was taken not as a beginning but as the final word' (*Capitalism, The Family and Personal Life*, New York: Harper & Row, 1976, p. 96). Maxine Molyneux highlights Engels' centrality to pervasive policies and attitudes in the socialist states that stress the importance both of women's entry into wage labour *and* their continued 'appropriateness' for domestic work (Molyneux, 'Socialist Societies Old and New: Progress Towards Women's Emancipation', *Feminist Review*, 8, 1981, pp. 9–10).

27  Barrett and MacIntosh, *The Anti-Social Family*, p. 40.

its larger determinations of social change exerted pressure *on* the family's integrity. This is the emphasis of John d'Emilio in his still persuasive essay, 'Capitalism and Gay Identity'. D'Emilio argues that the system of family-based production that was characteristic of New England villages from the seventeenth century on was gradually broken up during the nineteenth century by the emergence of urban capitalist production and the development of 'free labour'. This generated greater autonomy for workers, even as it exposed them to new forms of exploitation. Over time, it also facilitated, not merely same-sex contacts, but self-conscious, mostly urban communities based on same-sex desire as early as the late eighteen hundreds.[28]

Miranda Joseph has reservations about this narrative. She suggests that it evinces a tendency to link homosexuality with the exchange value that both superseded historically, and has subsequently masked, a use value thereby associated with the traditional, pre-capitalist family. The result is that 'gays ... become the scapegoats in a romantic or populist anticapitalism where only the abstractness of money and the impersonal corporation are seen as evil.'[29] She points out various problems with this way of representing the use/exchange value distinction, given that the family contributes to the order of exchange value through the reproduction of variable capital (i.e. the workforce), that it

28 John d'Emilio, 'Capitalism and Gay Identity', in *Making Trouble: Essays on Gay History, Politics and the University*, New York: Routledge, 1992, pp. 3–16. More recently, Didier Eribon has argued that the city has become 'the refuge of gay people in the twentieth century': *Insult and the Making of the Gay Self*, trans. Michael Lucey, Durham, NC: Duke University Press, 2004, p. 19.

29 Miranda Joseph, *Against the Romance of Community*, Minneapolis: University of Minnesota Press, 2002, p. 165. Zaretsky, who is supposedly the source of d'Emilio's romantic anti-capitalism in *Capitalism*, is also explicitly critical of romanticism.

consumes goods, and that many businesses are still family-run. These are all crucial points, and I shall return to them. However, d'Emilio does not argue that same-sex *desire* was determined by capitalism's breakup of traditional family production, but rather that certain kinds of communities and identities were facilitated by it. Moreover, d'Emilio is aware of the dangers of romanticism, and critiques such forms of thought in very much the same terms as Joseph: his conclusion is that lesbians and gay men have been stigmatized as a result of the destabilization of the family that is one consequence of capitalist development. As part of the project of legitimating sexual autonomy, he argues, socialists must demand 'structures and programs that will help to dissolve the boundaries that isolate the family, particularly those that privatize childrearing'.[30] D'Emilio therefore writes within a tradition of lesbian and gay liberation that saw the effectiveness of struggle as contributing to, and dependent on, more general social transformation and enhanced freedoms.

D'Emilio's focus on the growth of communities is significant, though: he affirms the capacity for same-sex desire to ground non-individualistic, relational values. However, his argument suggests that such communal life was facilitated by a prior autonomy that has traditionally been negatively associated with the atomization and anonymity of modernity. Hence, urban dwellers have been convicted of 'an absence of common feeling, an excess of subjectivity'.[31] What appears as lack of community for some, though, may be experienced by others as precisely the freedom to seek out company on something other than a highly circumscribed

---

30  D'Emilio, 'Capitalism and Gay Identity', pp. 13–14.
31  Raymond Williams, *The Country and the City*, London: Chatto & Windus, 1973, p. 215. Williams is here drawing attention to the tendency, not subscribing to it.

basis. For such figures, their sensations are the inverse of urban *anomie* in every sense. Mark W. Turner, for instance, suggests that 'modernity opened up a space, both real and conceptual, for the cruiser to inhabit',[32] and compares him or her to the Baudelairean and Benjaminian *flâneur*: in urban conditions, random sex became an abstract possibility latent within the flux of everyday life. Thus, the city generated a distinctive experience and sensibility. Speaking of twentieth-century contexts, Henning Bech suggests that the stimulus of the city consisted in an 'altogether special blend of closeness and distance, crowd and flickering, surface and gaze, freedom and danger' that combined with the homosexual's sense that 'sexuality is his innermost nucleus'.[33]

Bech, moreover, considers the qualitative nature of the kinds of contacts sought in such ways precisely in terms of their inversion of the value normatively placed on 'relationships' – the euphemism is instructive – as the antidote to the impersonality of modernity:

they are *not* long-term, *not* binding, *not* personal – and that is *not good*. They are *alienated*, not authentic: there is no giving of self, only enactment of a role and maintenance of distance; they are *reified*: the other person is treated as a thing to be used and disposed of, and only appearance counts in selling and buying;

---

32   Mark W. Turner, *Backward Glances: Cruising the Streets of New York and London*, London: Reaktion, 2003, p. 8. The *flâneur* tradition also occurs to Ross Chambers in describing Alan Hollinghurst's novel as an instance of 'loiterature': 'Messing Around: Gayness and Loiterature in Alan Hollinghurst's *The Swimming Pool Library*', in *Textuality and Sexuality: Reading Theories and Practices*, Manchester: Manchester University Press, 1993, p. 207.
33   Henning Bech, *When Men Meet: Homosexuality and Modernity*, Oxford: Polity, 1997, pp. 119–120. Bech is speaking of the homosexual as a figure who has become conscious of himself as such, no doubt through the processes of internalization described by Foucault.

they are *instrumentalized*: it is a matter of merely pursuing purely selfish interests and making the other person into a means for them, instead of both persons becoming a common end for each other; they are *fetishized*: only the surface of the other person, or only a part of him, is given attention and worshipped – that whole vocabulary of invectives and distancing phrases, formulated by the last couple of centuries' theoreticians and poets as fascinated and frightened witness to the development of the capitalist market, the state bureaucracies and the modern city. In short: these meetings are purely and simply the negation of what they should be; there is, so to speak, *nothing* left.

Yet obviously something does go on; and something, at that, which cannot be reduced to the mere trading of commodities.[34]

In this remarkable passage, Bech evinces a relish for and defiant insistence on the alienated, reified, instrumentalized and fetishized quality of such meetings that itself indicates the extent to which their erotic appeal is determined by the more general negative valuations of them: it is in the breaking of taboos that they acquire their thrill, the particular quality of freedom that makes them viscerally appealing. Even so, Bech ultimately feels the urge to challenge the adequacy of normative judgements by asserting a redemptive 'something' about these contacts. More than the 'nothing' of their material and objectifying forms, there is that paradoxically intangible, yet human, *substance* to them after all: needs of some sort are being expressed and satisfied.

The qualitative characteristics of such encounters are formed by contrast with the values of partnership, family and home that, in their idealization, are (still) represented as places of satisfaction,

---

34  Ibid., p. 112.

stability and repose. These, then, are spatiotemporal dynamics, both material and ideological, and they have crucially determined same-sex desires and the experience and representation of them. In the transition from country to city, and then again, in the related and intensified distinction between private and public, same-sex desire inhabits – if that is the right word – the latter. It is a desire exiled from home, rest, and a wholeness lost subjectively and/or historically, but that might be restored or won again – for Engels and much of the socialist tradition, through communism. It is dynamic and circulatory, restless and abstract, and for all of these reasons imbued with a specific intensity that informs both the denigration of it and the fantasies that perpetuate its appeal. Of course, and precisely because of the historical regulation of space and its persistent legacies, this determination of desire has been overwhelmingly the experience of men, whose sexuality is said by just about everyone to be most in need of constraint. It is for this reason that any consideration of the alleged progressiveness of capitalism necessitates consideration of diverse features of gender ideology as this governs perceptions of gay male sexuality in particular.

## Commodification and masculine desire

The intensity of desire between men as determined by its non-domestic status is also what has made it especially commodifiable. This is David T. Evans' argument in relation to those gay spaces that are mostly private, in terms of ownership, but more or less public in terms of access: bars, clubs, saunas and the like. Evans claims that traditions of cruising under conditions of illegality necessarily generated an objectifying sensibility among men who had sex with men that was continuous with the desires that were subsequently promoted on the commercialized scene.[35] His argument focuses on the partial decriminalization of sexual acts between men in Britain in 1967, though it has a more general relevance. The point is that British law did not mark any attempt on the part of the state to legitimate such acts, but merely established the limits of the state in relation to acts and desires defined as private – which is to say, both pertaining to the individual and to be pursued behind locked doors. Hence, there was no attempt to reform attitudes, and the principal sphere of civil society in which gay sociality was able to develop was the commercial scene, given that the market as such is indifferent to what is bought and sold. The consequences, however, were not neutral: 'As gay men claimed their leisure and lifestyle market, the market claimed them, colonized and exploited gay sexuality.'[36] An intensified objectification of the body and 'virile' pursuit of sex, Evans claims, were the consequences of this process, as was a pronounced depoliticization over time resulting from the new-found possibility of satisfying private desires.

Evans, though, makes an observation whose implications determine in large part what I am concerned with here and in the subsequent section. He suggests a continuity between contexts pre- and postdecriminalization, despite the widely noted stylistic transformations from camp codes of interaction to masculinized ones, especially on the leather scene.[37] Both are objectifying and self-objectifying, since effeminacy, in its 'cool detachment',

---

35  David T. Evans, *Sexual Citizenship: The Material Construction of Sexualities*, London: Routledge, 1993, pp. 98–99.

36  Ibid., p. 100.

37  See, for instance, most recently David M. Halperin's exploration of these in *How to be Gay*, Cambridge, Mass.: Belknap, 2012, pp. 46–59. Halperin, however, emphasizes that masculine investments frequently were, and continue to be, serious rather than parodic, as we have tended to tell ourselves they are.

differs from supposedly true (nurturing, sympathetic, reparative) femininity, and complements a stylized masculinity that is itself 'studiedly and specifically homosexual'.[38] Indeed, movement between, or combination of, the two is straightforward enough for the muscle Mary, who is for that reason a significant figure. The social determinations that have produced him are worthy of detailed consideration. Here, I focus on this hybrid figure's masculine aspect; I turn to his feminine one below.

Evans' intention is not to critique 'promiscuity' or any specific form of sexual encounter, but to cast a sceptical eye on the notion that markets simply respond to demand. Nonetheless, critiques of commerce along these lines can sound moralistic. Jonathan Dollimore notes ambivalent representations of the scene as a stock feature of queer fiction across the twentieth century: even postdecriminalization, the scene is represented as 'exciting, commercially vibrant, and *exploitative*'[39] (my emphasis). Larry Kramer's *Faggots* (1978)[40] is one striking instance, and the sense in that novel that just about anything has become possible by the late seventies all too obviously explains Kramer's latterly very powerful commitment to gay marriage as a 'solution'. Alan Hollinghurst's *The Swimming Pool Library* (1988), by contrast, is more nuanced and complex. Its remarkable achievement is to mount a non-moralistic critique of the scene, and of cruising in particular,[41] by

---

38   Evans, *Sexual Citizenship*, pp. 99–100.

39   Jonathan Dollimore, *Sexual Dissidence: Augustine to Wilde, Freud to Foucault*, Oxford: Clarendon Press, 1991, p. 57.

40   Larry Kramer, *Faggots*, New York: Random House, 1978.

41   Perhaps this explains why Emma Liggins finds that it endorses 'promiscuity' in 'Alan Hollinghurst and Metropolitan Gay Identities', in *Posting the Male: Masculinities in Post-war and Contemporary British Literature*, Daniel Lea and Berthold Schoene, eds, Amsterdam: Rodopi, 2003, pp. 159–170.

registering the pornographic quality of the pervasive eroticism the novel both conveys and relishes (rather in the manner of Bech).[42] It is worth exploring in more detail for this reason.

The novel's narrator, Will Beckwith, acknowledges few constraints on the realization of his sexual desires, though the novel suggests that the compulsive nature of these is at odds with his initial sense of himself as autonomous and free in ways consolidated by his class privilege (his family's wealth was made through the brewing industry, and he will inherit his grandfather's aristocratic title). The increasing narrative sense of him as being in reality controlled rather than in control, though, culminates in the revelation that he has been manipulated all along by former colonial administrator, Lord Nantwich, himself now a pornographer.

This trajectory itself exemplifies the novel's critique, which relies on the affective pull of a complex form of nostalgia for a historical and/or subjective past prior to the emergence of, or individual entry on to, the scene, with the consequence that the kind of self-consciousness generated by gay existence entails a loss of former 'innocence'. Importantly, such innocence is not associated with any disavowal of eroticism, but rather evinces either an unselfconsciousness about it, or a wariness of transforming it into direct sexual gratification. Will Beckwith looks back on the 'lubricious innocence'[43] of public school sex in the swimming pool library that gives the novel its name.

---

42  I have argued much of what follows at greater length, but in very different terms, in 'Desire as Nostalgia: The Novels of Alan Hollinghurst', in David Alderson and Linda Anderson, eds, *Territories of Desire in Queer Culture: Refiguring Contemporary Boundaries*, Manchester: Manchester University Press, 2000, pp. 29–48.
43  Alan Hollinghurst, *The Swimming Pool Library*, London: Chatto & Windus, 1988, p. 141.

Indeed, 'innocence' is everywhere invoked in terms that register its necessary violation, even through the very articulation of it as such, since to be conscious of innocence is to be culpably apart from it. When Will enters a porn cinema he wonders of one pensioner in the audience whether he could

> look back to a time when he had behaved like these glowing, thoughtless teenagers [on screen], who were now locked together sucking each other's cocks on the hay? Or was this the image of a new society we had made, where every desire could find its gratification?[44]

However, the past in its various forms is not simply idealized: Nantwich's diaries ultimately recount his arrest and imprisonment, reminding us that earlier times were also directly repressive.

Thus, the temporal logic of the novel combines at just about every moment a dialectical tension between progress and decadence that nonetheless does not suggest the possibility of a 'higher' resolution. Instead, it determines a particular, persistent, bittersweet affect, registered in the very opening of the novel in its description of the setting as at one and the same time Will's *'belle époque'*, and 'the last summer of its kind there was ever to be'.[45] The unstated reason for this has to do with the spread of HIV that is silently taking place: the ubiquitous scent of these halcyon days, commodifying the risk and danger associated with male sexuality, is 'Trouble for Men'.

The novel's treatment of temporality is problematic, though, in relation to colonialism, given that it tends to reinforce Nantwich's

44  Ibid., p. 51.
45  Ibid., p. 3.

claim in the present that gay men were preferred for posts in the empire because '"we were prone to immense idealism and dedication"'.[46] Such idealism is exemplified by his platonic relationship with his manservant, Taha, whom he loves and takes back to England, only for Taha to be murdered by racists while Nantwich is in prison. Thus, the empire is largely exonerated of a racial brutality that is rather associated with non-cosmopolitan, probably working-class, attitudes (and, as if to confirm this association, Will is attacked by skinheads on the council estate of his former black lover). Back in the Sudan, by contrast, we find Nantwich at one point, drunk, maudlin and doting on Taha's beauty, reflecting that he '*was* my responsibility made flesh: he was all the offspring I will never have, all my futurity'.[47] Such moments suggest that in the repressive past it was nonetheless possible for a self-conscious same-sex eroticism to mediate social relations positively, though the humanity of this relation is dependent both on its non-instrumentality and an investment in the future that generates social-paternalist feelings.

In the contemporary world, by contrast, relations are reductively sexualized: the reader is shocked to discover that one of the stars of Nantwich's porn films is Taha's son, Abdul. From the outset, moreover, Beckwith's own sexual fetishisms are informed by former colonial and class power relations, but the principal irony is that these appear impoverished when compared to the real thing, at least to the extent that we are made aware of these through Nantwich's conduct and reflections in the diaries. Moreover, it is commodification that facilitates such reductivism: when Will enters a sex shop, he notes 'mighty black jobs'[48] among

---

46  Ibid., p. 241.
47  Ibid., p. 210.
48  Ibid., p. 48.

the dildos on offer. *The Swimming Pool Library* therefore risks a form of conservatism in its critique of the market by appealing to an eroticized colonial paternalism as one instance of 'humane' relations eroded by a commercialization that determines the freedoms of the present, and exploits the 'innocent' past for the thrills generated by its sexualization.

The persistence of older forms into the present in the novel raises other complex matters on which I need to touch in thinking about the ways that same-sex desire has been conditioned by its exclusion from the domestic. Continuity in Hollinghurst's novel is also evident in the extensive, if degenerate, patronage the elderly Nantwich exercises. He even manages to consolidate through this relation something that perversely resembles a family. However, it is a family without women, and it is often remarked that the novel as a whole is intensely homosocial.[49] Indeed, the scene appears to be continuous with, at the same time as it sexually reifies, the kinds of contact facilitated by specifically male institutions: public schools, men's clubs and gyms, boxing clubs, even just the freer habitation of public space. The only woman's voice in the novel is that of Beckwith's sister on the end of a telephone. Here we must confront a persistent problem, then, that attends any tendency to elide lesbian and gay interests, or to assume a general queerness: the sense that patterns of male same-sex desire are quintessentially masculine and therefore objectionable from a feminist perspective.

An instance of this is provided by Adrienne Rich, who once objected to the perceived political affiliations between lesbians and gay men in her elaboration of an alternative filiation through what she described as a 'lesbian continuum'. In the process, she highlighted

---

49  See, for instance, Chambers, 'Messing Around', pp. 212–215.

the 'qualitative differences in female and male relationships – for example, the patterns of anonymous sex among male homosexuals, and the pronounced ageism in male homosexual standards of attractiveness'.[50] In a somewhat similar spirit, Michèle Barrett and Mary MacIntosh concede to defenders of the family that

> prostitution, pornography, and sexualization of the media, many facets of the male gay scene and ... the pre-marital sex of teenage years all reflect a predatory, dehumanized male sexuality. Yet they are so unpleasant because they are forbidden, rather than forbidden because they are unpleasant.[51]

This, though, is to lump together a large number of things on the basis merely of their exclusion from the family, and thereby to risk complicity with normative standards of what is unpleasant. Moreover, it presumes that this unpleasantness exists in some sense for the participants as well as the judgemental outsider, since the suggestion is that the mere removal of taboos would, perhaps spontaneously, result in a more humane male sexuality across all these spheres: *this*, they suggest – not further marketization – would be progressive.

One hears such claims less frequently these days, at least as regards cruising, in part because they are plainly untrue. Cruising affords pleasures that may have emerged from the legal proscription of same-sex desire, but it is surely a mistake to regard such 'promiscuity' as the perverse consequence of a repression whose annulment will guarantee cruising's disappearance. The specific qualitative pleasures it offers are bound up in all sorts of

---

50  Adrienne Rich, 'Compulsory Heterosexuality and Lesbian Existence', in *Adrienne Rich's Poetry and Prose*, New York: Norton, 1993, p. 218.
51  Barrett and MacIntosh, *The Anti-Social Family*, p. 31.

ways with the detachment of sex from commitment. To speak of this as dehumanized is tacitly to uphold the values of one side of the masculine/feminine division as structured by the public/private dynamics that have tended to keep women domesticated.[52] Henning Bech is ultimately complicit with this logic, though he valorizes the other side of that division. He provocatively rejects the 'assumption [that] sexual attraction of men to men might *as well* be an attraction to women', not on biological, but cultural, grounds, and further claims that 'an analysis of male homosexuality that doesn't acknowledge this difference of masculinity is indeed – homophobic'.[53] This, though, confirms the reification of the qualities associated with masculinity as properties of men exclusively, even though there are plenty of women who enjoy 'dehumanized' sex.

The specific problem that determines attitudes in this area is that of how women might enjoy greater sexual freedom with men, should they wish to, without either being subject to misogynist condemnation or finding their desires subsumed and subordinated by men's sexual demands. The specificity of that problem, though, gets lost in a universal imperative rendered in abstract terms: the necessary *domestication* of men. This is a logic that clearly emerges out of the history of patriarchal relations, perpetuating rather than displacing it. Gay cruising also emerges out of those structures, and honours them to the extent that it is conceptualized and invested in as masculine,[54] but part of its distinctiveness arises from the

---

52 Warner makes a similar point about a certain feminist distrust of the public, though not in relation to sexuality ('Sex in Public', p. 58).

53 Bech, *When Men Meet*, pp. 70–71.

54 By this, I mean 'pertaining to men'. I am aware that such a definition has been challenged by figures such as Judith Halberstam, who argues for an autonomous tradition of female masculinity in her book on that topic (*Female Masculinity*, Durham: Duke University Press, 1998).

fact that, without prey, there is no predation, merely (or hopefully) mutual pleasure. In cruising, after all, it is easy to say no.

This is not to suggest that cruising as it is practised is free from power relations. Indeed, Hollinghurst's novel suggests that it may thrive on them.[55] Nonetheless, it also both problematizes any simple grasp of power's dynamics through its questioning of Beckwith's mastery of his situation, and highlights the reifying qualities of commodification through its transformation of social and erotic relations into a self-conscious thing: *the* sexual.[56] To see all of this, and 'promiscuity' too, as symptoms of a masculine desire simply to be repudiated or superseded is to fail to recognize that such desire has also been predicated on the positive freedoms that were historically conferred on men by virtue simply of being men. The expansion of freedom is not served by confiscating privileges that have been unequally distributed, but to say this much is obviously not to equate the cruising sensibility with freedom as such.

## Prefiguration and decadence

And so, back to the muscle Mary in his other aspect. If gay desire is masculine in the way we have just discussed, gay personae are feminized because associated with the breakdown of the ideally

---

55 Alan Sinfield explores the notion that power is sexy in *On Sexuality and Power*, New York: Columbia University Press, 2004.

56 Both Rosemary Hennessy (*Profit and Pleasure: Sexual Identities in Late Capitalism*, New York: Routledge, 2000), and Kevin Floyd (*The Reification of Desire: Toward a Queer Marxism*, Minneapolis: University of Minnesota Press, 2009) theorize sexuality as a form of reification, but draw different political conclusions from this fact. I consider their arguments in my conclusion rather than in this chapter.

disciplined bourgeois manliness[57] that once dominated family life. The process is helpfully summarized by David F. Greenberg and Marcia H. Bystryn, who point out that, besides 'sharpening the division of labour and strengthening the ideology of the family', capitalism in its earlier phases had also functioned to reinforce subjective resistance to male homosexuality specifically 'by intensifying competition between men, by fostering an ethic of self restraint antagonistic to sexual expression ... and by giving rise to an ideology which reinterpreted deviance in medical terms'.[58] Such manliness was individualized and self-contained, yet conformist and 'respectable'; it still hasn't disappeared entirely, at least as an ideal. However, Greenberg and Bystryn point out that gay liberation eventually emerged out of the more general radicalism of the counterculture in conditions of relative affluence that had produced a relaxation of the disciplinary imperatives that characterized capitalism's emergence.[59]

The trajectory of lesbian, gay and queer movements also needs to be understood in relation to this ostensibly progressive, 'feminizing' expansion of goods and their various promises of satisfaction. One way of illustrating this is through Dennis Altman's account of the emergence of lesbian and gay movements

---

57   Herbert Sussman notes the distinction between masculinity and constraining, bourgeois manliness in *Victorian Masculinities: Manhood and Masculine in Early Victorian Literature and Art*, Cambridge: Cambridge University Press, 1995, pp. 10–11.

58   David F. Greenberg and Marcia H. Bystryn, 'Capitalism, Bureaucracy, and Male Homosexuality', in Steven Seidman, ed., *Queer Theory/Sociology*, Oxford: Blackwell, 1996, pp. 85–86. Greenberg expands considerably on each of these points in his monumental work, *The Construction of Homosexuality*, Chicago: University of Chicago Press, 1988, pp. 347–396.

59   Greenberg and Bystryn, 'Capitalism, Bureaucracy, and Male Homosexuality', pp. 100–101. See also Greenberg, *The Construction of Homosexuality*, pp. 455–464.

and subcultures. Here, he is writing in the early seventies of what he perceived (somewhat prematurely) as the increasing collapse of WASP hegemony as a result of socio-political challenges:

> the counterculture does not repudiate the advances of technology – stereos, motor-bikes, the pill. What it does do is reject the cult of hard work and consumerism; the latter, one might note, has been a very important part of the traditional gayworld. Largely perhaps because of social insecurity, homosexuals have long sought to buy respectability by conspicuous consumption; at the same time, within the gayworld the whole process of sex barter tended to enhance the importance of material possessions.[60]

It is difficult not to read this in light of the socio-economic transformations that have taken place since. Clearly, Altman felt it was plausible at this time to suggest a distinction between the embrace of technology, on the one hand, and conspicuous consumption, on the other.[61] This may look naïve to us, given the extent to which the discourse of 'innovation' has been appropriated and fetishized in neoliberal times as propaganda for the market and alibi for the disciplining and redisciplining of workers. Particularly striking, though, is the way in which this distinction is mapped on to 'the gayworld'.[62] Read retrospectively, that world therefore seems prefigurative of a more general consumerist

---

60 Dennis Altman, *Homosexual Oppression and Liberation*, revised edition, London: Allen Lane, 1974, pp. 161–162.
61 The category of 'conspicuous consumption' was coined and distinctively theorized by Thorstein Veblen (see *The Theory of the Leisure Class*, New York: Modern Library, 2001, pp. 52–73), but I discuss it here in the looser sense indicated by Altman.
62 Altman takes the term from Martin Hoffman's *The Gay World*, New York: Basic Books, 1968.

future and appropriation of the counterculture, though Altman here presents it as regressive, and in two respects that are seen as continuous with each other: the development of a lifestyle, *and* its distinctive kinds of sexual relations. And yet the passage makes a very different kind of sense once one registers the cumulative symbolism of those countercultural phenomena Altman highlights as somehow distinct from the logic of consumerism: motorbikes, stereos and the pill. If the latter represented an advance for women, it nonetheless facilitated the masculine heterosexual freedoms connoted by the other items listed, and these are collectively distinguished as technology; the gayworld is rather given over to frivolous trash. Masculine heterosexuality rebels against conformity (with or without a cause), while gay people abjectly buy legitimacy. In this frame, the distinction now appears ideological, more a matter of what is perceived as a commodity, since *conspicuous* consumption relies on other forms being *in*conspicuous, which is to say tacitly normative.

The concerns raised here have to do with the kind of critical discourse we employ when we speak about commodification. The Marxist critique of the commodity has to do with the ways in which, through its self-presentation in terms of exchange value, it obscures consciousness of the exploitative social relations of production. Thus, as Marx says, commodities appear to take on lives of their own.[63] However, Marx not only *doesn't* have a particular kind of commodity in mind in making this argument, part of the point he is making is that the dominance of exchange value subordinates specific, or use, value. His, then, is not a moral critique of the commodity: indeed, as we have seen, he thought the expansion in the range of goods

---

63  On commodity fetishism, see Karl Marx, *Capital*, vol. I, trans. Ben Fowkes, Harmondsworth: Penguin, 1976, pp. 163–177.

facilitated by capitalism was unambiguously a good thing. Strictly speaking, then, from a Marxist perspective, a pint of beer or a football is every bit as much a commodity as a shirt or lipstick; Marxism's alleged gender-blindness may be positive in this respect.

It is the moral critique of commodification that results in qualitative distinctions of the sort that appear to determine Altman's account of the gayworld. This is an old one and has to do with rival accounts of class legitimacy focused on the categories of leisure and corruption. J. G. A. Pocock highlights the extent to which the category of manliness, with its classical origins in the discourse of virtue, was central to eighteenth-century debates, as the middle classes began to claim rights to citizenship. The landed classes' established view was that their authority was disinterested because they were possessed of leisure and autonomy, and were therefore not governed by particular interests, as was the case with those engaged in trade. The commercial classes' case, by contrast, was that trade brought clear benefits to all, despite the self-interested motivations behind it, and that, in any case, the pursuit of trade was typically carried out with a self-discipline demanded by the (protestant) work ethic.[64] Over the course of the nineteenth century, as the latter perspective became increasingly hegemonic, it was leisure that came to seem suspicious, especially as it was conjoined to unearned wealth and the consequent undisciplined potential for revelling in luxury: *this* was now everywhere derided

---

64  J. G. A. Pocock, *The Machiavellian Moment: Florentine Political Thought and the Atlantic Republican Tradition* (Princeton: Princeton University Press, 1975), esp. pp. 462–467. Pocock's argument is more complex than I can do anything like full justice to here. The relevance of this history to foundational US convictions is also clear, given that, in Pocock's words, 'the forces of change and modernity had crossed the Atlantic somewhat in advance of the governmental imperative that compelled their recognition [in England]' (p. 467).

as effeminacy.[65] Moreover, the masculine commitment to the work ethic in opposition to luxury and effeminacy is one that has repeatedly consolidated the attachment of workers to the system – and even the class – that exploits them, and has simultaneously inhibited the development of a truly libertarian socialism.

Alan Sinfield points out that homosexuality becomes inseparable from the category of effeminacy as a consequence of the Wilde trials of 1895, the most sensational of the nineteenth century. Of course, Wilde identified with the popularly despised leisure-class persona and outrageously polemicized in favour of aestheticism and decadence. The consequence of his spectacular conviction by the courts was that through it 'the image of the queer cohered'.[66] From this point on, it became virtually impossible to hear a posh, English accent, especially when uttering an aesthetic judgement, without discerning a homosexual sensibility also being intoned. Wilde's persona and others in the subsequent decadent and/or leisure-class tradition lurk behind the camp sensibility, though it also draws on subcultural traditions dating back at least as far as the molly houses of the early eighteenth century.

Even the word 'gay', as it relates to sexuality, invokes this tradition, though it emerges out of the renewal of decadence that emerged in the 1920s and 1930s after its temporary suppression in the wake of the Wilde trials. It begins, Sinfield writes elsewhere, 'as the in-word of a leisured and artistic group (Coward specifically); is gradually extended through that subculture; and then onto queers generally; and eventually – in the face of some protest – into the straight

---

65  See, for instance, my comments in *Mansex Fine: Religion, Manliness and Imperialism in Nineteenth Century Britain*, Manchester: Manchester University Press, 1999, pp. 26–27.
66  Alan Sinfield, *The Wilde Century: Effeminacy, Oscar Wilde and the Queer Moment*, London: Cassell, 1994, p. 121.

world'.[67] This condensed history of its development is suggestive also of the multiaccentuality[68] of the term – which is to say, not simply its variety of meanings, but the extent to which these are embedded in social tensions and conflicts of the sort I have been tracing. These become more complex as the term is disseminated and used in circles beyond elite groups, while still maintaining some reference to them. Gay liberation's resignification of the term used more or less discreetly by the Coward set in order to assert defiant identity facilitated its separation from any necessary connection with effeminacy, but the situation was always more complex than this.

After all, the masculinization of gay life that took place in the early seventies was accompanied by a newly militant campness (evident, not least, in the Stonewall riots themselves, with those celebrated Latino drag queens in the vanguard). Gay liberation therefore licenses all sorts of combination of cultural and political identification and sensibility, including, at times, a purposeful disidentification with normative gender (as in 'sloppy drag' and genderfuck strategies). Still, the residual, elite and effeminate associations of 'gay' are preserved, even as they are disrupted or distinctively elaborated within an emergent formation. That preservation, moreover, accompanies, and is reinforced by, the purposeful marketization of gay subcultures in the decades subsequent to gay liberation,[69] such that it is possible to view this development as part of a continuous

---

67 Alan Sinfield, *Out on Stage: Lesbian and Gay Theatre in the Twentieth Century*, New Haven: Yale University Press, 1999, p. 109.
68 The term is V. N. Vološinov's: see *Marxism and the Philosophy of Language*, trans. Ladislav Matejka and I. R. Titunk, Cambridge, Mass.: Harvard University Press, 1973, pp. 23–24.
69 The indispensable sources charting this are Alexandra Chasin's *Selling Out: The Gay and Lesbian Movement Goes to Market*, Houndmills: Palgrave, 2000, and Katherine Sender's *Business, Not Politics: The Making of the Gay Market*, New York: Columbia University Press, 2004.

tradition stretching back to Wilde. Will Beckwith in Hollinghurst's novel may be a butch gym-goer, but he is also a leisure-class figure, albeit in a way ironically indebted to his bourgeois-puritanical grandfather's wealth and title. At one point, Beckwith remarks on 'the camp, exploitative, ironical control of my own speech'[70] by comparison with that of his black partner, Arthur.[71] Will Self's justification for writing an imitation of Wilde's *Dorian Gray* for neoliberal times was that he saw the original as pre-figurative of a contemporary gay life he sees defined by its commodified and privileged narcissism.[72] In both instances, though with different emphases, the libertarianism of the sixties and seventies has been ideologically collapsed back into a history of elite libertinism.

The moralistic critique of the commodity that focuses primarily on conspicuous consumption therefore suggests that other forms of consumption are more 'natural' precisely because they accentuate a man's sense of his masculinity, or because they are family-oriented. This is not to say that conspicuous consumption does not determine distinctively inflected kinds of gay snobbery. Indeed, Katherine Sender suggests that the marketization of gay subcultures has produced sexual-aesthetic transformations of them, and analyses these in terms of a subcultural capital that determines integration or exclusion.[73] But there are also specifically straight ways of mediating status through taste that express a disdain for

---

70  Hollinghurst, *The Swimming Pool Library*, p. 64.

71  Joseph Bristow's claim that the novel represents a dissolution of effeminate traditions therefore seems to me misplaced: see *Effeminate England: Homoerotic Writing After 1885*, New York: Columbia University Press, 1995, p. 174.

72  See my consideration of Will Self's *Dorian: An Imitation*, London: Viking, 2002, in '"Not everyone knows fuck all about Foucault": Will Self's *Dorian* and Postgay Culture', *Textual Practice*, 19(3), 2005, pp. 309–329.

73  Sender, *Business, Not Politics*, pp. 218–226.

the meretricious as 'too gay'. Hence, 'gay' often signifies a decadent excess that serves to naturalize shifting heterosacramental
norms of compatibility and absolve men in general of any sense of
guilt for their own increasing narcissism. Elsewhere, for instance,
Sender argues that the television series *Queer Eye for the Straight
Guy* assumes 'that after seeing themselves through borrowed
queer eyes ... reformed heterosexuals will have had just enough
training in romantic, female-friendly, hygienic living to function
effectively in the straight world'.[74] 'Just enough' is exactly right:
queers are over the top. Humorously so, no doubt, but mainstream
audiences are likely to see in the Fab Four's assertions of superior
wisdom an essential triviality and absorption in a world in which
commodities are mistaken for ends rather than means.

As Ann Pelligrini has put it, 'in the discourse of heteronormativity, gays have lifestyles, everyone else (an everyone else that
need not be further identified because we know who and what
we are) has lives'.[75] Thus, the visibility of gay life as commodified
requires a specific optic that overlooks forms of commodification
centred on the family. This is one consequence of the barrage of
intensely sentimental propaganda that promotes and prescribes
the family as both sacred and natural – simultaneously above and
below artifice – and thereby sustains a whole set of assumptions
about the relations between it and gay life as governed by mutually
opposing impulses, tastes and sensibilities: (selfless) reproduction
versus (selfish) desire, satisfaction (wholeness) versus pleasure

74   Katherine Sender, 'Queens for a Day: *Queer Eye for the Straight Guy*
and the Neoliberal Project', *Critical Studies in Media Communication*, 23(2),
2006, p. 135.
75   Ann Pelligrini, 'Consuming Lifestyle: Commodity Capitalism and
Transformation in Gay Identity', in Arnaldo Cruz-Malavé and Martin
F. Manalansan, eds, *Queer Globalizations: Citizenship and the Afterlife of
Colonialism*, New York: New York University Press, 2002, p. 142.

(incompletion), intersubjectivity versus objectification, depth versus surface.

Pelligrini's comment, however, was offered as a reproach to Donald M. Lowe, who offers a technologically utopian defence of sexual consumption. He suggests that the lifestyles pioneered by lesbian and gay groups have now expanded beyond their circles to the degree that such consumption

> has in effect led to polysexuality, challenging and subverting the heterosexuality at the heart of the repressive regulation of sexuality. In other words, we are witnessing the destabilization of the opposition between the heterosexual norm and its other, the 'homosexual vice'.[76]

Others make similar claims. In 1982, Dennis Altman revised his opinion of the gayworld by describing as 'the homosexualization of America' both the growth of visible and distinctive urban lesbian and gay communities, and the fact that 'more and more people, especially those who are young, educated and urban, are behaving in ways long thought typical of homosexuals'.[77] Anthony Giddens speaks of '*plastic sexuality*, severed from its age-old integration with reproduction, kinship and the generations' as having been 'the precondition of the sexual revolution of the

---

76 Donald M. Lowe, *The Body in Late Capitalist USA*, Durham: Duke University Press, 1995, p. 132.
77 Dennis Altman, *The Homosexualization of America*, Boston: Beacon Press, 1982, p. 35. Jeffrey Escoffier distinguished between a closet economy, a liberation economy and, finally, a territorial economy in 'The Political Economy of the Closet: Notes Toward an Economic History of Gay and Lesbian Life Before Stonewall', in Amy Gluckman and Betsy Reed, eds, *Homo Economics: Capitalism, Community and Lesbian and Gay Life*, New York: Routledge, 1997, pp. 123–124.

past several decades'.[78] Hence, 'the "biological justification" for heterosexuality as "normal," it might be proposed, has fallen apart'.[79] Henning Bech perhaps unconsciously echoes Altman when he claims that, though male homosexual existence is a specifically modern phenomenon, its once-defining traits have become more generalized: 'a "homosexualization" takes place, which does not however involve erotic preference to the same degree'.[80]

There is clearly truth in all this, but gender codes still continue to govern differences between cross- and same-sex relations and also to be erotically significant (in the narrow, non-Marcusean sense). Moreover, the importance of reproduction continues to be invoked as the trump card distinguishing proper from fake marriage. Hence, when opposition to gay marriage in Britain was not advanced on the grounds that same-sex relations are simply unnatural and/or immoral, the claim was rather that it would reduce the meaning of marriage to a lifestyle choice. According to this logic, lifestyles are legitimate enough; they are just not very profound or a part of the truly human community. Consequently, they threaten the integrity of those institutions that secure it. The Anglican Archbishop of York, John Sentamu, opposed gay marriage, but liberally declared himself in favour of civil partnerships, sustaining this distinction through appeal to a social pluralism that is legitimate so far as it 'does not degenerate into a fancy-free individualism'. Reserving a separate, higher status for marriage is important because, as a norm, it 'helps define who we are, what we value and *how we build for our future*. This is why it is spoken of as essential to our social

---

78   Anthony Giddens, *The Transformation of Intimacy: Sexuality, Love and Eroticism in Modern Societies*, Oxford: Polity, 1992, p. 27.

79   Ibid., p. 178.

80   Bech, *Between Men*, p. 196.

fabric, as the bedrock of a hospitable and diverse society'.[81] Such Anglican platitudinarianism is finely calibrated to offend as few as possible while nonetheless defending the status quo: 'bedrock' sounds firm and necessary, but for no discernible reason is said to underpin an accommodating pluralism Sentamu himself has reason to find appealing.

Thus, the excess of gay lifestyles persistently features as prefigurative, evidence of what the future portends through a logic discernible in the present. The family will protect against this excessive exposure which queers of various sorts have embraced. This is also why supporters of gay marriage consider it the ultimate recognition of their humanity. Those on the left who object to the normalizing implications of 'equalmarriage' often suggest that it evinces conformist pressures typical of neoliberalism. This, in turn, is problematic for reasons that demand further consideration.

## Neoliberalism, neoconservatism, normativity

There is a pronounced tendency in queer thought to suggest that neoliberalism has resulted in a new normativity that prescribes conventionally middle-class lifestyles for lesbians and gay men. In taking issue with lesbian and gay aspirations towards respectability, for instance, Michael Warner suggests that neoliberal and neoconservative are equivalent terms.[82] Alexandra Chasin, meanwhile, dismisses 'the fantasy that the market is amoral',[83] and Kevin Floyd

---

81  Sentamu's remarks, dated 17 May 2012, come in a clarification of comments he made for an interview in *The Daily Telegraph*: see 'A Response on Marriage and Civil Partnerships', http://www.archbishopofyork.org/articles.php/2481/a-response-on-marriage-and-civil-partnerships Emphasis added.

82  Warner, *The Trouble With Normal*, p. 77.

83  Chasin, *Selling Out*, p. 231.

speaks of 'neoliberal efforts to limit the horizon of struggle against "homophobia" to the right to get married and own property'[84] – implicitly, that is, to acquire respectability. Thus, queer politics are envisaged as continuous with the counterculture, and possibly as thereby possessing an obvious affiliation with anti-capitalist politics. It seems to me that such intuitions rely on a problematic conflation that results from an assumption that the system is more integrated and coherent than it has been for quite some time.

Floyd's point reflects the influential arguments of Lisa Duggan, who coined the term 'homonormativity' to describe 'a politics that does not contest dominant heteronormative assumptions and institutions, but upholds and sustains them, while promising the possibility of a demobilized gay constituency and a privatized, depoliticized gay culture anchored in domesticity and consumption'.[85] Central to Duggan's case is that neoliberalism reinforces class dominance and other forms of hierarchy along with it:

*The goal of raising corporate profits has never been pursued separately from the articulation of hierarchies of race, gender, and sexuality in the United States and around the globe.* Neoliberals, unlike many leftists and progressives, simply don't assume that there is any important difference between material goals and identity politics. They make use of identity politics to obscure redistributive aims, and they use 'neutral' economic policy terms to hide their investments in identity-based hierarchies, but they don't make the mistake of fundamentally accepting the ruse of liberalism – the assertion of a clear boundary between the politics of identity and class.[86]

---

84  Floyd, *The Reification of Desire*, p. 68.
85  Lisa Duggan, *The Twilight of Equality: Neoliberalism, Cultural Politics, and the Attack on Democracy*, Boston: Beacon Press, 2003, p. 50.
86  Ibid., p. 15.

Duggan makes a powerful case, but qualifications are necessary. Certainly – and this is substantially Duggan's point – capitalism has reinforced and exploited traditional or existing forms of discrimination or hierarchy. Thus, women have traditionally been paid less than men for doing equivalent work, and continue to find it more difficult to advance their careers. Capitalism also perpetuates the immiseration of those who are already poor, including those who are so because of entrenched or systemic social discrimination. The only conceivable way that the legacy of apartheid might finally be brought to an end in South Africa, for instance, is through a colossal redistribution of wealth and property that might look something like socialism; it would certainly be incompatible with the neoliberalism of today's African National Congress.[87] Capitalism also requires the disciplining of labour markets, and this may further fuel the stigmatization of groups who, for whatever reason, are disproportionately dependent on state support. Much racism is directed to those ends, as Duggan points out. In the UK, disability groups claim to have been targeted, and even stigmatized, by governmental austerity measures.[88]

There is a difference, however, between arguing that neoliberal dogma about unfettered markets is ill equipped to address social injustice that is not strictly class-based, and claiming that such dogma requires it. Part of the problem here is that Duggan's argument is focused on state politics. Though she does distinguish between neoliberal and neoconservative politicians,

---

87  An excellent account of postapartheid South Africa is offered by Patrick Bond in *Elite Transition: From Apartheid to Neoliberalism in South Africa*, London: Pluto, 2000.

88  See, for instance, 'Disability Cuts Will Have Devastating Consequences, Says Charity Chief,' *Society Guardian*, 12 July 2011, p. 5.

she nonetheless claims that they 'flexibly combine apparently con-tradictory positions, in a kind of productive incoherence designed to appeal and appease'.[89] This is a crucial insight, but the word 'apparently' suggests that politicians are actually being consistent rather than attending to contradictions forced on them by having to appeal to electorates or implement policies. Neoconservatives face the problem that, if the free markets they broadly support are corrosive of norms because people's desires are not spontaneously good, those markets will serve to undermine the moralism and family values they also hold dear. Meanwhile, the neoliberal belief that free markets and small government underwrite individual liberty tends to promote anarchic individualism *and* immense concentrations of wealth that undermine social cohesion, leading either to countermeasures in the form of authoritarian control, or concessions to those who in sufficient numbers feel left out.[90] Wendy Brown, meanwhile, puts a rather different case: although neoliberalism and neoconservatism are distinct political rationali-ties, neoliberalism's erosion of democratic norms has facilitated the growth of neoconservative sensibilities.[91] All of this suggests that the relations between neoliberalism and neoconservatism are complex and dynamic, but it doesn't provide a justification for col-lapsing them, and there are good reasons for not doing so.

Elsewhere, Brown effectively puts the counterargument to Duggan's case: 'Capitalism,' she writes, 'neither loves nor hates social differences. Rather, it exploits them in the short run and

---

89  Duggan, *Twilight of Democracy*, p. 14.
90  On these contradictions see, for instance, David Harvey, *A Brief History of Neoliberalism*, Oxford: Oxford University Press, 2005, pp. 79–81.
91  Wendy Brown, 'American Nightmare: Neoliberalism, Neoconservatism, and De-Democratization', *Political Theory*, 34(6), 2006, pp. 690–714.

erodes them in the long run.'[92] This sounds plausible on the basis of what I have argued so far, but is itself unsatisfactory for a number of reasons. First, the consolidation or erosion of social differences under capitalism relies on human intentions and agency within it, acting nonetheless on its terms: capitalism doesn't *necessarily* do either of the things that Brown suggests. Women, for instance, would not have won greater equality without feminism. Second, capitalism also reifies social differences by consolidating them as lifestyles, and the extent to which this process serves either to erode or merely reconfigure stigma is one of the things I am concerned with in this book. Finally, it is significant that Brown forgets about the social differences that are ultimately ineliminable from capitalism without it ceasing to exist altogether: class differences. These may be ameliorated, of course, but the history of capitalism in the postwar west suggests that such tendencies may be intolerable.

With all the reservations I have expressed here, the assumption that capitalist, or even class, power necessarily operates through normativity seems to me problematic. Michael Piore makes a plausible argument about the effects of flexible specialization on the lesbian and gay movement, claiming that the capacity of capital these days to focus on niche markets and difference has resulted in the emergence of a lesbian and gay entrepreneurial class that 'has an interest in preserving a distinctive gay culture'.[93] Nonetheless,

---

92 Wendy Brown, 'Women's Studies Unbound: Revolution, Mourning, Politics', *parallax*, 9(2), 2003, p. 9. See also Ellen Meiksins Wood's more detailed consideration of a similar perspective in 'Capitalism and Human Emancipation: Race, Gender and Democracy', in *Democracy Against Capitalism: Renewing Historical Materialism*, Cambridge: Cambridge University Press, 1995, pp. 264–283.
93 Michael Piore, 'Economic Identity/Sexual Identity', *A Queer World: The Center for Lesbian and Gay Studies Reader*, New York: New York University Press, 1997, p. 505.

Piore worries that the resulting concentration of wealth and influence in such a class will lead both to its dominance in lesbian and gay political organizations, and a consequent narrowing of the political scope and agenda of those organizations in ways that reflect its preoccupations.[94] The situation Piore describes, then, is contradictory: class identification may promote conformity – though even here it's not clear why this is *necessarily* the case – but market interest cuts against this. One example of the market catering to difference is provided by Joshua Gamson: he suggests that the now defunct US LGBT media corporation, PlanetOut, created 'out of the fragmented, divided, complicated subgroups [it recognized] a sort of mass market, to gather them together in layers ... a strategy made all the smoother by new technologies'.[95]

The relevant point here is that many entrepreneurs, whatever their own lifestyles may be, have a powerful interest in self-consciously resisting conservatism specifically. Let us consider only the most obvious area in which this is the case. Pornography is the largest and probably most diverse element in the field of sexual commerce identified by Rubin, and one that clearly suffers from initiatives like zoning laws. The US trade organization for the porn industry, to which many gay businesses have been affiliated, styles itself the 'Free Speech Coalition'. At one time, its website announced its goals as being:

> One, to be the watchdog for the adult entertainment industry guarding against unconstitutional and oppressive government

---

94   Ibid., pp. 505–507. Piore's anxiety clearly relates to Duggan's claim.
95   Joshua Gamson, 'Gay Media Inc.: Media Structures, the New Gay Conglomerates, and Collective Sexual Identities', in Martha McCaughey and Michael D. Ayers, eds, *Cyberactivism: Online Activism in Theory and Practice*, New York: Routledge, 2003, p. 273. This is despite its tendency nonetheless to promote minoritarian, even essentialist, identities.

intervention; Two, to be a voice for the industry telling the truth about the adult entertainment industry not only in the vital role it plays as an economic contributor, but also in its contribution to quality of life in a healthy society; and finally to provide business resources for our members to facilitate successful businesses in this ever-changing and challenging business environment.[96]

This is an impeccably neoliberal statement that aligns non-interventionist government with freedom, and cites this as fundamental to economic, social and even individual well-being. Constitutionality, vitality, health: these are the mutually reinforcing bodily tropes that define a properly functioning nation in terms of its competitive virility (despite the studiedly neutral language here, the underpinning assumption seems to be that the consumer of pornography will be male). Indeed, the discourse of health here is tacitly wrested from its moral appropriation by both neoconservatives and pro-censorship feminism. The final sentence seeks to dispel the specific controversies over pornography through appeal to the language of exchange value – pornography is a 'business environment' just like any other – though the subsequent reference to innovation also testifies, would you believe it, to the moral qualities of perseverance necessary for success. Pornography directly subjects sexual representation to the performance principle.

It is worth dwelling for a moment, though, on what is meant by 'innovation' in relation to pornography in order to grasp the qualitative transformations that have taken place in recent decades, since these touch acutely on the ways in which capitalism

---

96  See http://www.freespeechcoalition.com/about-us.html (accessed 15 August 2011).

reifies sexuality. Innovation here means: more technologically facilitated explicitness and realism (through high-definition recording, for instance); more competitive pressure to be kinkier, filthier, more brutal (moral terms whose deployment is used within the industry itself to testify to its own taboo-challenging radicalism); more niche marketing (and therefore greater specification and reification of 'tastes'); and more convenience for consumers. This latter emphasis is absolutely crucial, since it highlights the increasing importance of the internet and direct transmission to computer, thus obviating the need for, and embarrassment of, having to traipse all the way to those areas targeted by people like Giuliani in New York. Moreover, technological shifts towards more compact and portable cameras have done away with the necessity for studios, facilitating home production and the casualization of labour; hence the emphasis on so-called 'amateurs'. The transformation that is taking place in this respect is important and has a bearing on the presumption that neoliberalism promotes respectability.

Marcuse regarded the intrusion of such phenomena as television into the home – its direct transmission of propaganda and advertising, and its facilitation of subjective identification with celebrities – as a form of deprivatization: it eroded the (repressive) individual autonomy conditioned by familial privacy. Yet, we are more accustomed to thinking of such processes as themselves privatizing because they reinforce the self-contained qualities of home and individual life,[97] isolating individuals from public and collective space – even as they pass through it, wearing headphones and tapping away at a smartphone, for instance.

---

97 Raymond Williams speaks of 'mobile privatization' in 'Problems of the Coming Period', *Resources of Hope: Culture, Democracy, Socialism*, London: Verso, 1989, p. 171.

Technological developments in recent decades have reinforced both deprivatization, as Marcuse understood it, and the latter sense of privatization, and have even generated an illusion of agency through the facilitation of greater choice and interactivity: penetration of the individual consciousness is facilitated through greater reinforcement of the individual from – and even the redefinition of what constitutes – the external world. Thus, we can personalize our deprivatization and even carry it round with us – thereby becoming freer and freer and freer and freer. We are certainly, in such freedom, largely oblivious of the costs in terms of human labour and environmental degradation of making such proliferating, endlessly innovative, soon-to-be-obsolescent devices.[98]

Take, for instance, developments in internet and phone technology that have facilitated sex sites. 'What you want, when you want it' is the prosaic, but utopian, tagline of the dating site, gaydar, promising nothing less than abolition of the deferral of satisfaction that Freud recognized as the condition of existence for human society as such. The notion is quite precisely, and simultaneously, reifying (*this* is what you want), and infantilizing (you want and must have it now) in ways characteristic of consumer capitalism more generally. Of course, once you turn off your computer and have to travel across real space in real time, you appreciate the fantasy entailed by falling for this claim. But sites such as gaydar have had to change, threatened with obsolescence by apps such as grindr, which render the scene immanent to any and every space, thereby intensifying the sense of sex as an ever-present possibility, not least through the

---

98 This point is highlighted by Jim McGuigan in *Cool Capitalism*, London: Verso, 2013, pp. 116–128.

phone alerts that demand frequent attention. Those of us who can afford, but may be inclined to resist, such technologies on the grounds that we resent being defined by the idea of our sex compulsion for someone else's profit are made to feel both that we are missing out *and* convicted of a sanctimonious virtue we never suspected we harboured. After all, grindr is just a bit of fun, and all the more obviously harmless because that affable old fruit, Stephen Fry, endorses it (or, at least, he did before getting married). Many people today will have several apps of this sort on their phones, especially if they travel frequently.

These kinds of development help to illustrate the extent to which, if neoliberalism and neoconservatism are distinct but tensely overlapping phenomena politically, this is also the case at the subjective level. Let us take a particular example in the form of the scandal over Andrew Sullivan's failure to live up to his own moralizing discourse about how gay men should assimilate. If it is appropriate to view Sullivan as a neoconservative, he is a special, reformist kind, believing in lesbian and gay integration into the familial and patriotic life of the US through the extension of the right to marriage and join the armed forces. This would end public discrimination, as he understands it, but would also have a moralizing effect on those so integrated.[99] It is significant, I think, that Sullivan is English: there is a Burkean, organicist conservatism to his arguments that confounds US absolutism and makes him appear something of a maverick. Thus, he seems liberal to intransigent US neoconservatives because of his stance, such as it is, on gay issues, and he has not proved a staunch Republican voter. However, he is an unimpeachable

---

99  This is Sullivan's 'conservative' argument in *Virtually Normal: An Argument About Homosexuality*, London: Picador, 1995.

free-marketeer in relation to defining issues such as public healthcare and welfare.[100]

In 2001, Sullivan was revealed by Michelangelo Signorile to have placed an anonymous personal ad on the website, barebackcity. com, under the username RawMuscleGlutes, soliciting bareback sex and expressing an interest in 'bi-scenes, one-on-ones, three-ways, groups, parties, orgies and gang bangs'. Signorile defended his own apparently moralistic conduct in revealing this on the grounds that Sullivan was a hypocrite; Sullivan responded by bemoaning the death of privacy.[101] The problem with Sullivan's stance, however, is that he had already made his 'private life' the business of anyone who might want to offer bi-scenes, one-on-ones, three-ways, groups, parties, orgies or gang bangs – or, indeed, simply peruse his (OK, anonymous) profile.

Paul Robinson offers a partial defence of Sullivan, suggesting that, if he is hypocritical, he is at least openly and consistently so, given that he has written about the attractions for him of circuit parties.[102] But this still accounts for the situation in terms of a kind of personal integrity that seems beside the point, because subjective incoherence is systemically determined. The tension is between

---

100  On being named one of *Forbes Magazines'* twenty-five most influential liberals in 2009, Sullivan attributed his perceived liberalism to the fact that 'many on the Republican right just *read* everything I write through an anti-gay prism' and that 'conservatism has become a religious movement' ('Forbes Definition of "Liberal,"' *The Daily Dish*, 24 January 2009 (accessed 20 September 2011)).

101  The controversy is detailed in Paul Robinson, *Queer Wars: The New Gay Right and its Critics*, Chicago: University of Chicago Press, 2005, pp. 77–79. Richard Goldstein also refers to this in *The Attack Queers: Liberal Society and the Gay Right*, London: Verso, 2002, p. 9. Sullivan's defence, originally published only on Andrew.Sullivan.com, seems now only to be available at http://mailman.lbo-talk.org/2001/2001-May/010374.html (accessed 10 January 2012).

102  Robinson, *Queer Wars*, pp. 64–70.

Sullivan's consciously held conservative beliefs, about which there is no reason to suspect he is not serious, and those desires and fantasies stimulated by the market (in this case, a sex site) that relies precisely on the sense of sex as an abstract possibility: someone – or perhaps everyone – out there might be paying you attention. Hence, the terms of the debate between Signorile and Sullivan strike us as curious because almost reminiscent of a different era. Almost, but not quite, since the controversy testifies to the persistent tension between the systemic incitement to desire and fantasy, and resistance to it, often through a belief that such desire might, even should, be constrained in principle.

Hence, Sullivan's 'hypocrisy' is probably shared to some degree by most people. A friend of mine jokes and worries in equal measure about his liking for designer underwear and the extraordinary levels of 'technological innovation' (no less) that go into its new fabrics, waistbands, 'profile' enhancements, and so on, but he has no illusions about what kinds of fetishism this entails. It is not only 'conservative' principles that are challenged by the marketization of sex, then. Rather, such marketization renders any form of resistance to or critique of it apparently 'moralistic' because judgemental of the desiring self that is construed as private – despite the *de*privatizing, market determination of desire's forms and intensities.

In this context, Sullivan's comments on circuit parties are interesting. Writing of this 'series of vast, drug-enhanced dance parties held in various cities across the [US]' as a 'resilient, if marginal, feature of an emergent post-AIDS gay urban "lifestyle"',[103] he claims that they are really

---

103  Andrew Sullivan, 'When Plagues End', in *Love Undetectable: Reflections on Friendship, Sex and Survival*, New York: Alfred A. Knopf, 1998, p. 10.

not about ... sex. And as circuit parties intensified in frequency and numbers in the 1990s, this became more, not less, the case. When people feared that the ebbing of AIDS would lead to a new burst of celebration of old times, they were, it turns out, only half right ... What replaced sex was the idea of sex; and what replaced promiscuity was the idea of promiscuity, masked, in the burgeoning numbers of circuit parties around the country, by the ecstatic high of drug-enhanced dance music. These were not merely mass celebrations on the dawn of a new era; they were raves built upon the need for amnesia.[104]

The attempt to discern a coherent meaning or communal sensibility in all of this seems to me spurious because it attributes such feelings to an authentic, if sentimentalized, need. Nonetheless, the focus on abstraction, on the *idea* of sex and promiscuity as dominant, and a galvanizing principle of whatever it is that actually happens, is insightful. It is an idea produced by specific conditions: the convergence in space of otherwise geographically dispersed individuals, similarly motivated and possessed of – or at least aspiring to – looks and bodies defined as 'desirable'; the disinhibiting and highly potent influences of music, alcohol and drugs conditioning subjective feelings of both awe and individual potential appropriate to the scale of the event itself. This intensified desire is governed quite precisely by the performance principle: normally taking place on a weekend, it is both release from graft and reward through consumption for that graft – the 'work hard, play hard' ethic, puritanically and self-righteously decadent, aggressively impatient with anything that might interfere with it as a right that has been earned. Given all this, it might seem

---

104  Ibid., p. 14.

obviously implausible that any actual sex could live up to the sense of it that hangs suspended in the air, as it were. Hence, the commitment at such parties to endurance rather than consummation. Indeed, Sullivan's account suggests what experience no doubt confirms: that the state of desire may be *more* important than sex, and therefore relatively autonomous of it, because capitalism thrives rather by abstracting, intensifying and generalizing our condition of desire.

In this description, Sullivan seems to shift between viewing circuit parties as marginal, because they are organized by and for the privileged, and, portentously, as harbingers of a new epoch. This is not necessarily contradictory: while hardly being representative, they may still alert us to more pervasive tendencies, such as the transformation and proliferation of Pride marches into *mardi gras*-type events, ultimately geared to clubbing. These may be distinctive in certain respects – greater sexual forthrightness especially – in relation to similar kinds of carnival, but are nonetheless in keeping with the bread-and-circuses, synthetic festival culture encouraged by neoliberal municipal entrepreneurialism and market states. If we place Pride in this overall context, it further attests to assimilation and the diversification of the dominant in ways that question whether, or in what sense, it can properly be called 'subcultural' at all. This is the category I turn to in chapter four, but I want first to elaborate on the qualitative dimensions of the shift I have noted here.

## Sex and the economy of fun

If capitalism is progressive for queers, that is because it renders sex profane, though this simultaneously reinforces sacramentalism by contrast as something 'beyond price'. That this pricelessness is itself commodified and sold to couples and families as the ineffable bond of which the mere commodity is a token is a further irony (thus: my partner deserves this holiday, and my children are worth these designer clothes, and we all drive around in an SUV to ensure our inestimable importance as a family is preserved at everyone else's expense). The idea that the family promotes community and selflessness under conditions of neoliberalism is simply absurd. Still, the value attached to the family may be reinforced by the commodified desublimation of its relations elsewhere, since its function always resided in the preservation of 'human' against exchange value. This dynamic, reinforcing conservatism, was identified in a general sense by Marx: the supposed realization of human potentialities through capitalism, he claimed, represents rather the 'sacrifice of the human end-in-itself to an entirely external end', thereby determining a nostalgia for older, more limited and limiting, relations and achievements, because 'the modern gives no satisfaction; or, where it appears satisfied with itself, it is *vulgar*'.[105] The perception of gay life as either masculine (aggressively, insatiably desiring) and/or effeminate (trivial in its commodity fetishism) has perhaps become the pre-eminent instance of the latter part of this dynamic.

Marcuse's category of repressive desublimation needs revising,[106] though, in keeping with the intensification of the performance principle we have witnessed in recent decades. Marcuse theorized it as a form of deprivatization because it was precisely sex's former quality of freedom from direct social control that lent it

---

105  Marx, *Grundrisse*, p. 488. Perhaps this does mark an anticipation of the category of 'false needs', after all.

106  Finn Bowring, by contrast, has offered a recent defence of the term in 'Repressive Desublimation and Consumer Culture: Re-evaluating Herbert Marcuse', *new formations*, 75, 2012, pp. 8–24.

its powerful attraction.[107] Consequently, with the increasing integration of the sexual into everyday life has come a diminution of its dangerous or threatening qualities, and a loss of its genuinely radical potential. This very process of integration, though – the sheer extent and apparent limitlessness of it – demystifies the psychoanalytic category of the libido, endorsed by Marcuse, as a kind of quantifiable force that has been stored up.

We should therefore speak in somewhat more Foucaultian fashion of contemporary levels of sexual awareness and desire as specifically instilled, or provoked, in us, and therefore of repressive *incitement*. 'Repression' here refers both to the specification and privileging of sex over other forms of sensuous experience, perhaps as the telos to which they point, and to sexual desire's government by the performance principle. It is worth re-emphasizing, however, that repressive incitement should not be understood as a generalized subjective condition, as if each individual might be said to be both repressed and incited in more or less equal measure. Rather, experiences of desire and repression are separated out, often radically so, both in individual lives and depending on one's relative privilege within the system.

Repressive incitement has turned sex into fun, but fun is not as innocent or unproblematic as it imagines itself to be, as Adorno highlights in one of his best short essays, 'Free Time'.[108] Our sense of leisure, he suggests, is a form of reification in itself, established by contradistinction from work. Thus, free time, in order to qualify

---

107 Marcuse, *Five Lectures*, p. 57.
108 Theodor Adorno, 'Free Time', in *The Culture Industry: Selected Essays on Mass Culture*, J. M. Bernstein, ed., London: Routledge, 1991, pp. 162–170. I prefer this translation to the one in *Critical Models: Interventions and Catchwords*, trans. Henry W. Pickford, New York: Columbia University Press, 2005, pp. 167–175, because of its pithier rendering of Adornian paradoxes.

as such, tendentially excludes from it anything that is qualitatively laborious: seriousness, concentration, even purpose. Indeed, so conceived, free time *is* distraction expanded to fill the period outside working hours as compensation for what people are subjected to within them. Moreover, the desire for escapism or release people express in such time is further consolidated by the production of commodities that supposedly match, but also intensify, those desires: 'What they want is forced upon them again',[109] writes Adorno, capturing brilliantly that sense of unfreedom that attends the persistent bid for the contrary.

Brilliantly, yet sanctimoniously. Even Adorno's own reflections are tempered by empirical findings of the habits of those from whom he maintained his distance: 'whatever the culture industry sets before people in their free time', he writes, 'is indeed consumed and accepted but with a kind of reservation, similar to how even ingenuous people do not simply take events in theatre or cinema to be real'. This is a weak and unsatisfactory admission, attributing to the undifferentiated masses a passivity even in their forms of resistance. Adorno acknowledges no critical resources on their part for addressing what it is they are made to consume: if the people are not quite consubstantial with their roles, the precise reasons for this are left vague and are only grudgingly acknowledged – a question merely of having 'real interests [that] are still strong enough to resist, up to a point'.[110] Like Jameson in speaking of postmodernism, Adorno has a tendency to read people's subjective dispositions off the products they consume. What this suppresses is any sense of the complexity and contradictory nature of experience as this is instead emphasized by Raymond Williams. He repudiated

---

109   Ibid., p. 165.
110   Ibid., p. 175.

talk of masses on the grounds that there are actually 'only ways of seeing people as masses'.[111] Williams was not, of course, making the banal and obviously ideological point that we are all individuals, and that abstraction away from this is invalid; rather, we should not presume 'the people' to be unintelligent or insensitive, as those who have an interest in their subordination do.

The problem with Adorno's formulation is therefore evident in his very use of distanciating pronouns: 'they' and 'them', the dupes, others with whom solidarity is impossible because they insist on roping you into their fun, and will stigmatize you if you resist. Readers of this book will recognize such dynamics, but it is necessary to insist against Adornian disdain, and in order to advance a democratic and socialist critique of consumption, that we are all implicated in the dialectic of need and domination he describes: 'what *we* want is forced upon *us* again'. A certain kind of consciousness of this may be pervasive, as Adorno's own findings suggest, even if it is not coherently understood or expressed. It is certainly present in Hollinghurst's novel, as well as in other works discussed in this book, especially in chapter four. The point is that we should not assume in advance that critical consciousness of the culture industry is only possible for an elite, or that the compensations offered by that industry will in all circumstances be sufficient to sustain the system's stability. Adorno, like Marcuse, was writing about Fordist capitalism and also took for granted its stability and durability.

The sense that capitalism is progressive, then, relies, first, on the isolation of the act of consumption from its implications for and determination by production, and, second, on a scepticism at the very least towards the critique of false needs. Capitalism may,

---

111   Williams, 'Culture is Ordinary', p. 11.

of course, challenge conservative norms – and no one acquainted with the history of the persecution of queers should underestimate its importance in doing so – but only by subordinating all other values to the singular norm of exchange value, and reinforcing the sense of desire and fulfilment as a wholly private phenomenon that may only be interfered with by a (self-)scrutiny that will always appear alien (or 'higher'), and therefore moralistic. In one sense, desire *is* private, since I will never be able to feel yours directly under any kind of reconfiguration of society, language or culture. Hence, on a political level, the critique of individualism opens up to authoritarianism to the extent that it merges with scepticism towards the category of the individual as such. Even so, the desire for some specific *thing*, and the intensity with which I feel it, is socially determined.

Only by being puritanical – indeed, more or less monastic – can we avoid commodification to any great extent, but perhaps critique and activism may still be directed towards expanding the possibilities for what Kate Soper has described as an 'alternative hedonism' that would aspire to displace the version of the good life predicated on models of consumption that necessitate exploitation and are ecologically unsustainable. She speaks of 'a new erotics of consumption or hedonist "imaginary"'[112] that we might speculate should aspire to the dereification of sexuality (as essence or source of ultimate fulfilment) by rendering sexual pleasure both commonplace, to the extent that it is desired, and continuous with other pleasures, as queers at their most imaginative have supposed it should be. Hedonism can never be a substitute for political struggle in the self-sacrificial sense, but it must surely be an indispensable supplement to it if utopian critique is to be a

---

112   Soper, 'Alternative Hedonism', p. 571.

part of the means of achieving a world in which anything like the free development of each is the condition for the free development of all, rather than only ever the posited and deferred end. Such critique must seek to transcend the mutually sustaining, utterly contradictory and profoundly ideological opposition between a sacramentalism that, even now, remains presumptively hetero, and the market.

These questions of ends and means therefore necessitate further interrogation of the category of culture itself, and the claims that have been made for its radical or dissident potential.

# 3

## Feeling Radical:
## Versions of Counterculture

The New Left's torment – the torment of all radical
student movements – was that relatively privileged
people were fighting on behalf of the oppressed:
blacks, Vietnamese, the working class ... Yet to give up
the revolutionary dream would have been to confront
a situation without precedent in the history of the
modern left. The working class was conservative,
more or less, the privileged were radical. What could
be made of that?

(Todd Gitlin)[1]

In the Preface to *Utopia Limited*, Marianne DeKoven provides a
biographical frame for her project of charting the transition from
late modernity to postmodernity that she claims began in the
sixties. As someone who matured in those years and was caught
up in their ferment, she speaks of having become assimilated
to a bourgeois lifestyle (family, home, career), as well as having

---

1 Todd Gitlin, *The Sixties: Years of Hope and Days of Rage*, New York:
Bantam Books, 1987, p. 381.

been seduced by popular culture and become a (critical) member of the Democratic Party. From the perspective of her sixties self, she has become entangled with, or 'complicit' in, the system. Ultimately, this is something she welcomes. In the wake of 9/11, the utopian activism of the sixties – especially in its more violent manifestations – seems to her 'retroactively contaminated by the all-or-nothing fanaticism of contemporary fundamentalisms'.[2]

The comparison of groups like Weatherman with religious fundamentalism is not inappropriate, but this kind of abstract equivalence is surely misleading and tendentious as a way of dismissing utopian aspirations *per se*. Furthermore, the emphasis on postmodernity here serves to mask the market utopianism and fundamentalism of dominant capitalist neoliberalism,[3] and also to distract attention from the objectively greater violence of US imperialism, to which both Weatherman and 9/11 were, in their different and indefensible ways, responses.

DeKoven's biographical reflections appear to complement her emphasis on the postmodern as positively focused on localized, even subjective, experience: they position her. In another sense, though, her narrative makes certain implicit claims to representativeness, since it is simultaneously invoked to chart the emergence of a postmodern sensibility. However, it seems to me worth pausing over the relation between the universal and

---

2   Marianne DeKoven, *Utopia Limited: The Sixties and the Emergence of the Postmodern*, Durham, NC: Duke University Press, 2004, p. xv.

3   Interestingly, similar anti-utopian sentiments are expressed in Ian McEwan's post-9/11 novel, *Saturday*, through a stance that is hostile to post-modernism, but sees no alternative to the way things are in the west. See David Alderson, '*Saturday*'s Enlightenment', in Rachael Gilmour and Bill Schwarz, eds, *End of Empire and the English Novel Since 1945*, Manchester: Manchester University Press, 2011, pp. 218–237.

particular in her narrative, because the familiar feel it will have for many of us has at least as much to do with its social specificity as any of its more generalizable features.

This is because it is a tale told by, and mostly to, other academics and students, with whom it will therefore resonate. It is the narrative of someone for whom success within the system was not merely a possibility, but rather a likely consequence of the period in which she claims to have been least complicit with it, her student days. The very experience of being a student has a curious, socially detached and *un*specific feel to it, as if one were temporarily suspended from the forms of social determinism to which everyone else is subject. Potentially, at least, this facilitates experimentation in ways of living, perhaps encouraging feelings of purity that are unavailable to those necessarily caught up in some way in perpetuating the system more directly through their daily lives of labour and consumption. In Humanities disciplines, study itself encourages a critical perspective on everyday life. And yet, being a student is also the prelude to the later social position one acquires, partly as a result of that experience. In the case of the academic, there is a sense of continuity, of never quite having left one's student days behind either institutionally, or possibly in terms of convictions. The academic career is the experience of a certain concretization of study and lifestyle into a very curious kind of job, even if the qualities of that process depend on the shifting internal constitution of the university and its relations with the larger society.

DeKoven's status as a student was therefore as crucial to her emergence out of sixties radicalism as it was in conditioning it in the first place: the developments she traces through her own biography are in no straightforward sense allegorical of the history to which they relate, but rather provide a specific instance of the trajectory from radicalism to middle-class life that, as I note in chapter one, Alex Callinicos claims determined postmodern sensibilities. It may, however, be characteristic of the experiences of the radical left in the US especially, given the exceptionally prominent, though not wholly unique, role the student movement played within it: Students for a Democratic Society (SDS) was the most prominent organization on the New Left there, and the counterculture was first theorized as such by Theodore Roszak as primarily campus-based.

But, before going on to a more detailed consideration of the counterculture and its legacy, it might be helpful to set both DeKoven's narrative and the discrete history of the sixties left in a larger temporal framework. What that period witnessed was the breakdown of the carefully constructed Democratic New Deal coalition that gave peculiar definition to the term 'liberal' in the US through its combination of state intervention in the economy and establishment of welfare programmes, as well as support for trades unions and limited concessions to minority groups. However, it was also complicit with the persistent denial of citizenship to black people in the South, and it was the emergence of a more militant civil rights movement from the mid-fifties that began the process of destabilizing Democratic Party hegemony through the offence support for those rights gave to Southern white voters. Many of those whites turned to the fierce free-marketeer and Cold Warrior, Barry Goldwater, in 1964, because of his opposition to the Civil Rights Act. Though Goldwater lost by a landslide to Lyndon Johnson, that particular shift in voting patterns was to be consolidated in future years, as Republicans appealed to populist concerns over 'law and order' (frequently enough code in the US for anxieties over race), the youthful rejection of patriotism and the breakdown of traditional morality.

The New Left that emerged at the start of the sixties also broke with Democrat hegemony in key ways, and with effects quite disproportionate to its numbers. First, it turned its back on the anticommunism that had largely united the postwar left and right in the US. This facilitated sympathies with Cuba on the part of some, at least, but also, more widely, opposition to the Vietnam war, and even, in the polarizing conditions of the late sixties, identification with the National Liberation Front. Second, and in spite of disapproval of some within its ranks, the New Left also came to be associated with the phemomena often problematically distinguished as countercultural. These sought to revolutionize the whole American way of life, to which, as we saw earlier, theorists frequently claimed the working class had been assimilated both economically and in terms of tastes and lifestyle.

Working-class integration into Fordist capitalism was facilitated through the imposition of the Taft–Hartley Act of 1947, and consolidated through the unification of the two trade union organizations, the American Federation of Labor and Congress of Industrial Organizations (AFL–CIO) in 1955,[4] an initiative pioneered by the arch anticommunist, George Meany, who served as the amalgamated institution's President until 1979. In the words of Fredric Jameson, this merger

> secured the expulsion of the Communists from the American labour movement, consolidated the antipolitical 'social contract' between American business and the American labour unions, and created a situation in which the privileges of a white male labour force take precedence over the demands of black

---

4  Michel Aglietta, *A Theory of Capitalist Regulation in the US Experience*, trans. David Fernbach, London: Verso, 1987, pp. 192–193.

and women workers and other minorities [who] will thus be 'liberated' from social class ... to find new modes of social and political expression.[5]

In other words, it defined the labour movement as one focused primarily on the interests, narrowly conceived, of the white, male working class. Right through to the end, Meany ensured that the AFL–CIO remained strongly supportive of the Vietnam war. At its most potent, the union represented a power bloc within the system, rather than a challenge to it, while in the seventies and eighties it declined in membership, as well as political influence relative to business, as unions were increasingly marginalized as 'special-interest' groups under neoliberal conditions.

The politics of the period were not only determined by public events, however. They were also, and perhaps as importantly, a response to developments in the private sphere that consolidated the importance of the family under the affluent society: from the start, Ford had promoted the family,[6] and Fordist production was geared to supplying it with commodities, advertising was directed at it, hopes for fulfilment were invested in it,[7] and Elaine Tyler

---

5  Fredric Jameson, 'Periodizing the Sixties', in Sohnya Sayres, Anders Stephanson, Stanley Aronowitz, and Fredric Jameson, eds, *The Sixties Without Apology*, Minneapolis: University of Minnesota Press, 1984, p. 182.

6  Writing of the 'puritannical initiatives' of Ford, Gramsci wrote: 'It seems clear that the new industrialism wants monogamy; it wants the man as worker not to squander his nervous energies in the disorderly and stimulating pursuit of occasional sexual satsifaction' ('Americanism and Fordism', in *Selections from the Prison Notebooks*, ed. and trans. Quintin Hoare and Geoffrey Nowell Smith, London: Lawrence and Wishart, 1971, pp. 304–305).

7  Aglietta touches on these aspects with special reference to the commodities of standardized housing and the car (*A Theory of Capitalist Regulation*, pp. 159–161).

May has argued that it generated a sense of security against the dangers modernity brought with it, ranging from cosmopolitan degeneracy to cold war conflict and the bomb.[8] Todd Haynes's film, *Far From Heaven* (2002), explores the faultlines of the fifties family ideal through a post-countercultural lens that renders the Whitakers' self-conscious modernity archaic. Nonetheless, the so-called permissiveness of the postwar middle-class family was also held responsible for sixties radicalism by many, including those who participated in it, even though the rebellions were also pervasively interpreted as directed against the family – at sex roles in general, but the authoritarian father in particular. The Oedipal revolt of the son against the latter also conditioned much of the distinctive sexism of the sixties. 'The family' was often quite self-consciously at the centre of the struggles that took place, and of the sense that the personal was political, in ways that helped shape the emphases of gay liberation. Defence of the supposedly traditional family became central to the right's agenda.

The counterpoint to sixties radicalism was therefore the strategically savvy conservative reaction against it emerging out of Goldwater's campaign and focused on making audible by inciting 'the silent majority' (Nixon's term). In the seventies, moreover, Republicans increasingly appealed to individual economic interests in the face of stagflation through the promise of tax cuts that were understood as 'legitimately' to be paid for by axing those aspects of Johnson's Great Society project mostly perceived as benefiting poor blacks. But, of course, the Reaganomics of the eighties were designed principally to soak the rich – William C. Berman

---

8  See Elaine Tyler May, 'Cold War – Warm Hearth: Politics and the Family in Postwar America', in Steve Fraser and Gary Gerstle, eds, *The Rise and Fall of the New Deal Order*, Princeton: Princeton University Press, 1989, pp. 153–181.

calculates that, through various means, 'anywhere from $120 billion to $160 billion per annum was transferred in the decade of the eighties to the wealthiest 5 percent in America'[9] – while reconfiguring capital–labour relations through attacks on unions, forms of deregulation (e.g. health and safety) and a recession that cowed workers and culminated in a recovery based substantially on low-paid, non-unionized labour. State intervention under Reagan took the familiar US form of military Keynesianism, but on an unprecedented scale in (relative) peacetime through his sponsorship of an arms race that finally bankrupted the USSR and severely constrained subsequent governments. In 1989, Francis Fukuyama was able to argue that history appeared to have ended, culminating in the triumph of western liberal democracy.[10]

The US radicalism of the sixties must be understood in relation to these dynamics rather than as just one manifestation of a more abstract modernity. The social specificity of the student experience played a crucial role in this respect by transforming both perceptions of who might be the agents of progressive change, and, qualitatively speaking, what that change might bring, with all kinds of positive and negative consequences. Political sensibilities, including those manifest in queer theory, continue to be conditioned by that transformation, since the political imaginary from left to right in the US remains powerfully governed by relations to the fifties and sixties.[11] Of course, those sensibilities have also been determined by the rise of neoconservatism and neoliberalism, the emergence of a

---

9  William C. Berman, *America's Right Turn: From Nixon to Clinton*, second edition, Baltimore: Johns Hopkins University Press, 1998, p. 106.
10  The essay, originally published in 1989, was extended as *The End of History and the Last Man*, London: Allen Lane, 1992.
11  See Bernard von Bothmer, *Framing the Sixties: The Use and Abuse of a Decade from Ronald Reagan to George W. Bush*, Amherst: University of Massachusetts Press, 2010.

diversified dominant, and, on a theoretical level, the hegemony of postmodern and poststructuralist discourses that have reinflected countercultural dispositions in an antihumanist fashion.

Finally, something must be said about SDS. It was established in 1960, and over time became a substantial organization in terms of numbers and geographical coverage. The diversity it embraced was partly one consequence of its size, but also emerged out of its principles. The defining document of SDS, the *Port Huron Statement*, has been described by one historian of the organization as the most widely circulated document of the US left in the sixties.[12] It both captured and consolidated the mood of students by articulating and helping to shape a certain structure of feeling. Todd Gitlin highlights this quality in his recollection to Maurice Isserman that, on reading it, he thought, "'My God, this is what I feel." I wouldn't even say "think" because my thoughts were too inchoate.'[13] Gitlin also conveys something of the conditioning that facilitated this response, when he remarks that the tone of the *Port Huron Statement* was one of radical disappointment that America did not live up to its best ideals[14]: students initially became dissidents as good Americans. Nonetheless, confidence in the nation state was increasingly undermined as the sixties progressed, both by the escalating war in Vietnam and the state's willingness to meet protest with extraordinary levels of force. In these conditions, liberalism – the apparently naïve sense the system might be basically decent – became a dirty word on the left, just as it did, for very different reasons, as a result of the right's counterhegemonic project.

---

12   Kirkpatrick Sale, *SDS*, New York: Vintage, 1973, p. 69.
13   Maurice Isserman, *If I Had a Hammer ... The Death of the Old Left and the Birth of the New Left*, New York: Basic Books, 1987, p. 214.
14   Sale, *SDS*, p. 70.

However, the New Left was not a coherent phenomenon united around an agenda, or even key principles. Was it reformist or revolutionary, socialist, anarchist or left-liberal? It comprised all these tendencies, as well as others that were uncertain of their purposes in spite of a manifest subjective commitment. 'I'm not sure there is a New Left, and if there is I'm not sure I'm in it', wrote Casey Hayden in 1964,[15] though she was involved in SDS through its Economic Research and Action Project (ERAP) and the Student Nonviolent Co-ordinating Committee (SNCC). She also pioneered feminist critiques of men's dominance of the movement. The category of 'radical', the preferred term of sixties activists, is instructively unspecific in terms of positive commitments. All sorts of things can be described as radical. Moreover, to the extent that 'the system' came under attack, there was a frequent lack of specificity about what it consisted in, though capitalism and imperialism were invoked with greater frequency in the late sixties. Of his famous demand that the system be named, and simultaneous failure to do so, in his speech to the 1965 anti-war movement, SDS leader, Paul Potter, subsequently suggested that this was 'because capitalism was for me and my generation an inadequate description of the evils of America – a hollow, dead word tied to the thirties ... I wanted ambiguity, because I sensed there was something new afoot in the world'.[16]

Given the difficulties, therefore, of trying to pin down something at least about sixties movements, convictions and sensibilities, I want to turn to Theodore Roszak's manifesto. There are drawbacks to doing so, as this was itself a polemical intervention, rather than a descriptive or sociological study; it sought to influence activists, to make them more self-conscious and thereby to fashion

---

15   Casey Hayden, 'Raising the Question of Who Decides', in *Takin' It to the Streets: A Sixties Reader*, New York: Oxford University Press, 1995, p. 82.
16   Gitlin, *The Sixties*, p. 185.

something determinate out of more general, inchoate tendencies, without defining anything so 'reductive' as an ideological position. Indeed, it was significantly for him 'a counter culture', not 'the counterculture' the world has subsequently come to know and love or hate (and, for all sorts of reasons, I have been unable to resist this apparent reification). In what follows, I consider key features that serve to highlight more general dynamics that have had lasting consequences. I trace these in subsequent sections through analyses of both cultural texts and queer theory that seem to me to evince dispositions governed by countercultural assumptions. This may appear an odd strategy, but it seems to me an appropriate way of attempting to signal the persistence and transmutation of political *sensibilities*, rather than ideas as such.

The primary emphasis of the chapter, then, is on the US context, but the counterculture achieved global influence, not least in parts of the world in which revolutionary possibilities were bound to socialist traditions of one sort or another that were stronger, because more deeply rooted, than in the US. In such places, the relationship between countercultural movements and socialist ones was often deeply antagonistic. But out of that antagonism, and because of the determination to pursue some kind of relationship in spite of it, some remarkable possibilities opened up. In the final section I turn to Manuel Puig's novel, *The Kiss of the Spider Woman*, in order both to situate it in that context and to challenge what are now dominant postmodern interpretations of it that assimilate it to a historical narrative of superseded revolutionary hopes and possibilities. The point of concluding the chapter with this admittedly abrupt shift of focus is to attempt to resist that more negative evaluation of the counterculture that suggests it was in one way or another predisposed to reinforce the commodifying imperatives out of which it emerged.

## Theorizing the counterculture

The very need for the category of counterculture, claimed Roszak, occurred to him as a result of his experiences with the European left and its sense of superiority in relation to US counterparts on the grounds that the latter were not socialists. Far from wanting to deny this political difference, Roszak makes it the basis of his claim that US movements were actually superior to European ones, since they had fewer illusions about the actual or potential agency of the working class. Not only could the working class no longer bear the weight of such expectations, but it was rather a specifically reactionary force that had consistently sided with the establishment.

The counterculture, by contrast with socialist movements, had emerged out of a quite different constituency: youth. Though Roszak acknowledged that its consciousness as such was indebted to the market reification of age difference in the postwar period, he did not believe this constrained its potential. That was in part because he had in mind a socially circumscribed, relatively privileged section of the youthful: 'just as the dark satanic mills of early industrialism concentrated labour and helped create the class consciousness of the proletariat', he wrote, 'so the university campus, where up to thirty thousand students may be gathered, has served to crystallize the group identity of the young'.[17]

This comment about the institutional basis for the movement effectively condenses Roszak's larger argument and simultaneously highlights both its distinctiveness and limitations. The allusion to William Blake's 'Jerusalem' is no mere cliché, as Blake is a

---

17 Theodore Roszak, *The Making of a Counter Culture: Reflections on the Technocratic Society and Its Youthful Opposition*, Berkeley: University of California Press, 1968, p. 28.

consistent reference point in the book. The reasons for this are not difficult to discern. For one thing, Blake had been an inspiration on the romanticism of the Beat poet, Allen Ginsberg. Though himself a radical in the eighteenth-century sense of that term, Blake was also a critic of the rationalism that dominated the self-consciously progressive outlook of his time.[18] That is why conservative critics have subsequently found it possible to appropriate him for an idealist project.[19] When Roszak combines Blake's famous phrase about industrialism with the category of class consciousness associated rather with Lukács, the effect is both to highlight consciousness as such and to suggest the limitations of its proletarian form: the working class was reactionary because it was a product of the system. Over time, it came to see its interests as served by the expansion of that system, at least as Roszak understood it. The university, by contrast, facilitated dissent by making available the arguments of previous generations of radicals, thereby encouraging students to become critical of the modern university's role in preparing them for their position in 'the technocracy'.

This latter term, widely invoked at the time, is not reserved by Roszak for a class within the system, but defines the system as a whole. It was not a euphemism for capitalism either, even if it referred to 'the social form in which an industrial society reaches the peak of its organizational integration'. Rather, it was a form of rationality governed by 'such unquestionable imperatives as the demand for efficiency, for social security, for large-scale co-

---

18   See, for instance, Heather Glen's powerfully dialectical reading of *Songs of Innocence and of Experience* in *Vision and Disenchantment: Blake's* Songs *and Wordsworth's* Lyrical Ballads, Cambridge: Cambridge University Press, 1983, pp. 110–223.

19   This is the tradition against which E. P. Thompson argues in *Witness Against the Beast: William Blake and the Moral Law*, Cambridge: Cambridge University Press, 1993.

ordination of men and resources, for ever higher levels of affluence and ever more manifestations of collective human power'.[20] The technocracy was totalitarian, not primarily through its deployment of force, but through the integration that resulted from its scientific sponsorship and regulation of comfort. The counterculture's enemies in this account, then, were reason and conformity, forces that had generated a specifically existential alienation, not to be confused with the Marxist sense of that term.[21]

One can certainly hear Frankfurtian echoes in all of this, but Roszak provides a critique of Marcuse specifically that focuses on the supposed limitations of the latter's materialism. Roszak claims that this establishes a political agenda in Marcuse's work that is ultimately continuous with the dominant one of the greatest comfort for the greatest number, albeit within the constraints imposed (according to Marcuse) by necessary, basic repression and the inevitability of death. By contrast with Roszak, for whom the spiritual represents a potential dimension of experience in its own right to which art provides access, Marcuse values the arts for their prefigurative possibilities in relation to a non-alienated future: 'they guide us toward the secular future', writes Roszak, 'never toward that ever-present sacramental dimension of life designated by Blake "the real and eternal world of which this Vegetable Universe is but a faint shadow"'.[22] Though he claims to take seriously Marcuse's desire to eradicate domination, Roszak sees in the commitment to *historical* transcendence merely another mode of repressing the spiritual.

---

20  Roszak, *The Making of a Counter Culture*, p. 5.
21  Indeed, Roszak offers a critique of Marx's understanding of alienation in the *Economic and Philosophical Manuscripts*, and of their importance to Marxist humanists (ibid., pp. 89–98).
22  Ibid., p. 119.

Indeed, the Soviet regime is consistently invoked as that to which Marcuse's politics point,[23] and the distinction between capitalism and then extant communism is held to be less significant than their technocratic comparability. Thus, when Roszak interprets Marcuse's claim in *Eros and Civilization* that labour itself may be satisfying as suggesting that 'work can become play, and the harshly disciplined body, a "thing to be enjoyed"',[24] the implication is that this is akin to Soviet propaganda about happy workers and the like. Indeed, it surely goes beyond this, indicating that Roszak found legible in the discipline characteristic of workers' bodies their internalization of authority and regimentation. Roszak therefore appropriates the category of progress for a form of idealism that is conventionally contemptuous of labour, establishing this as definitive of countercultural oppositionality. Reasons are not hard to find, since the very discourse of culture is one charged with contempt for materialism and utilitarianism, which it has a tendency to conflate. The inflections of that discourse had mostly been elitist and conservative, especially under conditions of increasing political democratization and cultural industrialization.[25]

The radicalism of Roszak's project, therefore, lay in its equation of utilitarianism, not only with materialism, but also reason as such, and its consequent undialectical rejection of modernity. He simply overlooks Marcuse's admittedly controversial point that

---

23  Marcuse's *Soviet Marxism: A Critical Analysis* (London: Routledge & Kegan Paul, 1958) is overlooked by Roszak.

24  Roszak, *The Making of a Counter Culture*, p. 109.

25  This is the tradition to which Francis Mulhern gives the name 'kulturkritik' in *Culture/Metaculture*, Abingdon: Routledge, 2000, pp. 18–21. It is, of course, an aspect of the tradition classically highlighted by Raymond Williams in *Culture and Society 1780–1950*, London: Chatto & Windus, 1958.

different kinds of reason are possible,[26] and that utopian hopes may be sustained by the conviction that a different future might result from an end to the mind/body dualism Roszak's argument specifically sustains. The alternatives to technocratic rationality Roszak invokes are those of the supposedly harmonious non-western and/or pre-modern societies and spiritualities he idealizes at various points, though he also recognizes that there can be no simple return to the past.[27]

Roszak's romantic individualism both exemplified and encouraged the redefinition of the political that was taking place. He considered the latter to be definitive of the US left, interpreting the SDS slogan, 'one man, one soul', as suggesting that 'at whatever cost to the cause or the doctrine, one must care for the uniqueness and dignity of each individual and yield to what his conscience demands in the existential moment'.[28] The counterculture's central value therefore lay in its 'personalism'. Others highlight this quality in various ways. Stanley Aronowitz, for instance, has suggested that SDS was 'the most articulate expression of what became the leading theme of the ideology of the sixties: the attempt to infuse life with a secular spiritual and moral content, to fill the quotidian with personal meaning and purpose'.[29]

Personalism was evident in the SDS ideal of participatory democracy. Politics, claimed the *Port Huron Statement*, in language that may once again be regarded as either euphemistic or evasive,

---

26  Marcuse was famously challenged on this point by Jürgen Habermas in 'Technology and Science as "Ideology"', in *Toward a Rational Society*, trans. Jeremy Shapiro, London: Heinemann Educational, 1971, pp. 81–122.

27  Roszak, *The Making of a Counter Culture*, pp. 264–266.

28  Ibid., p. 61.

29  Stanley Aronowitz, 'When The Left Was New', in Sohnya Sayres, Anders Stephanson, Stanley Aronowitz, and Fredric Jameson, eds, *The Sixties Without Apology*, Minneapolis: University of Minnesota Press, 1984, p. 18.

should be 'the art of collectively creating an acceptable pattern of social relations' and have 'the function of bringing people out of isolation and into community, thus being a necessary, though not sufficient, means of finding meaning in personal life.'[30] Moreover, participatory democracy was not only the political ideal to which SDS aspired: the organization also sought to advance its own causes through those means. At best, this meant arriving at decisions by consensus; at worst, it resulted in chaos and a lack of coherent purpose, because of challenges to the right of anyone to make decisions on behalf of the organization as a whole and therefore on others' behalf. SDS was therefore anarchistic in tendency, and the political became personal because individual dispositions were regarded as authoritarian if too peremptory or assertive. This was so from the start, and was crucial to the differentiation of New from Old Left, as became clear in the famous bust-up between SDS and Michael Harrington of the League for Industrial Democracy over the wording of the *Port Huron Statement* and the attendance at its framing of a member of the Communist Party. SDS stuck to its principled rejection of anticommunism, but it was substantially Harrington's confrontational and inflexible – or, as he would have seen it, principled – *persona* that offended. Ironically, he came to be thought of by some as a 'Stalinist'.[31]

Marianne DeKoven goes so far as to suggest that 'the central impulse of the SDS articulation of participatory democracy is ... directed not primarily toward the reconstitution of society, though

---

30  'The Port Huron Statement', in James Miller, *Democracy is in the Streets: From Port Huron to the Siege of Chicago*, New York: Simon & Schuster, 1987, p. 333.
31  'I know now what it must have been like to be attacked by Stalinists', Casey Hayden said of the confrontation (Miller, *Democracy is in the Streets*, p. 140).

that is in some sense the ultimate goal, but rather towards the reconstitution of self'.[32] In this, it also portends a postmodern 'politics of the subject'. To the extent that this was the case, SDS may be regarded as having inverted socialist priorities, not merely by relating, but actually collapsing means and ends. Brecht's lament that 'we/ Who wished to lay the foundations of kindness/ Could not ourselves be kind' appears to have been well known in SDS circles,[33] but the words seemed best to characterize the Old Left it aspired to supersede. Tom Hayden thought them appropriate for characterizing the Maoist Progressive Labour Party (PLP) that ultimately took over and oversaw the demise of SDS.[34] What, SDS appeared to ask, were the obstacles to achieving kindness, community and personal meaning right now? Often the question was more rhetorical than analytic.

Part of the problem was the openness of SDS, as reflected in the *Port Huron Statement*. This was clearly strategic, for all the best reasons, designed as it was to attract the well-intentioned in general. But the strategy recognized and accepted a specific taboo: the unpronounceability in positive terms within 'American' discourse of the category of socialism (never mind communism). Certainly, Tom Hayden argued that the explicit declaration of any such conviction would be self-defeating, and that it was necessary instead to speak in a national idiom.[35] The problem with this,

32  DeKoven, *Utopia Limited*, pp. 132–133.
33  Kirkpatrick Sale notes that it was pinned to the wall of the Newark Community Union Project office (*SDS*, p. 150). The translation cited is H. R. Hay's: 'To Posterity', *Selected Poems of Bertolt Brecht*, New York: Harvest, 1947, p. 177.
34  Miller, *Democracy is in the Streets*, p. 312.
35  Harrington remarked on his discussions with Hayden that 'He'd say "I agree with you. But where I disagree with you is that you use the word 'socialism,' which is a European word, which simply cuts off your American audience"' (quoted in ibid., p. 54).

however, is that language is not neutral, and socialism – *if* that was ever really the aspiration – is not the kind of thing you might slip past people unnoticed by calling it something else.

Not all movements of the sixties, however, privileged the self, a fact recognized in Roszak's argument when he laments a growing militancy that embraces outright violence (he mentions Black Power as one instance of this, though he probably had the Panthers more specifically in mind). In such movements, the 'humane spirit' of the New Left and counterculture at its best gave way to 'the age-old politics of hatred, vindictiveness, and windy indignation'.[36] This is not the place to get into discussion of tactical legitimacy here, but by focusing on 'spirit' in this abstract way Roszak neglects to consider the different contexts in which militancy emerges. After all, self-realization is a possibility only in certain privileged conditions, and the assertion of dignity as a property of the individual in the face of its pervasive social denial requires particular oppositional strategies that bear scrutiny.

Dignity's denial to particular persons has conventionally been the basis of political movements' appeal to a future transformed by a self-sacrifice in the present that is itself the means of asserting both individual and collective (moral) value. Black Pride was one expression of this principle; the work ethic has been important historically to working-class movements through the essentially social claim that labour is the source of all value. The difficulty here is that what counts as dignified is normative, whereas a great deal of the countercultural emphasis on authenticity, experimentation and self-realization was directed at challenging conformity virtually in principle, usually on the presumption that this was middle-class or bourgeois. These latter terms were crucial

---

36  Roszak, *The Making of a Counter Culture*, p. 61.

to countercultural discourse precisely because their significance appeared self-evident.

Arthur Marwick speaks of a 'Great Marxisant Fallacy' as having suffused sixties movements in the west with a sense that

> the society we inhabit is the bad bourgeois society, but that, fortunately, this society is in a state of crisis, so that the good society which lies just around the corner can be easily attained if only we work systematically to destroy the language, the values, the culture, the ideology of bourgeois society.

A belief in this principle, he claims, united the otherwise disparate 'activists, student protesters, hippies, yippies, Situationists, advocates of psychedelic liberation, participants in the be-ins and rock festivals, proponents of free love, members of the underground and advocates of Black Power, women's liberation and gay liberation'.[37] I clearly do not share Marwick's hostility to Marxism, but his observations here go some way towards explaining the sense – precisely the feeling or intuition – that there was a certain coherence to actually highly diverse groups and movements between whom there were often also powerful tensions, not least in relation to what would now be termed 'normativity'. Nonetheless, the hostility to bourgeois society was frequently based on a rhetorical sleight of hand, since 'bourgeois' effectively displaced, while tacitly continuing to connote, several terms as if they were synonymous: conventional, authoritarian and capitalist. Countercultural claims to forms of avant-garde radicalism relied heavily on this linkage, obscuring capitalism's 'progressive' destruction of convention.

---

37  Arthur Marwick, *The Sixties: Cultural Revolution in Britain, France, Italy, and the United States, c. 1958–1974*, Oxford: Oxford University Press, 1998, p. 10.

Hence, the potency of revisionist work such as Thomas Frank's on cool, mentioned in chapter one. Building on those arguments, Joseph Heath and Andrew Potter argue that the anti-authoritarian attitudes of the counterculture have now become an obstacle to establishing necessary state and suprastate economic regulation, and that its 'alternative' modes of living have themselves become forms of cultural capital.[38] They speak of the counterculture as a kind of bohemianism, a tradition analysed by Elizabeth Wilson and Jim McGuigan as emerging out of a middle-class fractional hatred for the inauthentic bourgeois world on which it is nonetheless dependent in various ways. It quite specifically does not hold the social potential to force a movement beyond that world.[39]

To the extent that these revisionist claims seek to write off the counterculture – and this is variable – they are overstated. After all, the marketization of youth was pervasively recognized at the time.

---

38  Joseph Heath and Andrew Potter, *Nation of Rebels: Why Counterculture Became Consumer Culture*, New York: HarperCollins, 2004. To be clear, Heath and Potter are not socialists: their case is that strong regulation is necessary to establish the kind of ideal market conditions that will generate many of the outcomes that descendants of the counterculture would approve of, though they are also hostile to what they regard as forms of countercultural mysticism and irrationalism. Thus, they embrace both capitalism and the state, by contrast with both left and libertarian right. Contradictorily, they hold that the counterculture thus amounts to something like an ideology in the crudest, mystifying sense, while being bluntly dismissive of Marxist critiques of consumerism because they view ordinary consumers in neoclassical fashion as wholly rational actors. Finally, they show no interest in the exploitation that takes place in production. The arguments are further elaborated in the jointly authored *Rebel Sell: How the Counter Culture Became Consumer Culture*, Mankato: Capstone, 2006, and Andrew Potter's *The Authenticity Hoax: Why the 'Real' Things We Seek Don't Make Us Happy*, New York: Harper, 2011.
39  Elizabeth Wilson, *Bohemians: The Glamorous Outcasts*, London: I. B. Tauris, 2003; Jim McGuigan, *Cool Capitalism*, London: Pluto, 2009, pp. 47–58.

Roszak acknowledged it, and Marcuse had noted it as early as the mid-fifties in *Eros*, as we saw in chapter one. The latter's sense of it clearly informed his theorization of repressive desublimation. Jean-Luc Godard famously labelled sixties youth 'the children of Marx and Coca-Cola' in the film, *Masculin/Féminin* (1966), a European perspective that acknowledges commercialized cool as a form of Americanization.

The counterculture was therefore often grasped at the time as a paradoxical phenomenon whose potential value lay in its capacity to differentiate between its enabling conditions and its political aspirations. Others who belonged to it, though, rejected any belief that such a tension was necessary. Rebecca E. Klatch's remarkable account of both New Left and New Right in the sixties, based on personal accounts from some of those involved, demonstrates that the indeterminacy of SDS politics led to affiliations that appear to have been contradictory. While SDS incorporated elements that were sceptical of the emphasis on subjective experimentation, or dropping out, that became increasingly prominent from the mid-sixties, the conservative Young Americans for Freedom (YAF), established by William F. Buckley in 1960, came to be increasingly divided over the course of the decade between traditionalists and free-market libertarians. The latter were purged in 1969, the same year in which SDS collapsed as a result of the split between Progressive Labour and Weatherman. Market libertarians in YAF shared anti-statist sentiments with members of SDS; they opposed conscription, supported civil rights, experimented with drugs and participated in sexual libertarianism. Gus DiZerega, who was simultaneously secretary-treasurer of YAF and chair of SDS at the University of Kansas in 1967, claims never to have found his position contradictory 'because I was in each for very clearly defined reasons ... My support of the right had solely to do with economics ... My support of the left had to do with everything else'.[40]

However peculiar or marginal positions such as DiZerega's were, they represented a clarity and consistency in their anti-state convictions that were lacking in more intuitive radicalism. This consistency, moreover, serves to highlight the contradictions of others on the left in their focus on norms and their transgression. If the counterculture prided itself on rejecting bourgeois lifestyles, the avowedly 'straight' PLP regarded the counterculture itself as typically bourgeois in its self-indulgence. Consequently, the PLP's members dressed neatly, wore their hair short and lived in working-class areas. But Barbara Ehrenreich suggests that this strategy was also predicated on problematic assumptions about the relations between class and lifestyle: she records two Ivy League militants adopting this strategy only to be confronted with workers who resembled hippies and assumed the students were undercover narcotics agents.[41] The point may be overemphasized, of course, but the cultural legibility of class through subjective (self-)discipline could not easily be taken for granted.

The PLP's commitment above all to class solidarity may have been exceptional, but the assumptions about working-class cultural conservatism that informed its strategy were commonly held. Fredric Jameson makes a similar point to Marwick, but with a distinctive emphasis, noting that in the sixties

40  Rebecca E. Klatch, *A Generation Divided: the New Left, the New Right, and the 1960s*, Berkeley: University of California Press, 1999, pp. 216–217.
41  Barbara Ehrenreich, *Fear of Falling: The Inner Life of the Middle Class*, New York: HarperCollins, 1989, p. 123.

the new binary opposite to the term 'bourgeois' will no longer be 'proletarian' but rather 'revolutionary', and the new qualifications for political judgements of this kind are no longer made in terms of class or party affiliation but rather in terms of personal life.[42]

The linguistic substitution Jameson notes was significant in all sorts of ways. It was one consequence of talk of the bourgeoisification of the working class, but it was also symptomatic of harsher attitudes: of a disdain for that class, and an identification of it with reaction such as we have seen in Roszak's arguments. This was increasingly pervasive over the course of the sixties and seventies, as Ehrenreich has documented in extensive detail.[43] As she notes, this disdain had acquired strong 'scientific' legitimacy through influential sociological studies that alluded to Frankfurtian models of the authoritarian personality. Seymour Lipset argued that those who were relatively 'lower class' in any given society were likely to exhibit more authoritarian tendencies than the more privileged, owing to their experience of peremptory familial authority and lack of intellectual stimulation, including the kind of formal education that distinguished the New Left.[44] In his history of the category of homophobia, Daniel Wickberg argues that such convictions were crucial to its development by progressive psychologists: in such writings, 'the profile of the homophobe is very much in line with the opposite of the liberal's own self image'.[45]

---

42  Jameson, 'Periodizing the Sixties', p. 189. Specifically, though, Jameson is alluding to Maoism.

43  Ehrenreich, *Fear of Falling*, pp. 97–143.

44  Seymour Martin Lipset, *Political Man*, London: Heinemann, 1959, pp. 97–130.

45  Daniel Wickberg, 'Homophobia: On the Cultural Construction of an Idea', *Critical Inquiry*, 27(1), 2000, p. 55.

There is one important further dimension to this erosion of confidence in working-class agency in the US. In his 1965 essay on Castroism, Regis Debray remarked that 'when one considers the places where socialism has triumphed and the size of the populations involved, one is forced to inquire who is peripheral to whom and whether this idea of a *centre* still has any meaning'.[46] This spatial conundrum was also, of course, a temporal one about who was the most politically *progressive*, because revolutionary, without being the most *developed* in industrial terms. Indeed, this disparity contributed to the distinctive dialectic that emerges in the sixties critique of modernity as such, encompassing Roszak's overtly romantic argument, as well as Debray's. It appeared that resistance to capitalism/modernity required a more or less greater distance from it, since to be located at the heart of it, as with the US or more generally western working class, was to be assimilated to it.

The assumption persists. It surely conditions Jameson's pessimistic deployment of Williams's categories of dominant, residual and emergent in his arguments about a postmodernity whose achievement has been to colonize other spatio-temporal zones – a form of creeping American one-dimensionality – and thereby foreclose resistance. But that sense is also more pervasive in critiques of his work that find it 'too totalizing' and seek to prove this by invoking the kinds of marginal experience that apparently escape such 'purification'.

Jameson has also suggested that anti-colonialism, having initiated the sixties as a distinctive period, offers an instructive figurative means of grasping its dynamics. Elaborating on a

46  Regis Debray, 'Castroism: The Long March in Latin America', in *Strategy for Revolution: Essays on Latin America*, London: Jonathan Cape, 1970, p. 27.

distinction made by Sartre in his preface to Fanon's *The Wretched of the Earth* about the world having been organized by colonialism into *men* and *natives*, Jameson suggests that

> the sixties was ... the period in which all these 'natives' became human beings, and this internally as well as externally: those inner colonized of the first world – 'minorities', marginals, and women – fully as much as external subjects and official 'natives'.[47]

The internal/external distinction here clearly highlights that, whatever forces determined their emergence, the sixties he is accounting for were primarily a western phenomenon. Between the west and those it looked to in certain respects as exemplars of liberation, there was frequently a profound gulf that had to do, once again, with development, the social positioning of radicals in the US, and their often dramatically different grasp of what constituted progress.

In fact, Jameson's comments serve to call attention to connections and forms of solidarity that were prevalent through analogical thinking that was current at the time. In defending the principle of Black Power (i.e. black self-organization) as the basis of SNCC operations from 1966, for instance, the organization observed that

> it is very ironic and curious that aware whites in this country can champion anticolonialism in other countries in Africa, Asia, and Latin America, but when black people move toward similar goals of self-determination in this country they are viewed as racists and anti-white by these same progressive whites.[48]

---

47  Jameson, 'Periodizing', p. 181.
48  'The Basis of Black Power', in Bloom and Bries (eds), *'Takin' It to the Streets*, p. 152.

Todd Gitlin sees this shift as having been productive of a greater diversification: 'As the old SNCC exploded [casting white activists out], it threw off centrifugal energies like a dying star ... Black nationalism, hippiness, feminism: the old movement unities were certainly breaking down.'[49]

Whether or not one accepts Gitlin's assertion that Black Power gave rise to an increasingly fissiparous left, there can be no doubt that the language of autonomy and self-determination conditioned other movements, including those that were radicalized by the events of Stonewall. In 1971, New York City's Third World Gay Revolution group demanded 'the right of self-determination for all Third World and gay people, as well as control of the destinies of our communities'. It went on to argue for

> abolition of the institution of the bourgeois nuclear family ... All oppressions originate within the nuclear family structure. Homosexuality is a threat to this family structure and therefore to capitalism. The mother is an instrument of reproduction and teaches the necessary values of capitalist society, i.e., racism, sexism, etc., from infancy on. The father physically enforces (upon the mother and children) the behaviour necessary in a capitalist system: intelligence and competitiveness in young boys and passivity in young girls.[50]

A similar point was made by the Gay Revolution Party in angry response to the Cuban regime's pronouncements on 'the social pathological character of homosexual deviations' in 1971: 'We are,

---

49  Todd Gitlin, *The Sixties*, pp. 168–169.
50  Third World Gay Revolution, 'What We Want, What We Believe', in Karla Jay and Allen Young, eds, *Out of the Closet: Voices of Gay Liberation*, New York: Jove, 1977, pp. 364–365.

and always have been considered the scum of the earth,' it argued, 'but we are you: we are everyone. The gay revolution is basic because it will destroy the sexual and social roles which are at the bottom of *all* exploitation, establishing mutuality of relationship between all people.'[51]

It would be easy to lampoon both these groups' theoretical naivety, as well as their ambitions. With our retrospective wisdom, the requirements of capitalism look rather different than they were presumed to be then, and gay radicalism (if not revolution) as it has turned out does not seem to challenge sexual and social roles as thoroughly as was once imagined it must. It is also difficult to convict the family of being comprehensively 'authoritarian', whatever its limitations in other respects may be. But the universalist impulse, the sense that the abject is not only external, but also internal to the subject ('we are everyone') is consistent with what many of us continue to believe, even if the threat queers pose is diminishing with the rapid diminution in disgust that is felt for us.

What interests me about these statements, to put it in terms indebted to Eve Sedgwick, is the conviction they evince that an extraordinary universalizing, revolutionary burden had been conferred on a minority ('we are everyone'). The simultaneous, and obviously contradictory, appeal to autonomy made by Third World Gay Revolution highlights the strategic and theoretical difficulties that gays, lesbians and queers have struggled with ever since. A logic of rights attendant on the sense of constituting a

---

51  Gay Liberation Party, 'Response to the Declaration by the First [Cuban] National Congress on Education and Culture', in Jay and Young, eds, *Out of the Closet*, p. 248. The 'Declaration by the First National Congress on Education and Culture' precedes this on pp. 246–247.

kind of ethnicity[52] has been persistently at war with the radical repudiation of any such liberal compromise; the two have been mutually reinforcing.

Even the sense, discernible in the rhetoric at least, that there might be solidarities among the diverse autonomies that were opening up was a difficult one to sustain. One gay SDS activist, Allen Young, brought up in a Communist Party household, tells of his increasing disenchantment with, and rejection of, Marxism as a result of his experiences as a delegate in the Venceremos Brigade that sought to enlist support for the Cuban regime. He speaks of a persistent machismo in Cuban society with which Castro's regime was complicit. For Young, revolution had to be simultaneously, and even immediately, subjective and objective, uniting the struggles of quite different parts of the world in a synthesis of his own authenticity with the experiences of the Cubans.[53] 'There is no valid separation of the personal and political,' he wrote. 'If you want to bring joy to the suffering masses, you must be engaged in the process of bringing joy to yourself.'[54] Putting things like that, though, accentuates the problem: the statement shows a preoccupation with the bringers of joy, not those to whom it is apparently brought.

The lesbian and gay liberation movements, then, formed part of the broader countercultural/New Left revolt, and by the early seventies found themselves targeted, along with the rest of those formations, by the resurgent conservative right. Nonetheless, the countercultural legacy has been profound. Subcultural milieux continued to expand, of course, but at the expense of apparently superseded revolutionary hopes: autonomy was pursued through

---

52   Alan Sinfield highlights this tendency, and follows through many of its implications in *Gay and After*, London: Cassell, 1998, pp. 18–44.
53   Allen Young, 'The Cuban Revolution', in *Out of the Closets*, pp. 206–228.
54   Ibid., p. 228.

necessity, and the result was the kind of 'homosexualization of America' (and elsewhere) described by Dennis Altman. That life became the focus of new forms of stigmatization mobilized against the 'permissiveness' autonomy facilitated, and, in such conditions, it is difficult to imagine a more fortuitous phenomenon for the right than the AIDS crisis of the eighties; so fortuitous, indeed, that it seemed a godsend. I consider one angry response to this particular stigmatization in James Robert Baker's novel, *Tim and Pete*, below, but I do so primarily as part of an attempt to illustrate in what forms the spirit of countercultural radicalism persists.

It does so in spite of the shift in theoretical terms that has taken place, and for which the substitution of Foucault for Marcuse may well stand as an appropriate symbol. The afterlife of the counterculture in the kinds of theory sponsored by Foucault may be glimpsed in the emphasis on desubjectification he developed while visiting the US in the seventies. Foucault spoke in celebratory fashion of the saunas he visited while there, and of the cruising and sadomasochistic practices he enjoyed. In one essay he wrote of the anonymity of these experiences in ways that recall both Marcuse's comments on the reification of the body and those of Henning Bech on the 'alienated' encounter:

> I think it is politically important that sexuality be able to function the way it functions in the saunas, where, without [having to submit to] the condition of being imprisoned in one's own identity, in one's own past, in one's own face, one can meet people who are to you what one is to them; nothing else but bodies with which combinations, fabrications of pleasure will be possible. These places afford an exceptional possibility of desubjectivization, of desubjection, perhaps not the most radical but in any case sufficiently intense to be worth taking

note of. [Anonymity is important] because of the intensity of the pleasure that follows from it. It's not the affirmation of identity that's important, it's the affirmation of non-identity ... It's an important experience in which one invents, for as long as one wants, pleasures which one fabricates together [with others].[55]

What Foucault means to indicate through reference to the political here is unclear. After all, sexuality *was* able to function in the way he describes, because saunas existed. It appears, then, that he is eliding the distinction between the political and the ethical in a way that reflects countercultural emphases on selfhood. He expresses himself in anti-humanist, rather than humanist terms, but the suggestion here is not fundamentally different from the emphasis on unpicking 'bourgeois' socialization commonplace in the sixties. What is different, of course, is precisely the context in which it takes place: saunas are a product of a highly developed, urban subcultural life facilitated by commercial privacy, and the experiences that take place within them are intensified by environments that are carefully designed to preserve the cruising sensibility and, maybe also, by the easy availability of the 'good drugs' Foucault commends elsewhere.[56] The romanticism of this account is perhaps another product of this cultivated intensity, but that makes it all the more unclear why Foucault considers this a form of *de*subjectification rather than a different mode of subjectification – if those are the terms we want to use – within the diversified economy of sensation

55   Michel Foucault, 'Le Gay Savoir', trans. by and cited in David Halperin, *Saint Foucault: Towards a Gay Hagiography*, New York: Oxford University Press, 1995, p. 94.
56   See Michel Foucault, 'Sex, Power and the Politics of Identity', in *Ethics, Subjectivity and Truth*, New York: The New Press, 1997, pp. 165–166.

and pleasure that was emerging.[57] In such statements, the anti-bourgeois romantic subjectivism of the subculture is ironically perpetuated through the progressive qualities of capitalism.

## Radical anger: *Tim and Pete*

Marcuse wrote 'Repressive Tolerance' in 1965 and dedicated it to his students at Brandeis University. I referred to this essay in the introduction, but didn't touch there on the notoriety it has acquired over the years. One recent instance of this is the claim made by Jeremy Varon in his remarkable account of Weatherman in the US and the Red Army Faction in Germany that the essay contributed to a climate on the left that gave legitimacy to the activities of such groups.[58]

Such arguments seem to me to place the blame unfairly on Marcuse, who was writing at a time before the intensification of violence on the part of both state and activists in the late sixties. He argues in the essay that the principle of tolerance in a pervasively unfree, but democratic, society draws on the rhetoric of formerly progressive forces that they be heard, but presses it into the service of reaction. Tolerance for the way things are is promoted, and protest made within the limits of the permissible reinforces

---

57  Lois McNay makes an analogous point, suggesting that the later ethics of Foucault are inadequate for dealing with a form of biopower, neoliberalism, 'that operates precisely through the proliferation of difference and the management of individual autonomy' ('Self as Enterprise: Dilemmas of Control and Resistance in Foucault's *The Birth of Biopolitics*', *Theory, Culture & Society*, 26(55), 2009, p. 68).

58  Jeremy Varon, *Bringing the War Home: The Weather Underground, The Red Army Faction, and Revolutionary Violence in the Sixties and Seventies*, Berkeley: University of California Press, 2004, pp. 42–44. Varon's treatment of Marcuse is actually quite nuanced. He differentiates, for instance, between the former's dialectical emphasis on negation, and the Weatherman's nihilism; see pp. 166–168.

the system by testifying to its reasonableness. Progress therefore may be served rather by going beyond the tolerance the system requires for its own operations, such that reactionary arguments and actions are actively suppressed; violently so, if necessary.

It is important, however, to establish that Marcuse's understanding of violence was broad, and incorporated Gandhian peaceful resistance and the principle of the General Strike on the grounds that in such cases quantity passes over into quality. The *effect* of them is violent.[59] Moreover, Marcuse subsequently went on to speak in favour of

> actions ... condemned by the Establishment and by the liberals as acts of violence ... the disruption of court procedures which clearly expose the class character of the administration of justice; the peaceful occupation of buildings which clearly serve the purposes of the military or of political control; the 'heckling' of speakers who clearly espouse the policy of war and oppression.

Other kinds of action were indefensible. That

> directed toward vague, general, intangible targets is senseless; worse, it augments the number of adversaries. For example: the slogan of the 'hot summer' in France, which led to idiotic actions of sabotage and destruction, mostly to the detriment not of the ruling class but of the 'people'; or the destruction of the buildings and offices of companies which, in the public mind, are not recognized as 'war criminals'; and so on.[60]

---

59  Herbert Marcuse, 'Repressive Tolerance', in Robert Paul Wolff, Barrington Moore Jr, and Herbert Marcuse, eds, *A Critique of Pure Tolerance*, London: Jonathan Cape, 1969, pp. 116–117.
60  Herbert Marcuse, *Counterrevolution and Revolt*, Boston: Beacon Press, 1972, pp. 51–52.

If we can see past the essay's perhaps unfortunate choice of terms, then, it articulates a genuine conundrum for the left: faced with the massive imbalance of economic, political, military and cultural forces, what action is warranted against modes of repression that tolerance renders normal and reasonable? These problems become especially acute when progressive forces find themselves in a minority in consequence of those conditions.

Marcuse's essay registers in its very style, but also accounts for, the frustration and anger many feel at the way injustice is systematically registered, yet negated, in everyday life. These conditions are also the focus of James Robert Baker's complex meditation on political violence in the context of the AIDS crisis, *Tim and Pete* (1993). The book acquired notoriety on publication because of its apparent willingness to entertain the possibility that violence might be acceptable when used against the anti-gay Republican right that had exploited the AIDS crisis to advance its moral agenda through the stigmatization of a minority experiencing a catastrophic pandemic. The book goes beyond this, however, to highlight the powerful continuities between the cultural values promoted by the culture industry as embodied in Hollywood and the policies of the right. The setting for the novel, appropriately enough in both respects, is Los Angeles: Ronald Reagan was a screen actor, and governor of California between 1967 and 1975 who endorsed state violence against New Left forces.[61] It was this kind of uncompromising persona that assisted him in his subsequent successful bid to become President in 1981. In the novel, he is the target for a militant group of HIV-positive gay men

---

61 'If it takes a bloodbath, let's get it over with. No more appeasement', Reagan said in 1970, after there had been several already, including the one for which he bore significant responsibility at People's Park, Berkeley, in 1969 (Gitlin, *The Sixties*, pp. 414–415 and 359–361).

intent on assassinating him for his record over AIDS specifically during his time in office.

The novel is not only critical of the right; it is also scathing about the sensibilities of those pacified 'mainstream homosexuals', by contrast with whom both Tim and Pete define themselves. The couple's troublesome journey across Los Angeles begins when Tim's date with Victor, an older Barry Manilow fan who still lives with his mother, goes predictably wrong, and he drops in on his ex-boyfriend, Pete, to ask for help in getting home. Victor is significant precisely because he is treated so slightingly. His relationship with his mother is indicative of his more general femininity, and his excessive fastidiousness appears to complement his crude, typically 'gay' sexual advances towards Tim: Victor refuses to let Tim smoke in his Jaguar convertible; at the beach, Tim's paleness and 'baggy 1940s swim trunks' contrast with Victor's tan and Speedos. Victor's age, fussiness, wealth, campness and forthright, yet calculated and even desperate, sexual approaches are totalizingly uncool.

By contrast with Victor, Tim and Pete inhabit a world of indie music, and are knowledgeable about literature, film of all kinds and critical theory; they avoid the gym and the institutions of the commercial scene. The narrative is ultimately a love story: it begins with Tim's dream and subsequent thoughts of Pete after a year apart, thereby signalling a kind of fidelity, and highlights the problems they experience getting across a highly decentralized and fragmented Los Angeles without a car,[62] initially to different destinations. The journey nonetheless ends with them back together.

---

62   Mike Davis's *City of Quartz: Excavating the Future in Los Angeles* (London: Verso, 1990) is alluded to in the novel, and provides an account of the spatio-political development of LA along these lines; see especially pp. 101–219.

Their travels are made still more difficult by the racial tensions still simmering in the wake of the 1992 riots sparked by the beating of Rodney King by LA policemen, events that also serve as an appropriate backdrop to the novel's debates about the justification for violent responses to oppression and discrimination. That Tim and Pete do manage to get back together is indicative of the high value placed on relationships as one mark of the novel's distaste for what it depicts as the compulsive sleaziness of mainstream gay life, though the distinction between this and the 'hot', spontaneous sex otherwise celebrated by the two protagonists is an awkward one.

There are differences between the lovers: Tim is older and middle class, whereas Pete is from a 'lower middle class or blue collar'[63] neighbourhood. Though fantasy is an important part of their sexual and political life, Pete is more to Tim than 'just a mechanic or a rock musician or a cute, butch guy in a Yale T-shirt with a hard-on'. This suggests that their attraction transcends erotically charged class differences, but the novel has difficulty establishing how: Pete is special to Tim above all because of the 'sensibility and humour'[64] that fuel his musical and lyrical creativity. Paradoxically, the authenticity of their relationship is therefore signalled through culture, and a similar paradox attends Pete's music: the anger which underpins it is raw, but it is given creative expression. The provocation of the novel is that his song celebrating Baader-Meinhof is the specific inspiration for the HIV-positive activists who plot to bomb a Republican family convention. The novel only gives an account of their preparations, somewhat disturbed by Tim and Pete's attempts to prevent them, and ultimately leaves open the possibility that they might have been successful.

---

63  Baker, *Tim and Pete*, p. 62.
64  Ibid., p. 38.

To be in the mainstream, then, is to be deluded about one's situation in the US in the 1990s, sedated by the culture industry in the midst of a crisis that is political as well as medical. The relationship between the right and mainstream gay men is frequently, and provocatively, compared by Pete to that between Nazis and submissive Jews during the Holocaust. For gay men to respond to their situation with violence would be to challenge the popular image of them as passive, and thereby feminized: referring to the aversion to violence of Tim's friend, Gregory, Pete suggests, '"He'd mince right into the cattle car – as long as they told him he could shriek at Bette Midler comedies once he got to Auschwitz".'[65] And yet, the novel is primarily a critique of dominant, repressive forms of masculine identification, about which it effectively articulates a number of theses.

The first is that masculinity is inculcated through the use of violence by fathers in disciplining boys: specifically it is used to beat out of them any temptation to establish sexual bonds with other boys, and thereby violently to police the otherwise precarious distinction between the desire to be a man and the desire for one. Pete's first boyfriend was driven to commit suicide by his father's violent response to finding them having sex. Pete initially sought revenge, but ultimately realized that '"he was just doing what any red-blooded American dad would've done. That's why I blame the whole culture now".'[66] Republican hegemony is defined by its universalization of a discipline associated with the working class.

The focus on fathers specifically, and the family in general, is especially important in the scene in which Pete drops in on his mum at work to discover her having sex with her boss, the Republican

65  Ibid., p. 198.
66  Ibid., p. 87.

politician, Gerald C. Bryer. The disgust registered at this scene renders it uncannily primal in the psychoanalytic sense. We get 'a nasty shot of [Pete's mother's] butt and glistening vagina' and of Bryer's balls which are 'gray like elephant skin'.[67] Though strictly speaking this is Tim's perspective, it is nonetheless aligned with Pete's through the smell of pipe tobacco in the office that reminds Tim of his own father. The father, then, is a role, not an individual, and the attack on Bryer, who bears significant responsibility for the culture in general, is therefore a repetition of Pete's parricidal impulse. But, once again, the distinctions between Tim and Pete are blurred: later, Tim finds that the remembered image of Pete feeding Bryer his own blood while claiming simultaneously that he is HIV-positive 'on a certain level of justice still does my heart good'.[68] That 'certain level' is a retributive one, the level ultimately of the terrorist gang.

The culture is also dominated by Hollywood,[69] and masculinity is mostly reinforced through cultural identifications with violent cinematic instances of it. This is why Tim and Pete take great pleasure in 'desublimated' fantasies of action movies, Westerns and the like. Politics represents an extension of the values of Hollywood, such that distinctions between the two are eroded. At one point, after inadvertently taking mescaline, Tim surreally notes 'the mulatto *Die Hard* building (where Ronald Reagan kept his office in the tip of the glassy glans penis) appeared to flex like a living cock. I looked away and rubbed my eyes, which made me see spinning swastikas.'[70]

---

67  Ibid., p. 42.
68  Ibid., p. 44.
69  Hollywood is a consistent feature of Baker's satire, as in his brilliant documentary-style account of the director, Shark Trager, in *Boy Wonder*, London: Futura, 1988.
70  Baker, *Tim and Pete*, pp. 165–166.

The problem the novel has to confront, then, is that violence is so closely identified with the reproduction of heterosexuality and the repression of homosexuality that it makes violence in the cause of gay liberation appear contradictory. Speaking of Glenn's gang, Tim suggests,

'It all seems so Neanderthal. I mean, *imagining* something violent as a kind of cinematic fantasy is one thing. But to actually start fooling around with weapons – it's so dim-witted and heterosexual. There's no getting past the moronic Chuck Norris/ Rambo connotations.'

[Pete:] 'Well, Glenn would say that if Rambo's coming through your door with a flamethrower, you'd better do something besides hold up a volume of Proust.'

'And, of course, you agree.'

'Well, what would *you* do?'

'It's a comic book situation,' I said.

'So?'

'So, I *would* hold up Proust. The flameproof volumes. Then, once Rambo had used up his fire, I'd rip out an extralong sentence and hog-tie him with it. Then I'd fuck him.'

'He'd probably like that.' Pete did a grunting Rambo impression: '*Yeah!* Fuck my greased up ass! Slam that cock right up there. Don't worry about hurtin' me! You can't hurt Rambo.'[71]

Desublimation is here imagined in the specific forms offered by a certain kind of gay pornography, with its own virtuoso masculine emphases on sex as, not only virility, but also capacity and endurance (the 'power bottom'; even 'passivity' is thus transfigured). The privilege accorded the phallus is hardly displaced, but rather more

---

71  Ibid., pp. 195–196.

directly equated with the penis. Similar qualities are evident in both kinds of film, then, despite the suggestion that the Hollywood one is based on sublimation.

In part, the novel registers that being gay does not in itself entail a break with the father: fantasies may still be dominated by his idealized image. Pete eventually confesses to Tim that their original breakup had to do with Tim's anger: it reminded Pete of his father.[72] The relationship between Glenn and his boyfriend, Joey, is said to be 'a dad-and-lad scene' that draws on Joey's experiences of abuse as a child.[73]

And yet, elsewhere, the misogyny evident in the treatment of mother's boy Victor, who embodies the pacified subculture, is maintained in the novel's focus on sex. In response to the scene with his mother and Bryer, Pete abuses her as a 'stupid fucking cunt' in a graphic synecdochic reduction of her to her unthinkingly conformist act (an affair with the boss). Pete makes little allowance for her relative powerlessness: what matters is that she has betrayed him in his campaign against fathers.

The ambivalence of the novel in this respect is crucial to its ending. Before Glenn's gang go out to attack the Republican convention, they have sex and shoot up drugs. Tim and Pete witness this from their hiding place, and Tim acknowledges that it reminds him of the kind of porn that excites him. The sex is deliberately unsafe, and after Glenn shoots up into the vein on Joey's cock, Tim thinks, 'I'm not exaggerating when I say I don't think I've ever seen anyone come for so long or so much'. Duration and quantity here are, again, conventional signs of masculine intensity; this is the climax of all climaxes. Tim's response is important:

---

72  Ibid., p. 68.
73  Ibid., p. 166. Sinfield notes this in *On Sexuality and Power*, New York: Columbia University Press, 2004, p. 19.

In the living room Dexter began licking the semen off Joey's chest. And that was too much. Even in the old days that bit in porno films had always seemed unnecessarily gross. But *now* – dear God.

And yet, in some other way that wasn't even entirely sexual, I was still excited. Watching through the window it *was* like looking at a silent porno tape (I always turned off the sound anyway, to lose the bad dialogue and music). And even though this was dangerous, disgusting, deadly, unconscionable – shooting speed! Swapping blood! Eating jiz! – these guys obviously didn't care anymore. They were already doomed, so what did it matter? And there was a terrifying but profoundly seductive freedom in that. They could do anything now, anything they wanted to, anything at all.[74]

While death is here linked to transgression, it is not as consequence or punishment for that transgression, but rather the opposite: as the fact that makes possible an absolute freedom that is at once repellent and profoundly attractive 'in some other way that wasn't even entirely sexual'. What thrills Tim is a form of desubjectification through the negation of internalized morality and responsibility (including subcultural safe-sex messages). This abandonment is nonetheless wholly consistent with the individualism of the system now given over to consumerist pleasure; here, pornography. But, of course, *absolute* freedom is itself the negation of meaningful freedom, and the repeated 'anything's of that final sentence echo dialectically with their opposite: to the extent that nothing matters to the gang any more, this is because they are already dead. The (sexual) excitement here is Tim's: Dexter and Joey are breaking taboos that are still significant for him.

---

74  Baker, *Tim and Pete*, p. 187.

Indeed, Tim's subjective ambivalence is crucial less because it is ambivalent than because it is subjective, since what appears to matter almost above all else in the novel is how one feels. In all of the debates about the legitimacy or otherwise of political violence, the focus is rather on who may or may not deserve what for the damaging and consequential offence they have caused. Pete becomes complicit with the violence because he suggests the convention in place of a target that might have resulted in the deaths of non-Republicans. When he gets the opportunity, the only person he attempts to save from the attack is his mother (thereby rescuing her from all those lascivious Bryers). Strikingly, no objection to the violence is offered on the grounds that it would inevitably lead to more intense scapegoating and be used to justify more repressive measures against those who remain; even subcultural responsibility is disavowed by the gang.

But then Glenn's political radicalism is an extension of his individualistic freedom of *expression*: it is a departure from his artwork in the sense of being an outrageous extension of it. In one notorious exhibition of that work for an AIDS charity prior to his involvement in the gang, for instance, he sprays the wealthy donors with blood, pretending it is infected, shouting, '"You've all got it now! Now you can *really* empathize! 'Cause you're all going to die too".'[75] That this is an incoherent, self-indulgent gesture – see how *I* feel – dignified as 'political' art through its transgression of formal 'bourgeois' conventions is not lost on Tim and Pete, but the novel nonetheless also emphasizes an aesthetic complicity between Pete and

---

75   Ibid., p. 162.

Glenn.[76] The difference is that Pete's anger finds expression in cultural form alone, something derided as 'catharsis' by Glenn[77]: Pete is wimpy, because creativity is quite conventionally feminized by contrast with action.

Baker himself, in responding to criticism of the novel, expressed his own ambivalence about political violence, but nonetheless spoke of the feelings of anger that prompted it as 'valid'. He acknowledged the need for pragmatism in real life, but claimed it was 'appropriate' to explore feelings unconstrained by such 'real world' concerns in a novel.[78] For Baker, then, the novel is the legitimate vehicle for the subjective expression of an anger that objectively would have been irresponsible, because the relative powerlessness of lesbian and gay movements in their minoritized situation would have left them vulnerable to further persecution in response. As in the case of Pete's song about Baader-Meinhof, legitimate anger is driven back – sublimated, one might say – into a form of cultural expression that is nonetheless authentic to one's situation.

Minoritarian anger in conditions of repressive tolerance is expressed by Lee Edelman at the persistent offence directed at queers in his book, *No Future* (2004). It seems to me to resonate instructively with Baker's preoccupations, since it commends resistance to the compromises demanded of queers socially, culturally and politically. Edelman confronts a logic I articulated

---

76  Sinfield plausibly views situationist experimentalism as the relevant context for these debates, and notes that ACT UP and Queer Nation were effectively part of that lineage that emerged from this: *On Sexuality and Power*, p. 80.

77  Baker, *Tim and Pete*, p. 221.

78  See Baker's web interview with Rich Grzesiak, 'Rage, Rant, Revolution: Kamikaze Writer Novelizes Aids in L.A.', http://www.axiongrafix.com/baker.html (accessed 29 November 2011).

above in discussion of political movements – the principle they have commonly articulated of self-sacrifice in the name of a better future – but by acknowledging this now as a dominant, rather than oppositional, imperative, and by couching his account in Lacanian terms. Renunciation, he suggests, is demanded of us by the cultural figure of the child who promises a harmonious future that is necessarily an illusion, since the division for which that figure anticipates a resolution is ultimately constituted by our accession to the Symbolic order. Because of their abjection within that order, however, queers are distinctively called to resist the illusions the Symbolic generates through their embrace of that very positioning, and thereby to identify instead with the death drive in order to achieve a certain *jouissance*.

Edelman's radicalism resides in his demand – and the book has the tone of a manifesto – that queers be authentic, albeit to a role determined for them by the Symbolic order, as distinct from some social identitarian principle. He claims, for instance, that 'queerness could never constitute an authentic or substantive identity, but only a structural position determined by the imperative of figuration',[79] but we apparently still have the capacity to be faithful to it, because 'we can ... make the choice to accede to our cultural production'.[80] This seems to reinstate the initially repudiated principle of authenticity, then, but it is only plausibly available to us if we allow that the queer is indeed culturally produced in the ways that Edelman claims she is.

In order to sustain a powerful degree of pessimism about political and historical possibilities, Edelman's argument is facilitated by a number of elisions. First, it is unclear how he

---

79  Lee Edelman: *No Future: Queer Theory and the Death Drive*, Durham, NC: Duke University Press, 2004, p. 26.
80  Ibid., p. 22.

perceives the queer. At some points, the queer is that figure who is unassimilable simply by virtue of the fact that any social order whatsoever is dependent on norms, with the result that certain forms of behaviour are discountenanced; not anything goes. Thus, we discover that 'the queer comes to figure the bar ... to every social structure or form'.[81] At other times, queers appear in some more specific sense to be sexually dissident figures, since the term designates 'all [those] so stigmatized for failing to comply with heteronormative mandates'.[82] This facilitates the sense in Edelman's argument that heteronormativity is a historically permanent state of affairs whose alleviation we delude ourselves into thinking possible through our assent to (heteronormative) reproductive futurism. This is despite the fact that he recognizes at one point that the sentimentalization of the child that governs the Symbolic's representations is itself historically determined.[83]

This elision of the universal (the principle that queerness is immanent to any and all orders) with the specific (those who fit the bill now) is bound to another between the Symbolic order – or, at least, what is claimed about it – and the social order, and therefore history. Thus, the Symbolic at times appears to 'install' optimism in a reality that is at least conceivable as distinct from it (e.g. 'fantasy alone endows reality with fictional coherence and stability'[84]), but at others it is conceived as constituting the field of sociality as such (as when Edelman makes a point about 'those queered by the social order that projects its death drive onto them'[85]). Edelman brilliantly demonstrates the pervasiveness

---

81  Ibid., p. 4.
82  Ibid., p. 17.
83  Ibid., pp. 10–11.
84  Ibid., p. 34.
85  Ibid., p. 30.

of reproductive futurism across even the most apparently well-meaning of cultural phenomena, such as Jonathan Demme's film, *Philadelphia*, but the question is whether he also establishes the integrity of a 'homophobic culture' that requires the kind of subjective resistance to temporality he prescribes.

Of course, Edelman acknowledges that change happens, though it is not clear why he thinks it does. Is it the result of the faith placed in the possibility of change and progress as a result of reproductive futurism, or is it determined ultimately by systemic conflict, as Marxists, for instance, would suggest? Whatever the answer to that might be, the change can never be enough. He writes:

> We might like to believe that ... the future will hold a place for us – a place at the political table that won't have to come at the cost of the places we seek in the bed or the bar or the baths. But there can be no *queers* in that future as there can be no future for queers, chosen as they are to bear the bad tidings that there can be no future at all.[86]

There are a number of things to note about this. First, it acknowledges that the social perhaps doesn't project the death drive on to all spheres ('the bed or the bar or the baths' are part of it, after all). Second, it reproduces that elision between the sexually queer and the more abstract queer who attends any and all orders by virtue of them being orders at all. And yet, if we can conceive of the order changing to the extent that the sexually queer might indeed become fully assimilated, such that queerness as a structural principle has to be fulfilled by others, that can only be because reproductive futurism is no longer operative.

---

86  Ibid., pp. 29–30.

The problems with Edelman's argument are overdetermined by a number of factors: that of understanding historical change within a framework that privileges signification, both in principle and in the form Lacan inherits from structuralism as primarily synchronic; the further one of relating the specificity of the *sexually* queer to the abstract condition of queerness; and, it has to be said, the fact that the very processes of human reproduction that do secure futurity will rightly be a central concern of any society whatsoever, and the possibilities for achieving it are not infinitely open, even if they need not be limited to the forms that are currently dominant.

There is a further determining factor at play in Edelman's pessimism about political possibilities. This results from being able only to conceive the spectrum as ranging from a liberal left he problematically equates with 'reason' as such through to the conservative right. It is pretty clear, in other words, that the claim to universality his argument necessarily makes refers quite specifically to the US, where politics is so spectacularly dominated by the span from progressive Democrat to evangelical Republican. The former imagines LGBT people as banally similar to everyone else, and therefore unjustly discriminated against, while the latter understands better, and consequently loathes, the perverse threat that queers represent. Given that no better options seem plausible, it is unsurprising that history appears unavailing.

I do not mean to suggest that things are radically different elsewhere at present. Rather, I want to observe that the apparently voluntaristic repudiation of reproductive futurism Edelman demands of queers in order that they maintain their authenticity not only does not preclude assimilation, it appears to dictate it. This is clear from the syntactical structure of his well-known verbal assault on the 'homophobic culture' variously encoded in everything from the pronouncements of the former Pope on homosexuality through to certain theatrical musicals:

> Queers must respond to the violent force of such constant provocations not only by insisting on our equal right to the social order's prerogatives, not only by avowing our capacity to promote that order's coherence and integrity, but also by saying explicitly what Law and the Pope and the whole of the Symbolic order for which they stand hear anyway in each and every expression or manifestation of queer sexuality: Fuck the social order and the Child in whose name we're collectively terrorized; fuck Annie; fuck the waif from *Les Mis*; fuck the poor, innocent kid on the Net; fuck Laws both with capital ls and with small; fuck the whole network of Symbolic relations and the future that serves as its prop.[87]

'Not only .... but also': we can, indeed must, thus be radical and 'realistic' at the same time. These conjoined tendencies seem to map on to the reified categories of private and public respectively: assuming that the kind of resistance Edelman has in mind is exemplified in subsequent chapters, it is significant that they comprise virtuoso critical readings of a range of literature and film. The inescapable logic of Edelman's argument is that our uncompromisingly radical queer authenticity actually *should* simultaneously counsel acquiescence in the way things are, because it refuses to be deluded into thinking they might be comprehensively different.

## The sixties with less hope: *Shortbus*

Personally, I think that everything is about love or the absence of love, and my work – specifically *Hedwig* and *Shortbus* – are about

---

87   Ibid., p. 29.

the question we have to ask is [sic] whether we're gonna be alone
or not alone. And that can mean sexually and romantically, or it
can mean politically. I felt less alone making this film.

(John Cameron Mitchell)[88]

John Cameron Mitchell's film, *Shortbus* (2006), sought to
embrace sexual explicitness in a way that nonetheless avoided
pornographic conventions. During filmed auditions for it released
on DVD, he responded to an inquiry from Sally Beamish, the actor
who plays Severin, about the aesthetics of the film: 'Pornography
is something that there's no connection to in this film.' And
he's surely right: there is plenty of nakedness, and even 'real
sex',[89] but these are not focused on 'gratuitously' by the camera;
neither is calculated to encourage excitement. The film, after
all, begins by splicing together three sex scenes that are among
the most explicit. The problem is that the participants are not
enjoying it – or, at least, they are not *really* enjoying it. James's
autoeroticism is part of a filmed suicide note, addressed to his
partner; Sofia and Rob are ostentatiously faking it (she, we later
learn, cannot have an orgasm, prompting feelings of inadequacy
in him); Severin is a bored, alienated sex worker and dominatrix,
dedicated to satisfying others' needs rather than her own. In each
case, sensationalism gives way to disappointment: James's fetal
act of contortion in sucking himself off is precisely symbolic of
an incapacity for appreciating the love his partner feels for him,
and he sobs uncontrollably after coming; the 'wild sex' Sofia and
Rob have lacks what is for the film the defining event; and, after
Severin's wealthy client has come over a Jackson Pollock painting

---

88 'Gifted and Challenged – the Making of *Shortbus*', DVD edition.
89 Nick Davis explores the paradoxes of this term in 'The View from the
*Shortbus*, or All Those Fucking Movies', *GLQ*, 14(4), 2008, pp. 623–637.

– a wonderful piece of art criticism this – she tells him that the last time *she* came it felt great because 'it was like time had stopped and I was alone'. The disappointing reality, however, was that 'time hadn't stopped and I wasn't alone'.

Though some of these characters are having sex with other people, then, none is *connecting*. Thus, even among those who are able to have an orgasm, no one's is as it should be: for all the diversity of relationship the film celebrates, it nonetheless places a sacramental value on lovemaking, and a virtually Reichian one on orgasm as its material sign. Not being able to have proper sex is its means of figuring isolation, since orgasm signals intensity, and penetration may be spiritual as well as physical.

Even in the 'sex not bombs' room of Shortbus itself, the emphasis is hardly on pornographically orgiastic possibilities. The majority of the volunteer 'sextras' of the film tend to be young and in good shape, as they say, but are not exclusively so, and the camera doesn't foreground them. The lighting is a fairly discreet deep red, connotatively 'hot' and intimate rather than clinically illuminating. The camera pans across the various couplings and triplings, only lingering on the partners the credits describe as 'the Beautiful Couple' in order to convey to us Sofia's fascination with them. Their sex is not ostentatiously energetic, but spontaneously devotional. The Beautiful Couple do not merely perform sex, in the inauthentic sense, but rather embody the film's humanistic grasp of sex's potential to overcome pervasive alienation.

The unsatisfactory nature of the characters' sex lives is paralleled by their problematic careers: Sofia is a relationship counsellor whose formal strategies for her clients' problems correspond to her own incapacity for orgasm (lack of spontaneity); her husband, Rob, meanwhile resents being dependent on her; James, a former hustler, is now a lifeguard in the sauna where he first comes face to face with a drowned man who inspires his own attempted suicide; Jamie is an actor, still best known for his childhood role playing a white boy who mistakenly thinks he is an albino in a black family; Severin's clients mistake even her genuine hostility towards them for insincere role play; Ceth is a model ('I hate it; it totally sucks'); and Caleb is a copy editor invested in the apparent perfection of the two Jamies' relationship because he hasn't got one of his own. And yet, because they are unsuccessful in, sceptical about, or merely bored by their work, they also exhibit a detachment from the system that underwrites their marginality to it in all senses; all, that is, except Sofia, whose comfortable, but earnest, middle-class lifestyle appears to be precisely her problem. She's just too fucking bourgeois to come.

Neither working nor stereotypically middle class, then, these characters are a loosely bohemian bunch, and seem for this reason to hold the potential, at least, to fit the former mayor's description of New Yorkers in general as 'permeable' and therefore sane. Others – outsiders – are, by implication, impermeable and insane. We are expected to supply our own candidates, but the post-9/11 context for the film strongly hints at home-grown warmongers, on the one hand, and Islamist terrorists, on the other, suggesting a doubly besieged quality to a liberalism/radicalism that apparently defines New York. Nonetheless, the film tends to avoid explicit political statement, and explores this question of permeability/impermeability through interpersonal relations within the curiously constituted space that is Shortbus itself.

Hence, not all of these characters initially fit the former mayor's description. James, for instance, is impermeable and depressed. He tells Caleb that he can't feel the love of his partner, Jamie, because 'it stops in my skin'. This is one consequence of his earlier career as a hustler, a time of reassurance to him he tells Severin, since the financial price set on him by others told him precisely what he was worth: actual love, then, disorientates him because it is incommensurable with exchange value. Ultimately, however, James's lack of self-esteem is a consequence of his incapacity to accept he is gay: 'Don't you see, I don't want to be this,' he yells at Caleb when Caleb insists on kissing him.[90] Not *do*, but *be*: for all its queerness, the film is still focused significantly on identity, if often in proliferating and intersecting forms, and it is only when he lets Caleb fuck him that James can accept what he *is* by becoming permeable.

This literalization of Derek's humanistic metaphor directs our attention back to the film's explicitness in a way that suggests some connection with pornography cannot be shrugged off that easily after all. When Justin Bond introduces Sofia to the 'sex not bombs' room, he tells her: 'It's just like the sixties, only with less hope.' And, indeed, the synecdoches that comprise the room's name – it precisely isn't 'love not war' – are suggestive of this fact, as is the finale's rather desperate insistence that 'we all get it in the end'. None of this is very 'spiritual'. It therefore 'realistically' tempers the emphasis elsewhere on transcendental possibilities, just as pornography 'demystifies' love.

The same applies to Shortbus itself: it is in some ways a club, in some ways more like someone's house party. It is private, then, even if it is finally traversed by a public parade that figures as part of the film's attempts to imagine a broader community. After all, the separation and isolation that are characteristic of New York as a city are accentuated throughout by the compartmentalized, box-like model buildings that represent it in order to facilitate the

---

90 The actor playing the role of James, Paul Dawson, also says that his character has 'this deep-seated feeling that a lot of gay people have that what they are is wrong or bad'.

camera's dramatic sweeps between particular locations. That way of figuratively conveying the city emphasizes the fragmentation that constitutes the condition of possibility for Shortbus, a utopian centre of convergence for people who otherwise lead diverse and disparate lives. Even so, the club's transformational power holds greater potential: Sofia's orgasm appears powerful enough to turn the lights back on across New York, as there is finally connection.

The film therefore aims to celebrate all that is at least potentially good about New York in the face of attempts to hijack patriotic sentiment for the aims of the political right, and thus implicitly offers its own defence of freedom, or permeability, as an American principle. 'Sex not bombs' may critique US imperialism, but it also suggests rejection of a terrorism carried out in the name of repressive religion. The opening, detailed shots of a model Statue of Liberty are as much homage as irony, and many of the film's most obvious elements of critique are similarly double-edged. When Ceth instructs Jamie to make more noise while rimming him, Jamie – registering the trickiness of the proposition – sings 'The Star-Spangled Banner' into Ceth's arse. Ceth joins in, using James's cock as a microphone, in mock grunge-rock mode. It's all beautifully irreverent, but not necessarily out of keeping with an attempt to reclaim sexual freedom as a specifically US value through rock music. Indeed, Mitchell confirms this when he says of this scene:

we are taking the piss a little bit there. But, at the same time, we are talking about the optimism of the US, the poss ... the ingenuity. I mean even the position the three of them are in is rather ingenious. There's resonances of the pursuit of happiness.

*Shortbus*, then, combines a commitment to transcendence that nonetheless identifies it as an immanent potential in the 'circuit board' that constitutes New York. If the symbolism of connection alternates with, and complements, that of permeability, the (rather self-congratulatory) sense that New Yorkers possess such potential is nonetheless presented through a socially specific kind of community, such that a gulf remains between the universal hope still expressed in the film, and the particular people whose queerness is freighted with such hope: they are representative because they are unrepresentative; they are what everyone might become with a bit more of the right kind of intensity. There surely remains something attractive about this utopianism, even if the investment it maintains in the anti-bourgeois potential of sex in relation to subjectivity is archaic, as the film's relationship to pornography tacitly acknowledges.

In its emphasis on community, Shortbus appears to emphasize the desirability of progressive social solidarity in the face of terrorist attack and right-wing political domination. But its solidaristic imaginary, if we can call it that, is problematic in its potential as much to divide as unite: *this* community will not spontaneously appeal to all, because it remains indebted to countercultural principles. Audiences for the film will be mostly those who frequent arthouse cinemas, even if multiplexes have now diversified in order to show 'independent' film, just as independent production companies have been bought up by the large Hollywood studios. 'Independent' is a marketable sensibility within the diversified dominant. This is not to say that nothing of value can be produced in that sphere, but its value will be circumscribed by its niche status.

Hence one of the problems with those versions of queer that self-consciously resist the so-called 'anti-social turn' articulated by Edelman through claims to greater political traction: solidarity is possible only with those who find themselves at variance with social norms. One proposal along these lines is offered by Judith Halberstam. It comes at the end of a flawed account and critique of David Harvey's discussion of time–space compression as productive of postmodernity that attributes to him a political concern only for the 'white working class'[91] (an identity he, as a Marxist, could only regard as a racist mystification). Halberstam suggests that Harvey fails to recognize that

> all kinds of people, especially in postmodernity, will and do opt to live outside of reproductive and familial time as well as on the edges of logics of labour and production. By doing so, they also often live outside the logic of capital accumulation: here we could consider ravers, club kids, HIV-positive barebackers, rent boys, sex workers, homeless people, drug dealers, and the unemployed. Perhaps such people could productively be called 'queer subjects' in terms of the ways they live (deliberately, accidentally, or of necessity) during the hours when others sleep and in the spaces (physical, metaphysical, and economic) that others have abandoned, and in terms of the ways they might work in the domains that other people assign to privacy and family.[92]

This represents another assertion, familiar from both Foucault and DeKoven, that postmodernity combines fact and value in ways Harvey's totalization, and the demand for supersession it implies, cannot grasp. It is worth interrogating more closely,

---

91  Judith Halberstam, *In a Queer Time and Place: Transgender Bodies, Subcultural Lives*, New York: New York University Press, 2005, p. 8.
92  Ibid., p. 10.

however, the value that is ascribed to these subjects. Note, for instance, the way in which Halberstam blurs crucial distinctions between, in her terms, optional, accidental and necessary modes of existence as a means of conjuring a kind of queer coherence out of considerable diversity. But why might we productively call these people 'queer subjects', and whose need is served by doing so? Would they welcome, or even recognize, this description of themselves? Perhaps the account rather testifies to the theorist's radical sensibility in discerning such potential in them. After all, what if any of them should do anything so drearily normative as get a 'regular' job, or have a family – optionally, accidentally or out of necessity – and thereby assimilate to the logics and spaces of reproduction and capital accumulation? Would they consequently be excluded from our solidaristic gaze? Halberstam's intentions here are clearly well meaning in their attempts to democratize the category of queer and express social concern for those who are disadvantaged, but the figures she lists here have had dropping out superimposed on them.

## The revolutionary's unconscious: *The Kiss of the Spiderwoman*

Manuel Puig's most celebrated novel has been widely discussed by critics. The consensus is that it is postmodern in technique, focus (its preoccupation with popular film) and political philosophy. Each, it seems, necessarily implies the others. The critical reception of the novel, then, may be said to resemble DeKoven's teleological project of discerning the nascence of postmodernity in late modernity, since the immediate context for it, as highlighted by the texts referred to in the footnote, is that of the counterculture and gay liberation movement whose influence had extended to the Argentinian left.[93] In my view, the postmodern account of the novel is one that that forecloses the sense of potential it conveys, in spite of its dismal conclusion.

The novel is principally concerned with the meeting in prison between a Marxist revolutionary, Valentín, and a figure often, but problematically, described as a homosexual by critics, Molina. The latter effectively seduces Valentín by recounting some of his favourite films in highly subjective terms that result from his identification with their heroines, as well as by more generally assisting Valentín's recovery from poisoning by the prison regime. The effect of Molina's strategy is to soften Valentín, who has initially insisted on the importance of hardening himself against any form of indulgence that might weaken his resolve. This is frequently taken as the sign of his commitment to revolutionary praxis that is masculine through its aspiration to change the world on the basis of an objective grasp of it (in the confinement of his prison cell with Molina, Valentín dutifully studies when he can). Thus, the dialectic established in the novel seems to be one between (feminine-homosexual) pleasure and (masculine-heterosexual) purpose. The success of Molina's strategy appears to prompt a dramatic shift in Valentín's sensibility that has implications for the way he regards his politics.

It isn't difficult, then, to see why the view of the novel as postmodern therefore also tends to see in it a rather one-sided perspective that sympathizes more with Molina than Valentín. Drawing on Lyotard's arguments in *The Postmodern Condition* and *Libidinal Economy*, Paul Julian Smith suggests that the novel privileges particular language games and narratives over the

---

93   An excellent account of this context is provided in José Maristany, 'Revolution and Sexuality in Argentina in the 1960s and 1970s', in Daniel Balderston and Francine Masiello, eds, *Approaches to Teaching Mañuel Puig's* Kiss of the Spider Woman, New York: MLA, 2007, pp. 101–109.

meta-narratives to which Valentín is committed as the means by which power is negotiated between the two.[94] Smith acknowledges that his own reading is an active one engaged in producing the meaning of the text, but one way of interpreting this is to suggest it demonstrates a certain disposition towards the text and its principal characters. Smith's is a philosophical, largely dehistoricized account, justified as such by his claim that these characters' confinement 'is particular (even peculiar), and cannot be made to bear the weight of all oppression in Argentina'.[95] To support this case, he highlights Molina's refusal to identify as a homosexual. But this isn't convincing: Molina *is* representative, but of a conservative, if transgressive, sensibility. Sexual libertarian ideas are articulated not through him, but in the footnotes.

Another reading of the novel sees it as anticipating the postmodern in a historical sense, and makes strong claims for its allegorical status. In *Postmodernity in Latin America*, Santiago Colas sees Puig's book as dominated by images of thwarted utopian impulses in the films that Molina relates, but also in both the persons of Valentín and Molina, and the very prison they inhabit. The paradox of Valentín's declaration at one point that their shared space constitutes their own personal idyll testifies to the dependency of opposing categories each on the other (here, inside/outside, freedom/imprisonment) that at least anticipates a postmodern scepticism toward the purity on which the concept of utopia supposedly relies.

---

94 Lucille Kerry adopts a similar strategy in *Suspended Fictions: Reading Novels by Manuel Puig*, Urbana: University of Illinois Press, 1987, pp. 184–235.
95 Paul Julian Smith, *The Body Hispanic: Gender and Sexuality in Spanish and Spanish American Literature*, Oxford: Clarendon Press, 1989, pp. 194–195.

Moreover, Colas suggests that this is determined by the novel's specific context: the failure of the revolutionary project in Argentina. This was fatally hitched to the initially politically ambiguous figure of Perón, who ultimately betrayed the revolution from within: on his return from exile in 1973, state and fascist paramilitary forces turned their guns on the very armed insurgents, the Montoneros, who had fought for that return. Moreover, Perón's return to a second, brief period in power was made possible by the impact on Argentina of the deepening global economic crisis of the 1970s that marked the conditions for the transition to post-Fordism/flexible accumulation: he was allowed back because he was considered the only person who might be capable of holding an already divided Argentinian society together at this time.[96]

This is a powerful argument, but one in which the novel's focus on sexuality specifically is relegated to more abstract propositions about the (im)plausibility of utopian convictions. The relevance of Molina's, and Puig's, homosexuality is said to reside in an awareness 'of the ways the [Peronist] movement could reproduce authoritarian exclusions',[97] and the relationship between Valentín and Molina exemplifies Colas's more general argument because of its dialectical quality, since each represses that which the other embodies: 'Molina is perceived by both characters as "female"; as sensitive, emotional, sensual and uninterested in politics. Valentín, on the other hand, is a hard-boiled Marxist revolutionary, highly rational and macho.'[98] By the end of the novel, each reforms the other.

The perception that reform is mutual seems plausible, but there

---

96  Santiago Colas, *Postmodernity in Latin America*, Durham, NJ: Duke University Press, 1994, pp. 76–117.

97  Ibid., p. 116.

98  Ibid., p. 85.

are grounds for resisting it. Alan Sinfield, for instance, observes that Valentín largely remains faithful to the principles of Latin American machismo by remaining the 'active' one; 'he just adapts his manly role slightly'.[99] This isn't because of a particularly strong attachment to that role on Valentín's part: Sinfield recognizes that Molina needs him to live up to this role in order to desire him at all. However, this is an unusual acknowledgement in criticism of Molina's complicity in his own subordination, indeed of his sexualized desire for it.

The things that condition the critical sympathy for Molina are no doubt, first, the fact that it is Molina's discourse that dominates the novel through his narration of the films, and, second, a certain correspondence between the figures of Molina and Puig himself, given the latter's camp persona and devotion to Hollywood film and screen actresses of the forties and fifties.

One consequence of this sympathy is that readerly hostilities towards Valentín can be very powerful. This is Francine R. Masiello's forthright summary of the novel in an early critical account of it:

Puig makes no attempt to conceal his sympathies for Molina who turns out to be the innocent hero of the novel. Meanwhile Valentín is described as an inept and rhetorical youth, responsible, in the final analysis, for the death of his friend. Puig draws attention to the characters' sexual identity, by no means incidental to the narrative structure or to the novel's thematic focus. The real revolution, Puig implies, comes not from class struggle, as Valentin would suggest, but rather from sexual

---

99  Alan Sinfield, *Gay and After*, London: Serpent's Tail, 1998, p. 49. Sinfield sees the novel as scrutinizing traditional Latin American roles from the perspective of a metropolitan one.

liberation, designed to free the individual from the constraints of bourgeois society. In this sense, prison detention serves as a pretext for labyrinthine explorations of sexual self-identity. Puig thus modifies a potential denunciation of institutionalised repression to focus instead on the personal reality of characters and the ideology of sexual politics.[100]

There are various problems with all of this. First, as Masiello acknowledges elsewhere in the same article, we are given no extradiegetic narration, only – in the cell at least – the voices of Valentín and Molina. Consequently, Valentín is nowhere *described* in any terms whatsoever: we have only what he says, his thoughts and dreams, and what certain documents, such as his prison report, say about him. Any derisive view of him as inept and rhetorical therefore once again comes back to readerly disposition. Responsibility for Molina's death, moreover, is surely one of the questions the novel raises: certainly it results from Valentín's proposal that Molina take a message to his revolutionary comrades, but Molina only agrees to the mission after first rejecting it, and possibly – others speculate – as a means of fulfilling his identification with tragic heroines. Moreover, Valentín and Molina are united in the repressive state institution of the prison, not merely because they are criminals of different sorts, but because it is assumed by agents of the state that Molina is weak, unprincipled, manipulable – in other words, that he is a typical homosexual, and therefore the perfect traitor (a correlation the novel invokes in order to undermine). It seems odd therefore to suggest that the state is more or less incidental to the novel's primary preoccupation with 'personal reality' (whatever that means). Moreover, if it is unclear

---

100 Francine R. Masiello, 'Jail House Flicks: Projections by Manuel Puig', *Symposium*, 32, 1978, pp. 16–17.

from what vantage point sexual liberation represents 'the real revolution' by contrast with Valentín's presumably bogus one, it is difficult to make any sense at all of the proposition that such a revolution might deliver the individual from bourgeois *constraints* if the bourgeois *society* that Valentín seeks to overturn remains in place. Indeed, Molina finds his fulfilment through an identification with quite specifically bourgeois ideals of womanhood, as Valentín rightly points out. However transgressive that identification may be, it nonetheless depends upon – indeed, it insistently reaffirms – the validity of those ideals for the category of 'woman' in which Molina includes himself.

Valentín is condemned by Masiello for the crime with which he more than anyone else in the novel reproaches himself. In harbouring desires that 'contradict' his politics, Valentín considers himself subjectively inconsistent, and is riddled with a guilt whose burden Molina helps to alleviate – or should that be accentuate? – by exploiting his desires for bourgeois womanhood. But a reading of the novel that merely brands and dismisses Valentín as hypocritical is both inattentive to its focus on him, and seems to rely on the belief both that it is possible to maintain a subjective purity in an objectively contradictory world, and that it is necessary to do so in order to harbour utopian ambitions.

Outside literary criticism, though, not all 'readings' of Valentín have been hostile. When the musical version of the novel first opened in Buenos Aires in 1995, the audience was apparently stunned into tearful silence when actors stepped to the front of the stage at the end carrying pictures of the Argentinian disappeared, among them the actor playing Valentín.[101] It would be a peculiarly, and

---

101   Suzanne Jill Levine, *Manuel Puig and the Spider Woman: His Life and Fictions*, London: Faber, 2000, p. 382.

determinedly, insensitive response to this gesture that claimed it represented a betrayal of the novel's questioning of Valentín's revolutionary authenticity and served to distract attention from *Molina*'s death. Nonetheless, such a response might cite the production's apparently rather chaste kiss between Molina and Valentín to highlight its marginalization of queer concerns. The difficulties of establishing whether the musical production or the hard-hearted response to it might be the 'truer' account surely point us to a different understanding of the novel than the one that seems to me to have prevailed: that, actually, it doesn't take sides, and steadfastly refuses any resolution of the conflict embodied by its two principal characters. This reading of the novel treats the relationship between Molina and Valentín as a complex, and open, dialectic.

Valentín is not the embodiment of some abstract revolutionary possibility, but a highly specific figure whose socio-familial background the novel insists on. He comes from a wealthy, landowning family whose dynamics condition his predisposition towards Marxist commitments. He is not a peasant, like the girlfriend in the guerrilla movement he wants to love but cannot help despising. Indeed, the italicized passages that give us a distorted picture of his life before prison, mingled with the fantasies that emerge out of and condition that life, suggest that his involvement with the guerrillas resulted from a desire to vindicate the reputation of his father as a good employer who was betrayed by his mother. They also present a figure who desires the celebrity that was possible for Latin American revolutionaries in cosmopolitan circles (the fate of Guevara). The real love of Valentín's life, Marta, is '*a desirable woman, a woman who understands a Latin American, a European woman who admires a Latin American revolutionary, a woman more preoccupied* nonetheless with Paris automobile traffic than with the problems of some colonized Latin American country';[102] her independence – including her sexual independence – is thus simultaneously attractive, and yet frustrating, to Valentín (she won't accompany him back home). Valentín's commitment to the objective principle of justice is therefore subjectively determined by an investment in a supposedly decent patriarchal familial and social authority (his father), and the contemporary form of masculine eminence available outside Latin America to its radicals. All women – his revolutionary peasant girlfriend, Marta, and especially his mother – disappoint him in one way or another.

And yet, in spite of these complications, Valentín is in prison, where his report indicates he continues to lead protests. He remains devoted to his cause, and will ultimately be tortured to death for it. In the prison dialogues, he highlights the ideological implications of Molina's own identifications, including the latter's willingness to overlook the overtly racist nature of the Nazi propaganda film with whose heroine Molina identifies. Smith suggests that:

> Molina is well aware that narrative is conventional: he knows that the Resistance were heroes in real life – it's just that they're not in the film ... this remark can be taken as acknowledging an awareness of the relativization of knowledge which need not imply the dissolution of all standards of value.[103]

In a truly objective sense, however – through the sheer space it takes up – the novel insists with Valentín on the racist dimensions of the film through the footnote from the studio book account of it that makes its propagandistic intentions clear.

---

102 Puig, *Kiss of the Spider Woman*, p. 125.
103 Smith, *The Body Hispanic*, p. 198.

The question of fascist identification, moreover, was a more urgent question than Smith makes it sound in the context of Argentina: the Peronist regime had provided sanctuary for Nazi war criminals, and Puig had been partially raised on German, Italian and Spanish film because of a Peronist embargo on Hollywood.[104] Perón's third term, in the 1970s, increasingly led to the liberation of fascist forces against the left, a trend consolidated under Isabel Perón. Valentín is therefore not making a historical point, but one of profound contemporary relevance and principle. And yet, seduced as usual, he ultimately allows Molina to continue to the end: the level of contradiction the novel insists on cannot be captured by a qualified insistence on relativism.

The unsympathetic perspective on Valentín views him as masculine, as we have seen. The point of critiquing masculinity, however, is not to suggest that certain modes of being and conduct are wrong in themselves, but to reject their privileged association with men. Once masculinity is reified as a set of traits to be either embraced or repudiated we are only ever a short step from pernicious essentialism of one form or another. There is nothing necessarily wrong with resolve, for instance; it is masculine only to the extent that it is considered a property of men, as that which typifies them by contrast with women. Thus, to view Valentín as masculine because he evinces certain properties normatively associated with men may well be to ignore the fact that he not only doesn't see those properties as typically male, but explicitly rejects male privilege, at least in theory. After all, if there is an overtly, if inconsistently, feminist voice in this text, it is Valentín's. When his former girlfriend takes over from him as the leader of his group, he expresses no reservations about her suitability. In other

---

104  Levine, *Mañuel Puig*, p. 267.

words, it may well be the reader or critic who reifies Valentín as 'masculine'. Molina certainly does, as we have seen, but Valentín resists.

Valentín's inconsistency once again proceeds from his subjective conditioning by a society he would like to see comprehensively transformed. The final conversation between Valentín and Molina illustrates the difficulties of being consistent, especially in the face of Molina's particular form of resistance:

[Valentín: ...] physically you're a man as much as I am ...

– Mmm ...

– Sure, you're in no way inferior. Then why doesn't it occur to you ever to be ... to ever act like a man? I don't say with women, if they don't attract you. But with another man.

– No, that's not for me ...

– Why?

– Because it's not.

– That's what I don't understand very well ... All homosexuals, they're not that way.

– Right, there's all kinds. But me, no, I don't ... I don't enjoy it any other way.

– Look, I don't understand anything about this, but I want to explain something to you, even if just bumble my way through it ... I don't know.

– I'm listening.

– I mean that if you enjoy being a woman ... you shouldn't feel any less because of it.

...

[Molina:] But if a man is ... my husband, he has to give the orders so he will feel right. That's the natural thing, because that makes him ... the man of the house.

– No, the man of the house and the woman of the house have to be equal with one another. If not, their relationship becomes a form of exploitation.

– But then there's no kick to it.

– Why?

– Well, this is very intimate, but since you're asking about it ... The kick is in the fact that when a man embraces you ... you may feel a little bit frightened.

– No, that's all wrong. Whoever put that idea in your head? It's absolutely wrong.

– But that's the way I feel.

...

[Molina:] Let's not talk about it anymore, because this conversation isn't getting anywhere.

– To me it is, I want to talk more about it.

– But I don't.

– Why not?

– Because I don't, and that's that. Please, I'm asking you ...[105]

Of course, Valentín begins here in a confused way by assuming the physical superiority of men, and, in his eagerness to demonstrate that he regards Molina as an equal, remarking on their similarity in this respect. The further assumption at this stage is that this superiority determines the 'dominant' role normally taken by the man in sex. Valentín also continues to view the homosexual as a type who might be explained, though he is nonetheless 'enlightened' enough to appreciate that not all homosexuals are 'submissive'. It is Molina, by contrast, who insists that patriarchal relations are natural, that these adequately account for his feelings,

---

105  Puig, *Kiss of the Spider Woman*, pp. 243–244.

and that his feelings cannot and must not be questioned. This is typical of the peremptory subjectivism that renders him quite as certain of himself as Valentín in his professed rationalism and objectivity, and, if anything, even more inflexible. In the sex scene that precedes this, Molina romantically believes himself to have become one with Valentín, but this final conversation 'isn't getting anywhere' because it is uncongenial to Molina, as conversation – rather than monological narration – tends to be. We may sympathize with the latter to the extent that Valentín's desire to understand suggests it is Molina who is in need of being understood, but Molina's resistance proceeds from an absolute refusal to interrogate patriarchal ideology. Molina's romance is shattered; the novel presents no achieved synthesis of the values either character embodies.

Indeed, by the end of the novel, we understand a great deal more about Valentín than we do about Molina, and this is one of the book's great ironies: the would-be analyst becomes the analysand. Molina steadfastly resists, because he has arrived at an intuitive scepticism towards, psychoanalysis that is borne out 'objectively' by the critiques of it elaborated in the novel's footnotes. But this resistance is also the product of an uncritical relation to filmic modes of characterization informed by psychoanalytic assumptions about femininity.[106] Valentín's initial mistake is to believe he sees through the films' personae to their real deficiencies; Molina's is to believe that he is escaping that analysis through a drive towards

---

106 Mary Ann Doane, for instance, argues that the attraction of the stars of women's films of the forties for female viewers was based on their positioning as narcissistic consumers. 'Narcissism confounds the differentiation between subject and object and is one of the few psychical mechanisms Freud associates specifically with female desire' (*The Desire to Desire: The Woman's Film of the 1940s*, Bloomington: Indiana University Press, 1987, p. 320).

total identification with their female characters. That identification finds its consummation in his death – or so various characters speculate, but not even this level of depth, or motivation, is disclosed to us about Molina for sure.

At the end, Valentín's death is not imminent. The conviction that it might be, encouraged by his consoling dream, effectively imposes a popular-filmic resolution on things, perhaps as if Molina were imagining it. However, the nurse who gives him morphine does so because otherwise Valentín will 'be in a lot of pain for quite a few days',[107] and in order to facilitate a recuperation that will facilitate further interrogation. At the end of the book, then, Valentín is enjoying a merely temporary respite from the electrodes, and Marta's final words to him – 'this dream is short but this dream is happy'[108] – thus take on more sinister implications, as indeed must the symbolism of Molina as spider woman. As Valentín knows at the outset, but is encouraged to forget, the contrast temporary utopias offer may play into the hands of his torturers, whose techniques thrive on contrast.

If the dialectic between Valentín and Molina is refused any premature synthesis, the footnotes that accompany their dialogue, providing various modes of commentary on it, do not resolve things either. Instead, they gesture towards future possibilities through their articulation of radical/Marxist psychoanalytic thought by figures such as Norman O. Brown and Marcuse. The final footnote takes the form of the invented words and ideas of Anneli Taub. Though there is an obvious irony to referencing a fictitious figure through this scholarly apparatus, there is no obvious way in which the substance of her argument is called into

---

107 Puig, *Kiss of the Spider Woman*, p. 275.
108 Ibid., p. 281.

question. It also articulates a dialectical position: Taub recognizes that homosexuality evinces 'revolutionary nonconformity', while the conduct of male and female homosexuals has been influenced by 'a slow brainwashing in which heterosexual bourgeois models for conduct participate'.[109] This explains their marginal relation to revolutionary movements, though this is now changing thanks to the emergence of women's and gay liberation movements. Taub concludes in anticipatory, rather than prescriptive, fashion: a different future is possible, but not for the novel's characters in the remorseless historical present into which they are released from their confinement in the cell.

The suggestion of various postmodern critics of the novel is that it teaches us that liberation is a chimera. It seems to me a mistake to regard the novel as teaching us anything so decisive. Rather, it suggests that the resources we might draw on for liberatory struggle are diversely distributed and configured, both socially and subjectively.

Indeed, this was, in a way, Marcuse's judgement about sixties radicalism in the US, which he never believed held the capacity to effect the revolution it at times aspired to:

> In the domain of corporate capitalism, the two historical factors of transformation, the subjective and objective, do not coincide: they are prevalent in different and even antagonistic groups. The objective factor, i.e., the human base of the process of production which reproduces the established society, exists in the industrial working class, the human source and reservoir of exploitation; the subjective factor, i.e. the political consciousness, exists among the nonconformist young intelligentsia; and the

---

109  Ibid., pp. 212–213.

vital need for change is the very life of the ghetto population; and of the 'underprivileged' sections of the labouring classes in backward capitalist countries. The two historical factors do coincide in large areas of the Third World, where the National Liberation Fronts and the guerrillas fight with the support and participation of the class which is the base of the process of production, namely, the predominantly agrarian and the emerging industrial proletariat.[110]

No aspect of that analysis bears greater emphasis than the reference to 'different and even antagonistic groups', and, indeed, the antagonisms went further than Marcuse here acknowledges, because the supposed coincidence of subjective and objective factors in the third world did not correspond to the revolution in subjective experience that was pursued among the objectively privileged in the west.

Subsequent history has eroded these distinctions to some extent, and for reasons that need to specified. First, the divisions Marcuse highlights were not wholly discrete. The extent of any overlap between them differs according to the social identities with which we are concerned. Queer constituencies, for instance, have always been heterogeneous. Second, in subsequent years, many pursued forms of solidarity of various kinds; it is simply not true to say that identity politics have consistently resulted in single-issue campaigning. One result of that pursuit has been that working-class movements and institutions, including trades unions, have become more self-consciously diverse in terms of membership

---

110   Herbert Marcuse, *An Essay on Liberation*, Boston: Beacon Press, 1969, p. 56.

and campaigning,[111] even if their general influence has dwindled. Finally, one must acknowledge the role that marketization has played for reasons outlined in the previous chapter, and not *only* for elites. Queer radicals often like to remind the organizers of contemporary *mardi gras*-style Pride events that Stonewall was a riot. True enough, but it was first of all a bar.

111  See, for instance, Duncan Osborne, 'Lavender Labour: A Brief History', in Amy Glucksman and Betsy Reed, eds, *Homo Economics: Capitalism, Community and Lesbian and Gay Life*, New York: Routledge, 1997, pp. 223–227, and the essays collected in Patrick McCreery and Kitty Krupat, eds, *Out at Work: Building a Gay-Labour Alliance*, Minneapolis: Minnesota University Press, 2001; also Steve Williams and Rishi Awatramani, 'New Working Class Organizations and the Social Movement Left', in Leo Panitch and Greg Albo, eds, *Socialist Register 2015: Transforming Classes*, London: Merlin Press, 2015, pp. 336–350.

# 4

## Subculture and Postgay Dynamics

Phrases such as 'lesbian and gay community', or 'LGBTQ community', tend to invite sceptical responses: 'so-called', someone will add. The implications are various, but they include the suggestion that individuals within those groups – and frequently gay men specifically – are only interested in sexual satisfaction rather than any collective or political purpose. 'Money', writes Simmel, 'has made it possible for people to join a group without having to give up any personal freedom and reserve.'[1] Sexual satisfaction is not a bad thing to be interested in, but the single-mindedness of that pursuit is clearly one consequence of the material developments explored in chapter two. Equally, however, it may be felt that the category of 'community' is felt to mask divisions. After all, what kind of community are we speaking of here, who is excluded from it, and who, if anyone, might be said to speak for it? Perhaps we should rather speak of communities? After all, we can always find more 'difference' if that is our inclination, but the logic of that quest directs us away from community altogether.

---

1 Georg Simmel, *The Philosophy of Money*, trans. Tom Bottomore and David Frisby, London: Routledge, 2011, p. 371.

The problem with the category of community is that it is one of those terms everyone feels obliged to express support for because it suggests cohesion rather than fragmentation and instrumental relations. Miranda Joseph, however, suggests it also functions as a kind of (Derridean) supplement to capital by generating the use values that are transformed into exchange value, even as community and capital are construed as autonomous and even opposed spheres and principles.[2] If part of the problem with community is therefore that it tends to suggest a cosy or romanticized view of a group and the relations that comprise it, a better term might be subculture.

For the most part, though, this is a category that is simultaneously ill-defined and taken for granted, rarely theorized, yet endlessly invoked. What, for instance, does the prefix in subculture refer to? Does it merely indicate a part of the larger culture, as in 'subset'? If that were the case, would it make sense to speak of groups such as golfers or cyclists as constituting a subculture? Intuitively, we might think not – and so, perhaps more importantly, might golfers and cyclists. Golf, after all, may be a minority pastime, but that minority is a mostly privileged one often keen to protect the exclusions of its sport as the very badge of privilege. It would seem more in keeping with usage to suggest that 'sub' also suggests subordination, but if it is the case that we need to think in terms of a diversified dominant, claims in this respect are likely to be very much less compelling than they once were.

Other assumptions nonetheless tend to persist in relation to subcultures that follow from this presumed subordination. Are they necessarily dissident or radical, or should they be? And if so,

---

2   Miranda Joseph, *Against the Romance of Community*, Minneapolis: Minnesota University Press, 2002, pp. 1–29.

does this mean that individuals who belong to a subculture, but do not consider themselves 'political', should be regarded as in some sense 'inauthentic' or suffering from a form of false consciousness? Subculture often appears to be used in terms analogous to counterculture, yet we have seen that the counterculture was a diffuse phenomenon, and was for the most part comprised of individuals and groups who were relatively privileged (or destined to become so). Members of the Birmingham School of Cultural Studies argued that subculture had class implications, representing 'a weakening of control over the youth of a subordinate class, [whereas the counterculture] was a crisis among the youth of the dominant class'.[3] Note, however, that both phenomena are defined as youthful.

Judith Halberstam seeks to avoid the latter emphasis in order to expand the term's relevance. She speaks of 'queer subcultures' as challenging normative temporalities, because 'for queers, the separation between youth and adulthood quite simply does not hold, and queer adolescence can extend far beyond one's twenties'.[4] The problem with this way of formulating things is that it suggests a continuing fetishization of youth through its extension, rather than any depriviledging of it altogether. Why not speak more positively of the potential expansion of certain qualities said to be characteristic of maturity: reflexivity over spontaneity, for instance, or sensitivity over aggression? The answer surely has to do with the extent to which youthful energy has been commodified and sold to us as desirable. The attempt to maintain one's youth may

3   John Clarke, Stuart Hall, Tony Jefferson and Brian Roberts, 'Subcultures, Cultures and Class: A Theoretical Overview', in Stuart Hall and Tony Jefferson, eds, *Resistance Through Rituals: Youth Subcultures in Post-war Britain*, London: Routledge, 1993, p. 62.
4   Judith Halberstam, *In a Queer Time and Space: Transgender Bodies, Subcultural Lives*, New York: New York University Press, 2005, p. 174.

actually be a burden; it will certainly be a losing battle. Indeed, it is one focused on by much of the cultural production I look at in this chapter. A great deal has been said about queer temporalities,[5] but we are fooling ourselves if we presume them to be free from more general pressures – indeed, their distinctiveness may result from a peculiar intensification of those pressures – or congratulate ourselves that they are necessarily more satisfying than others.

Halberstam also sees radicalism as bound to musical taste and identity, rather than a political commitment that is not necessarily associated with such things. That is in part because, following Judith Butler, she sees radicalism as performative rather than a matter of conviction: the punk she values 'has always been the stylized and ritualized language of the rejected',[6] and therefore subversive of norms.[7] She does not deal, however, with Dick Hebdige's argument in relation to punk specifically that style is always commodifiable, and has been so in this instance.[8] Still, Halberstam's project is one that celebrates subcultures that offer alternatives to what she sees as the increasing conservatism of lesbian and gay communities, since she prioritizes those that are 'nonheterosexual, nonexclusively male, non-white, and nonadolescent'.[9]

---

5   See, for instance, 'Theorizing Queer Temporalities: A Roundtable Discussion', *GLQ*, 13(2–3), 2007, pp. 177–195.

6   Halberstam, *Queer Time and Place*, p. 153.

7   Halberstam's later work continues this theme: discussing Edelman's work, she points out that 'The Sex Pistols made the phrase "no future" a rallying call for Britain's dispossessed' (*The Queer Art of Failure*, Durham, NC: Duke University Press, 2011, p. 107).

8   Dick Hebdige, *Subculture: The Meaning of Style*, London: Methuen, 1979, pp. 94–96. See also David Wilkinson's critique of the tendency to romanticize punk in 'Ever Fallen in Love with Someone You Shouldn't Have Fallen in Love With: Punk, Politics and Same-Sex Passion', in David Alderson, ed., *Queerwords*, special issue of *Key Words*, 13, 2015, pp. 57–76.

9   Halberstam, *Queer Time and Place*, p. 161.

Queer theoretical purists might object to Halberstam's argument on the grounds that it serves to reify a term, queer, that neither can nor should be pinned down, one that is in principle diffuse, anti-identitarian and illimitable to persons or spaces. Halberstam's formulation nonetheless shares with this abstract and idealist version of queer an avant-gardism that excludes those who don't consider themselves very remarkable; those who may be middle-class, middle-aged and fairly liberal, or black, working-class and conservative, for instance, but who nonetheless frequent the local scene and maybe read the odd lesbian or gay novel. Are such people's lives not also subcultural? Does their lack of radicalism render them inauthentic?

In briefly outlining here some of the problems associated with this category, I am freely drawing on the kinds of consideration informing what is surely the most extended and sophisticated theorization we have, especially in relation to sexually dissident groups, in the work of Alan Sinfield. That work has tended to be neglected within queer studies for a variety of reasons. For one, it emerges out of his powerful account of British postwar dynamics, though it certainly does not limit itself to consideration of British contexts. The most influential work, by contrast, comes out of the US academy and mostly reflects US traditions, conditions and priorities, as I suggested in chapter three. Sinfield's work is also argued from the tradition of cultural materialism, and therefore contrasts with the poststructuralism of queer theory. It is true that his version of cultural materialism evinces certain superficial similarities with such thought – anti-humanism, for instance, and a privileging of particulars over universals – but these emphases emerge from precise materialist arguments rather than any abstract value placed on difference.

Sinfield's account is first elaborated in the conclusion to one of the most important books in the British cultural studies tradition, *Literature, Politics and Culture in Postwar Britain* (1990), but it has been consolidated in other works since then, in part in order to engage with the diversification of lesbian and gay into LGBTQ movements and contexts, since his conviction is that in writing about subculture one should consider oneself actively engaged in its formation. This is not a matter of the archivism Halberstam proposes and executes in relation to subcultures that are presumed to be radical,[10] but rather of *critical* engagement and intervention. In this chapter, I outline his arguments in more detail, and discuss their relations with cultural materialism as developed by Raymond Williams before going on to suggest some reservations prompted by the kinds of historical developments and theoretical arguments I have pursued in previous chapters.

## Subcultural materialism

Sinfield's endorsement of subcultures emerges out of his rejection of the kind of universals that tended to be advocated by both left and right in the welfare capitalism of postwar Britain. Among the left of that period, he argues, culture came to be regarded as a good to which all had a right, rather like health or employment. Thus, just as the former was to be available to all through the National Health Service, and governments considered full employment a desirable goal to set for themselves, culture might also be state-funded, as it was through the Arts Council of Great Britain, established in 1946 and chaired by John Maynard Keynes himself.

For Sinfield, there were two problems with this perception of the importance of culture. First, the dissemination of culture that was

---

10    Ibid., pp. 169–174.

presumed to be good overlooked that culture's ideological features. Shakespeare's plays, for instance, have tended to be considered self-evidently great; they had stood the test of time. If they voiced awkward sentiments, such as a respect for traditionally constituted authority, they might nonetheless be said to transcend these because of a more abstract concern with 'the human condition'. Second, and from a position sanctioned by the investment in such art, this perspective disdained in principle the commercialism of 'popular' culture, and thought that distinguishing between the two was a straightforward matter. Sinfield argues that not only was this presumed dichotomy false to begin with, since art had for centuries relied on the market and had therefore been conditioned by it in one way or another – Shakespeare's drama is actually an obvious instance of this – but the presumption of any separation between art and mere entertainment became increasingly difficult to sustain as it came under manifest pressure in the postwar years. The apparent 'breakdown' that this seemed to herald prompted some to turn to the kind of postmodern arguments I have already explored, in some cases to celebrate this 'subversion', but, as I pointed out in chapter one, Sinfield indicates that this process masked a more general reconfiguration of power taking place at the same time.[11]

A number of things follow from this complex grasp of postwar dynamics. First, Sinfield regards the left's principled sniffiness about the popular and commercial as a mistake: not only did it represent a failure to engage large audiences, evincing instead a preference for improving them,[12] but it neglected the ideological dimensions of preconstituted 'good' culture as these were

---

11    Alan Sinfield, *Literature, Politics and Culture in Postwar Britain*, third edition, London: Continuum, 2004, pp. 321–329.
12    Ibid., p. 283.

becoming increasingly apparent under pressure from campaigns against sexism, racism and heterosexism. Nonetheless, Sinfield's conviction that an engagement with the popular is important is not one governed by any assumption that this will in and of itself challenge hierarchies or power. Rather, it reflects a scepticism towards the humanistic or romantic claims often made by left and right alike about established culture, and a pragmatic sense that the value of something resides more in what can be made of it than in its presumed essence.

It took the Thatcherite repudiation of the postwar consensus finally to call into question the various spurious universalisms promoted during that period. This is the principal conclusion Sinfield draws from that history:

> 'Man' is a powerful concept, but I cannot regret its loss to the left. A divided society should have a divided culture: an (apparently) unified culture can only reinforce power relations. In many situations it may be necessary, now, to defend the arts, as they have been inherited from welfare-capitalism, against new-right assault. But the idea of a universal 'good' culture is mystifying and oppressive, and a medium-term project should be to validate instead a range of subcultures. These are already in place, producing alternative stories, contributing to the solidarity and self-understanding of the groups that sponsor them. It is not a time for universals, but for rebuilding from that base.[13]

It should not be presumed, however, that in advancing such a position he is pitting subcultures that are presumed to be internally unified or coherent against a dominant only disingenuously committed

---

13   Ibid., p. 341.

to universals. Rather, he conceives subcultures as sites in which various divisions – of class, race, gender, and so on – are played out, because within them individuals acquire a sense of themselves in relation to others.[14] This in part informs his further rejection of any account of them as the repositories of an authentic radicalism:

> they are formed partly by and partly in reaction to [the dominant]. They redeploy its cherished values, downgrading, inverting or reapplying them, and thereby demonstrate their own incoherence. Their outlaw status may exert a fascination for the dominant, focusing fantasies of freedom, vitality, even squalor. So they form points from which its repressions may become apparent, its silences audible.[15]

This sounds rather like Foucault, and the influence is explicit: subcultures are never autonomous or to be thought of as 'external' to power, even if they possess distinctive resources to challenge power's norms. Indeed, subcultures are strung out across institutions (theatres, cinema, television, universities, bars and clubs, for instance) that will help determine the possibilities and purposes of whatever takes place within them. In validating subcultures, Sinfield is very far from proposing some kind of Great Refusal.

Moreover, he argues for the specific value of middle-class dissidence on the grounds that there are subordinated factions within that broadly defined class who may be an important

---

14 Michael Warner suggests something similar of what he calls 'counterpublics': 'participation in such a public is one of the ways by which its members' identities are formed and transformed' (*Publics and Counterpublics*, New York: Zone Books, 2002, p. 57). The term suggests his continuing indebtedness to countercultural notions.
15 Sinfield, *Postwar Britain*, p. 344.

resource for any radical project, including a socialist one, not least because of the relative freedom such positioning can offer for the purposes of thinking, writing and informing.[16] Indeed, Sinfield strikingly identifies the New Left as a middle-class subculture,[17] and the significance of that merits serious reflection. Hence the way he theorizes his own role as an organic, rather than traditional, intellectual; that is, as an intellectual of the LGBTQ movement, rather than merely an academic. One of the advantages of this, he suggests, is that it does not entail a distance from those one's work addresses. Equally, it does not presume 'that organic intellectuals will not cultivate a wider analysis of relations in capitalism and patriarchy; to the contrary, one task is to bring such an analysis to the subculture'.[18] Such a commitment clearly distinguishes subcultural engagement so conceived from any narrow conception of identity politics as affirmation.

The effects of all this are discernible in the writing itself, which engages with a breadth of work, academic and non-academic, left, right and middle of the road in a largely non-polemical but deeply principled way that also sets a high priority on lucidity. Through such means it aims to encourage subcultural cohesion, even as the subculture has arguably become queerer. Perhaps some would question whether it remains appropriate to speak of subculture in the singular at all, but that perspective relies on the view Sinfield disputes that subcultures should be relatively free from dissensus, as well as on an abstract postmodern conviction that plurality is desirable as such because the singular is evidently oppressive. Sinfield's work, by contrast, rather tends to assert the value of collectivity as a matter of principle.

16  Ibid., pp. 307–311.
17  Ibid., p. 295.
18  Alan Sinfield, *Gay and After*, London: Serpent's Tail, 1998, p. 158.

The specifically cultural materialist emphasis of these arguments is evident, first, in their account of the specific role culture and the conceptualization of it played in welfare capitalism, and, second, in an insistence that we must pay attention to the sites and institutions on which subculture is necessarily dependent. We are never merely lesbian, gay, queer or anything else, and insofar as we consider ourselves to be those things it is important that we grasp the complex social and economic determinations of them: this is the point of self-reflexive engagement.

If Sinfield provides good grounds for focusing on subculture, though, it is also important to remind ourselves that his project in *Postwar Britain* was a defensive one in relation to the defeats suffered by the left in the eighties, and was projected into the medium term. There are inevitably questions about what ends it might ultimately serve. 'It is not a time for universals, but for rebuilding from that base,' he wrote. Perhaps so, but rebuilding what exactly? The very sense that something required reconstituting is suggestive of a stalled project, but, as I suggested in chapter one, it may well have been that the unity aspired to by much of the left – the sense that there may be some *necessary* connection between socialist, feminist, black, lesbian and gay and other movements – depended on a presumption that 'the system' was indeed coherent in its evident disdain for them. Stuart Hall's point that Thatcherism was contradictory in its simultaneous appeal to national traditions and emphasis on economic individualism is crucial here.[19] Thatcher was more of a neoconservative than a neoliberal, as was Reagan. She looked back to the Victorian businessman and paterfamilias as an ideal,

---

19  Stuart Hall, 'The Great Moving Right Show', *The Hard Road to Renewal: Thatcherism and the Crisis of the Left*, London: Verso, 1988, p. 48.

or at least that is the impression she cultivated in public and pursued through her policies.[20]

It may be helpful therefore to make a distinction between Williams's categories of dominant, residual and emergent, and Sinfield's focus on subculture. The former are spatio-temporal categories, whereas the latter appears to be a relatively persistent structural one. Perhaps his observation that 'there have been and are societies where same-sex passion figures more amiably than ours. But I can think of none where it is unremarked – a matter of indifference'[21] is relevant in this respect. This does not mean that subculture is an ahistorical category, since it is bound to the institutions that in some sense 'host' it, but it does mean that, insofar as subculture is conceptualized as a more or less continuous process of elaboration, it will develop its own traditions. Nor does this mean that Williams's and Sinfield's categories relate to entirely distinct forces. Rather, their relation needs to be specified. Gay liberation, for instance, provides a clear enough instance of a once emergent movement that dramatically transformed subcultural perceptions, conduct and politics. It did, indeed, bring broader social critique to the subculture, but it also sought in its more radical manifestations to effect universal change, thereby challenging *dominant* universals (notably the value attached to the family). Its principal legacy as things have turned out has been more modest, both because the left ultimately did not prevail in the seventies and eighties, and

---

20  I once heard the gay Tory MP, Matthew Parris, remark on BBC Radio Four that Thatcher was more tolerant in private than she appeared in public, though I did not record when or on what programme. He seemed to be offering this as a partial defence of her, but actually it suggests that aspects of her 'conviction politics' were cynical and manipulative.

21  Sinfield, *Gay and After*, p. 197.

because the assumption that capitalism inherently favoured the heterosexual family was overstated.

One of the ways of understanding the distinction between Williams's terms and Sinfield's is through the category of intention. If dominant, residual and emergent forces evince collective forms of intentionality aimed at transformation, stabilization or conservation, subculture suggests a more diffuse set of purposes. In Sinfield's account, it is in part a protective formation.[22] If the diversified dominant thesis is helpful, however, one thing we may reasonably conclude is that dominant intentionality is now expressed more substantially through the subculture, and with less resistance, than hitherto. This, in turn, suggests assent to a claim I critiqued in my introduction: Fredric Jameson's argument that under postmodernity the dominant has effectively annexed both residual and emergent forces – and, we might add, subcultural ones. I want to attempt to give full weight to this case, but I also want to suggest that critique of the dominant's constitution of the subculture is not only far from absent, but has been pervasive, and constitutes a profound ambivalence within subcultural forms. Indeed, we have already seen a particular inflection of that ambivalence in Hollinghurst's *The Swimming Pool Library*.

In order to develop the case, though, I want to turn to what can still properly be regarded as a watershed in gay (if not lesbian) representation, *Queer as Folk*, in order to highlight the economic and institutional imperatives that governed this quite self-consciously 'provocative' portrayal of contemporary realities. I then consider one instance of explicitly leftist critique of the kind of world represented in that series in Mark Ravenhill's drama, though my

---

22  See comments in both *Postwar Britain*, p. 344 and *Gay and After*, pp. 197–199.

purpose in turning to that work is also to highlight some problems with the view that such subcultures may easily be rejected. The two instances are instructively of the same moment, and reflect on the expansion in commercialized forms that took place in the nineties. In both cases, I want to anticipate the subsequent discussion of the postgay in order to evaluate the project of subcultural work and the quite diverse challenges to its potential.

## *Queer as Folk* and the urban renewal of subcultures

Though first broadcast in 1999, *Queer as Folk* remains one of Channel Four's most commercially successful series. This was no fluke: a great deal of calculation went into ensuring this would be the case through related financial and symbolic investments in the series that have paid off in terms of institutional reputation, extensive video and DVD sales, and international takeup by other channels, each of these ensuring the series' substantial afterlife. A 'definitive collector's edition' was brought out in 2010, for instance: it now has the status of a classic in a way that testifies both to its original importance and the ways in which it has assisted in shaping subsequent standards of taste. Moreover, the original version was subsequently adapted for the US channel, Showtime, in a form that also broke new ground in its exclusive lesbian and gay focus and sexual explicitness, but was able to do so in the US because Showtime broadcasts to niche markets via cable; the diversification of the dominant takes on tellingly different national forms. My principal focus here is on the British version because I am interested in the very specific institutional and urban histories that not only made it possible, but also governed its modes of representation; in other words, with the material determinants of the diversified dominant.

Established by the Thatcher government in 1982 with a specific remit to produce experimental and minority programming, Channel Four's output was characterized by an ethos that defied conventional broadcasting commitments to neutrality in terms of content. It thus quickly became an institutionalized alternative – with all the eighties resonances of that word – to the establishment. The channel's apparent ideological commitments, though, went along with a structural dependence on independent programme production that its first Commissioning Editor for Independent Film and Video, Alan Fountain, notes prefigured transformations in TV production generally: 'it was the battering ram that began to change the economics of television companies and independent film groups ... television production became based on a small centre fed by hundreds of casualized producers'.[23] This was quite intentional on the part of government: in early campaigns by the Channel Four Group to persuade the Thatcher government that it should not be dependent on the production studios of ITV (Independent Television) companies for its programmes, the case was made that farming out work to independents would help 'diversify television production in Britain and perhaps at the same time, break the union's grip on the industry and alleviate the existing hidebound industrial relations'.[24]

Channel Four thus pioneered in broadcasting the deregulation

23   Alan Fountain, 'Opening Channels: Channel Four and After', in Sheila Rowbotham and Huw Beynon, eds, *Looking at Class: Film, Television and the Working Class in Britain*, London: Rivers Oram Press, 2001, p. 205; see also Colin Sparks, 'Independent Production: Unions and Casualization', in Stuart Hood, ed., *Behind the Screens: The Structure of British Broadcasting*, London: Lawrence & Wishart, 1994, pp. 133–154.

24   Stephen Lambert, *Channel Four: Television With a Difference?* London: BFI, p. 89. The union referred to here was the Association of Cinematograph, Television and Allied Technicians.

and outsourcing that were increasingly characteristic of the rest of the economy under flexible accumulation. Over time, according to Fountain, the ideological bearing of independent companies changed from alternative to entrepreneurial: being businesses themselves, 'the sense of critique dropped away'.[25] Under the professionalizing control of Michael Grade in the nineties, moreover, Channel Four's experimentalism focused increasingly on forms of sexual adventurousness that earned him the soubriquet 'pornographer-in-chief' from the right-wing, family-oriented newspaper, *The Daily Mail*, and tacitly reflected the left's negative fortunes.

Thus, by the time the new Executive Director, Michael Jackson, laid out his vision for Channel Four in 1999, he was going with the grain: it was now to be a specifically 'modern' channel that rejected 'worthy, but dull' programming in order to appeal to an apparently expanded and educated middle class that was 'libertarian' in outlook, and embraced 'freedom, permissiveness, hedonism, discernment, experimentation, ambition and individuality'. Thus, the minority to which Channel Four was to appeal from now on was a privileged and self-congratulatory one that was progressive, cool and no doubt sexy in all the ways that neoliberal capitalism facilitates for those who can best afford its pleasures.

At the same time, Jackson argued, the competitive environment brought about by digital technology meant that programming needed to be increasingly sensationalist. 'Television,' he wrote, 'used to be a small pond, and it was easy to create a significant ripple with a pebble. Competition has made it a raging sea; if you toss a pebble in now it has no impact. We need to toss boulders.'[26]

---

25  Fountain, 'Opening Channels', p. 206.
26  Michael M. Jackson, 'Four the Record', *Media Guardian*, 5 July 1999, pp. 2–3.

The perceived need for such sensationalism has ensured that terms such as 'controversial' are now positively value-laden, rather than descriptive, and used to anticipate reception. The taste for controversy assists in the reproduction of class differentiation. In Jackson's view, *Queer as Folk* was perfect for establishing the Channel Four brand ethos in this larger context: this was the calculation.

Comparison with an earlier instance of Channel Four's radicalism helps to illustrate these more general shifts in tone and sense of purpose. The lesbian and gay magazine series, *Out on Tuesday*, first broadcast in 1988, was made by Abseil Productions, so called after the lesbians who interrupted parliamentary debate about Section 28 of the Local Government Act in the same year. Its humour was therefore connected to an activism still perceived as necessary, such that even this may be said to have had a whiff of earnestness about it. *Out* sought genuinely to represent subcultural diversity and debate, assisted in this respect by its format, and it also tackled charged topics, such as the gay fetish for skinheads and its possible political implications.

*Queer as Folk*'s screenwriter, Russell T. Davies, by contrast, consciously suppressed any sense of obligation to be either representative or serious:

> I did feel this incredible pressure to be representative ... Lesbians, older gay men, monogamous gay couples, AIDS. And it's just too big, trying to represent an entire world – that's never going to create good drama. God it would have been bland and worthy.[27]

---

27  Russell T. Davies, *Queer as Folk: The Scripts*, London: Channel Four, 1999, p. 6. Admittedly, this passage comes in a generally self-ironizing portrait, but it nonetheless registers sentiments similar to those expressed in publicity for the series.

Why there should be anything inherently undramatic about these apparently fringe matters is both unstated and all too clear, since they are not on the whole central to the 'fun' projected as definitive of Canal Street life. Rather, this and other statements made by Davies in pre-screening interviews he gave reflected the sentiments he shared with Jackson: the politically correct demand to be representative and responsible would have inhibited any focus on the freedoms of the scene. The series is suffused with this anti-PC ethos through its contempt for anything like a positive-image agenda.

Consequently, it was the depiction of Stuart's sexual freedom that provoked viewers' complaints, generating the brand-defining controversy that was hoped for. These were relatively small in number, and came not on the whole from the usual moralists, but rather people like Angela Mason, then Chief Executive of campaigning group, Stonewall: 'as I saw it', she suggested, 'they really played to every prejudice and stereotype in the book ... I think it will be quite damaging and send a pretty awful message to the public about gay people'.[28] Mason's comments, notably in their revealing distinction between 'the public' and 'gay people', appear to evince something of the heteronormativity Eric O. Clarke claims is imposed on queers as a condition of public sphere representation[29] – except that Mason was complaining about the *excesses* of a form of public sphere representation, demanding accountability to those it claimed to represent in their desire to achieve legitimacy. The problem Mason perceived had in part to do with timing, since the screening of the first episode – in which underage, fifteen-year-old Nathan has sex with twenty-nine-year-old Stuart – came just prior to a House of Lords vote on equalizing

28   *Right to Reply*, Channel Four, 27 February 1999.
29   Eric O. Clarke, *Virtuous Vice: Homoeroticism and the Public Sphere*, Durham, NC: Duke University Press, 2000, pp. 29–67.

the age of consent at sixteen: not a trivial matter. Perhaps any position one might want to elaborate on the desirable relations between cultural representation, politics and censorship in such a context is always going to be less striking than the fact that what we had here was a reformist and assimilationist campaigning organization angrily condemning the greater 'radicalism' of a corporation for whom the transgressive representation of gay sex principally served its marketing need for sensation.

The series was not only significant for the way in which it served Channel Four's purposes, though. It also helped to boost the international prominence of the city of Manchester, and was facilitated by the city's transformation. This also bears scrutiny, since Manchester's success in this respect established it as a prototype of 'urban regeneration' for other cities, both in the UK and internationally, and the fact that its gay village has played a small but symbolically disproportionate part in the expansion of the leisure economy that has been a crucial aspect of the City Council's strategy since the late 1980s[30] has directly influenced other councils' decisions to encourage and promote similar spaces elsewhere. *Queer as Folk* has thus assisted in establishing Canal Street as a synecdoche for larger projects of economic and moral liberalization that have come to define modern life, and not only in capital cities.

Manchester's visibility is therefore linked to political shifts its council was instrumental in generating. Prior to the Labour Party defeat of 1987, many of the challenges to the Thatcher government came from a municipal socialism that aspired democratically to

---

30 Alan Kidd, *Manchester*, third edition, Edinburgh: Edinburgh University Press, 2002, pp. 234–250; Steve Quilley, 'Constructing Manchester's "New Urban Village": Gay Space in the Entrepreneurial City', in Gordon Brent Ingram, ed., *Queers in Space: Communities, Public Places, Sites of Resistance*, Seattle: Bay Press, 1997, pp. 284–288.

represent its various marginalized or oppressed communities, class-based or otherwise. Along with trades unions, left-wing local councils consequently became the focus of Conservative attacks, both ideologically, through key speeches, and through legislation that circumscribed their powers and autonomy. This was the period of the derided 'loony left'. The leadership of Manchester City Council that came to power in the 1980s after a period in exile from local Labour Party influence was of this ilk.[31] Figures within it, however, later put together Manchester's urban regeneration programme after the Labour Party's defeat in the 1987 election. From this point on, the Council sought to encourage local entrepreneurialism, court capital investment from outside, and itself bid competitively against other councils for funding for various projects, frequently in order to stage the kinds of event that would encourage a further influx of people and money. Whereas the City Council had previously rejected competition with other socialist councils, it now embraced an ethos of rivalry that has since effectively come to define the role of both local and national governments.[32] Manchester is now projected as the centre of a '"Northern Powerhouse" of economic growth, driven by a flourishing private sector and supported by innovative local government', and negotiated by council and business leaders with the Tory Chancellor, George Osborne.[33]

---

31   Hilary Wainwright, *Labour: A Tale of Two Parties*, London: Hogarth Press, 1987, p. 120.
32   See Steve Quilley, 'Entrepreneurial Turns: Municipal Socialism and After', in Jamie Peck and Kevin Ward, eds, *City of Revolution: Restructuring Manchester*, Manchester: Manchester University Press, 2002, pp. 82–88. More generally, David Harvey summarizes the trend in *The Condition of Postmodernity: An Enquiry Into the Origins of Cultural Change*, Oxford: Blackwells, 1990, p. 92.
33   HM Government, 'The Northern Powerhouse: One Agenda, One Economy, One North' https://www.gov.uk/government/uploads/system/uploads/attachment_data/file/414815/the-northern-powerhouse-tagged.pdf (accessed 10 March 2015).

This shift from municipal socialism to municipal entrepreneurialism also had an impact on the democratic features of the Council. An earlier focus on the *processes* of local government – on how to make the Council more accountable and representative, as well as less discriminatory – was subordinated to the overwhelming priority of achieving results defined in terms of income; in terms of performance, that is. Casualties included the Council's lesbian and gay subcommittees, which were wound up as a consequence of the centralization of policy decisions.[34] Instead, support for the lesbian and gay community was expressed through an explicit commitment to the development of the commercial scene on Canal Street.

The cosmopolitan diversity promoted by municipal entrepreneurialism takes on a particular character. Dereka Rushbrook for instance, has argued that 'queer and ethnic spaces are offered as equivalent venues for consumption at a cosmopolitan buffet in a manner which erases their individual histories and functions, as well as the different mobilities of the bodies that inhabit them'.[35] This draws our attention to tensions between the more integrated clientele of these spaces and those economically less 'mobile' figures condemned to a merely local existence, who nonetheless provide a place with its potentially marketable (and necessarily idealized) 'character'.[36] In *Queer as Folk*, Canal Street is represented as fairly insular, even 'provincial', despite being visibly the product

---

34   Quilley, 'Entrepreneurial Turns', pp. 85–89.

35   Dereka Rushbrook, 'Cities, Queer Space, and the Cosmopolitan Tourist', *GLQ*, 8(1–2), 2002, p. 188.

36   For a study that probes beneath such idealizations to outline contemporary structures of feeling in mostly working-class Manchester and Sheffield, see Ian Taylor, Karen Evans and Penny Fraser, *A Tale of Two Cities: Global Change, Local Feeling and Everyday Life in the North of England. A Study in Manchester and Sheffield*, London: Routledge, 1996.

of the capitalist investment that has produced a global homogeneity of gay spaces. That provincialism is evident in the pervasive northern English humour evident throughout: the title puns on a local saying ('there's nowt so queer as folk') even as it alludes to an international slogan of defiance ('queer as fuck').

Finally, urban regeneration is also evident in the way Manchester's spaces are inhabited. As the centre has become the focus of urban renewal, it has also become an increasingly populated, but gentrified, area, the site of new private accommodation and styles of living consonant with the city's cosmopolitan aspirations: the number of city-centre hotels rose from a mere seven in 1980 to thirty-five by 2001, just after the series was broadcast; its resident population grew from just 250 in 1988 to 15,000 by 2003.[37] Both have continued to rise, and the skyline is permanently populated by high-rise cranes. A discernible gay presence has accompanied this process, not merely because accommodation here is convenient for Canal Street, but because city centres are not governed by the same norms as suburbs that materially and ideologically appeal to families because of their histories: they are where houses tend to be sited – though increasingly they are also being turned into flats – along with the institutions typical of suburban life. Indeed, the lifestyles of many queers and the needs of construction companies to maximize profits are strikingly compatible: the majority of city-centre living spaces are highly profitable, single-bedroom apartments.

It is not only the distinction between city centre and suburb that is significant to the spatial reconfiguration of Manchester as this finds representation in *Queer as Folk*, though. What used to

37  Gwyndaf Williams, *The Enterprising City: Manchester's Development Challenge*, London: Spon Books, 2003, pp. 250–251.

be known as 'inner-city areas' – sites of poverty and even urban rebellion, especially in the form of the 'race riots' of the eighties – have been squeezed as 'city-centre living' expands into such territories, with predictably tense results. In Manchester, these can be seen in areas such as Hulme – whose name has sponsored a new type of citizen, 'the Hulmosexual' – and Salford. The perhaps overly schematic sense of these divisions that we get in *Queer as Folk* contrasts the 'vibrant' and liberal city centre (Stuart's flat) from the working-class areas of terraced streets (Hazel's house), as well as morally and spatially from the middle-class suburbs where Nathan's family lives.

*Queer as Folk* is generally celebratory of the scene. Throughout, Canal Street is neon-lit and densely populated, signalling the contemporaneity of the series and registering the extent to which the scene has been transformed from a discreet, marginal, down-at-heel, and often persecuted – not least by the police[38] – area into a licensed, confident, chrome-and-glass-dominated space. It conveys a sense of the excitement, possibility and freedom from moralistic judgement that are integral to it, and recognizable in similar cities across the world (the US version is set in Pittsburgh, but was filmed in Toronto).

Nonetheless, consciousness of the effects of commodification on desire is present right from Vince's opening voiceover in episode one: 'Cos you keep looking. That's why you keep going out. There's always some new bloke, some better bloke, just waiting round the corner.' The initial shots of Canal Street at this point provide us with a feel for the kind of world we are about to enter, but it also suggests problems. First, there is an irony

38   On former tensions between the gay village and Manchester police, see Quilley, 'Constructing Manchester's "New Urban Village"', pp. 283–284.

about the voiceover, given that its speaker is the least successful among the central characters at finding not only newer and better men, but even barely adequate ones. His 'shags' are more or less unenthusiastically embraced substitutes for his abiding desire for Stuart, and it is in part this unrequited love that humanizes him by comparison with the insatiable Stuart. This particular irony is compounded by the fact that, shortly after this, the camera comes to rest on the vulnerable figure of Nathan, whose welcome to the scene takes the form of a class- and age-fuelled contempt from Bernie about the 'bastards' and 'wankers' who populate the bars.

There is a certain ambivalence, then, at the heart of the series' representations of Canal Street that is productive of its dynamic. As Terry Eagleton has noted, 'every text can be seen as a "problem" to which a "solution" is to be found; and the process of the text is the process of problem-solving'.[39] The problem of *Queer as Folk* is that of how to reconcile the individualistic, commodified freedoms of the scene with a humanistically conceived commitment and reciprocity, and it is in the way that the series explores possible solutions to this problem through the various relations between its characters – relations that symbolize and dramatize aspects of the institutional and urban history outlined here – that it most obviously discloses its sensibility.

Stuart's freedoms are visibly those of the market, but to ambiguous effect. His loft apartment adjoining Canal Street is indicative both of the extent to which the scene is integral to his life and the fact that such integration is dependent on his ability to afford it. His job with a PR firm is also connected to both commodification and homoerotic desire. As played by

---

39  Terry Eagleton, *Criticism and Ideology: A Sudy in Marxist Literary Theory*, London: Verso, 1976, p. 87.

Aiden Gillen, Stuart comes across as a depthless, coolly affectless character rendered subjectively complex only by the occasional expression of vulnerability bound up with his sense of ageing. In general, though, the sexiness embodied by him is predicated on an objectifying and self-objectifying detachment of sex from emotion, and therefore with a virility that is characteristically masculine, in spite of the narcissism that attends it. He may well be said to evince a postmodern sensibility and disposition, but he is given class definition and objectified for audiences as a problematic figure.

If the scene's freedoms are presented as simultaneously exciting and alienated, the alternative to it must logically be wimpish and unsexy. It is embodied in Vince, who is from a rather sentimentalized working-class background and lives in Fallowfield.[40] The will-they-or-won't-they plot line represents the programme's doomed attempt to resolve its problem. The ending to the second series, in which Stuart and Vince are ultimately transported to the American deep South, is really only a displacement of this problem, however: freedom is now that of the wide-open spaces and individualistic ethic of the American road movie, while commitment is maintained through the couple's assaults on redneck homophobia.

Others' moral relations to the scene are also conveyed through their spatial relations to it in ways that determine the series' evaluations of them. Romey, the lesbian who has inexplicably chosen Stuart as the biological father to her child, is mostly associated with middle-class domesticity. She is, in the terms of the series, politically correct, and judgemental of gay male hedonism.

---

40 Approximately three miles from the city centre, Fallowfield is an area of largely terraced housing, these days substantially colonized by students.

The main foil for her is Hazel, who spontaneously bridges cosmopolitan and local values. Her centrality is paradoxically enabled by her atypicality: she is both working-class and a woman, without being a lesbian. Indeed, she is more of a gay man than a lesbian, since she is also strangely integral to the scene to which her son has introduced her. She is simultaneously distanced by virtue of her class and sex from the alienating commodification of the scene, but is non-judgemental towards it in ways again bound up with class, through her 'vulgarity' and *risqué*, politically incorrect humour. However, she is also possessed of a (stereo-)typically northern English working-class common sense and shrewdness that allow her to assert her superiority at crucial moments, and to act as a figure whose wisdom proceeds from experience rather than dogma.

Hazel's ideological significance often manifests itself in otherwise apparently trivial moments, the most important of which relates to Lance, a figure whose profound significance for the series resides in its intolerance and peremptory dismissal of him and the complexities he introduces. He thereby discloses for us precise limits to the programme's cosmopolitanism. Lance is a Ghanaian whom Romey decides to marry in order to prevent him from being deported. But, in the constitution of a queer family, Lance cannot be assimilated: visibly through his clothing, and professionally as a traditionally serious academic, but also racially – coming from a continent notorious in the west for its homophobia – he is distinguished from all that Canal Street represents.

Thus, it seems spontaneously in character for him to voice subtly moralistic perspectives at various points. At Vince's birthday party, he says that none of them are invited to the wedding because they would make the whole thing look suspiciously 'gay' to those whom it is designed to convince. Lance is thereby made to appear complicit with the heteronormativity of the immigration office that eventually deports him: queerness is made to seem dissident at *his* expense because he belongs neither to the local nor the 'legitimately' cosmopolitan worlds that generate the series' positive values. He simply does not belong, and is visibly and ideologically an awkward presence throughout.[41] Through him, too, Romey's left-wing principles are discredited and thereby established as residual, though in complex ways.

The marriage proposed by Lance not only threatens Stuart's paternalistic sensibilities, but also the security of Romey's girlfriend, Lisa (Lance's name has been put on the deeds to the house she shares with Romey). According to the script, she is a 'classic lipstick lesbian',[42] a fact that marks her out as Stuart's natural ally: she is a professional, and more cynical than Romey. '[Romey's] only doing the right thing,' Lisa says, 'she always does the right thing, she's saving a man from being deported. She's so bloody correct.' There is here that explicit acknowledgement that Romey's ideals are both admirable and an obstacle to ordinary life: the word 'correct' is both compliment and indictment.

The final resolution of this subplot is crucial because it ultimately enlists Hazel. Nathan agrees to Stuart's request that he send Lisa and Romey's love letters to the immigration office. The consequences disclose for us the 'truth' about Lance: the fact that he punches the immigration officer who questions him demonstrates that his educated, eloquent and even judgemental exterior masks an ultimately irrepressible instinctuality. (Significantly, the US series reworks this subplot, evincing greater

---

41    It seems implausible to me simply to ascribe the racism towards Lance to the characters, as Russell T. Davies has defensively claimed: see Glyn Davies, *Queer as Folk*, London: BFI, 2007, pp. 51–52.
42    Davies, *Queer as Folk*, p. 22.

sensitivity to racial representation: the figure of Lance is replaced by a non-violent, gay French man.)

When Romey confronts Stuart over the deportation at Hazel's house, the scene inside is complex. The audience knows that Nathan's account of his motives – that he did this to protect Stuart's paternalistic feelings – is false, but Romey's incomplete knowledge of events reduces her to an inarticulacy that ultimately forces her to condemn all that Stuart represents: 'It is your fault, it's all your fault! Cos you just ... shag!' But Romey is ultimately put in her place by Hazel:

> Romey [to Stuart]: And I chose you as the father.
> Hazel: You chose Lance as a husband, and look at him. Slightest bit of trouble, out come the fists. D'you want a man like that living with your kid?
> *Romey's already thought of this, but Hazel's the first to say it out loud.*
> Romey ... maybe not.[43]

Hazel's real-world astuteness is the only possible reproach at this stage to Romey's correctness.

The programme's antipathy towards PC does not result in it overlooking homophobia. Rather, its critique of discrimination comes to be expressed largely in defence of the freedoms of the scene, and in a style that is determined by that scene through Stuart's modes of defiance. Specifically, this consists in his intrusion of explicit sexual content into normally protected or discrete environments. Thus, his 'political' interventions are an extension of his egotistical and scandalous sexual assertiveness.

---

43   Ibid., pp. 205–206.

When he drives his vandalized car – 'queers' has been written on the side – at speed into Nathan's school grounds in episode two, and one boy shouts 'Come on, boys, give us a kiss', Stuart retorts: 'I'll give you a fuck, you tight little virgin, you won't be laughing then.' His later 'coming out' speech to his parents, taking the form of a list of reappropriated anti-gay insults, is a further instance of such scandalousness that is a refusal either to be humiliated or a good citizen. The disavowal of PC as a means of dealing with social issues, then, leads to an extension of the supposedly non-conformist, anti-PC world of 'fun'. It is only in this way that the programme can redeem politics of their worthiness.

*Queer as Folk*'s contemporaneity lay in the way it gave form to a certain sensibility determined by that cosmopolitan libertarianism encouraged by urban centres as they had developed since the 1980s and had been captured, in turn, by the ethos of Channel Four. This account of the programme should not be mistaken as some form of nostalgia on my part for an earlier left culture that was all too often characterized by guilt inducement at any and every perceived exclusion. Nor am I holding out hope for a return to the project of a municipal socialism whose limitations were demonstrated by precisely the history outlined here. As Alan Sinfield has put it, 'if socialism in one country was unattainable ... what were the chances for socialism in one city?'[44] Still, those leftist movements at their best aspired to contribute to the larger, truly global realization of democratic inclusivity and equality, values that are effectively denigrated by the strictly circumscribed cosmopolitanism of the series, most notably through its symbolic denial of citizenship to Lance.

It might be argued that there was no necessary reason why either

---

44  Sinfield, *Postwar Britain*, p. xxi.

Manchester City Council or Channel Four should have 'selected' the gay scene as a means of confirming their modern credentials in neoliberal conditions, but there was certainly a logic to it, since in doing so they assisted in confirming and intensifying the processes by which the market has established itself as 'progressive' because corrosive of norms. I have suggested that *Queer as Folk* represented a watershed in gay representation. It did not thereby mark a qualitative transformation or diversification of subcultural space, but rather achieved its effects through an insistence on the centrality of an expanded scene, and by consolidating a tendency – actually a material pressure – reductively to identify scene with subculture as such. Hence, the series' critics have a point: it *is* narrow. But it is also representative, in spite of Davies's disingenuous disavowals of any such purpose: it testifies to the narrowing of social, cultural, and, yes, erotic relations on an expansive and promiscuous scale.

## Postgay drama: Mark Ravenhill's *Mother Clap's Molly House*

*Queer as Folk* could hardly be described as 'postgay', and yet it acknowledges supersession in key senses: in relation to left politics as formerly conceived; in highlighting the comprehensive displacement of the 'twilit world of the homosexual' and its replacement with abundant possibilities for hedonistic fun; and in the status it confers on both a deindustrialized Manchester and a formerly PC Channel Four as modern. It thereby registers a shift in the very signification of the term 'gay' that is the focus of Mark Ravenhill's critique of it. In a typically pugnacious interview to mark the opening of his first major successful play, *Shopping and Fucking*, in New York in 1998, he suggested that 'gay people have had enough positive images. What those nellies need is some negative images to shake them up ... I've been laughed at for saying this before, but if you can have postfeminism, why can't you have postgay?'[45]

The superficial linguistic similarity between these two terms, however, masks a clear difference of purpose: Ravenhill's drama consistently associates commodification and depoliticization directly with a gay existence characterized by an infantilized state of sex and drug addiction, and it is this he critiques. Postfeminism, by contrast, has been accused of embracing commercially generated images of femininity, and thereby prematurely abandoning a political project. 'What does it mean to "celebrate" their sexuality by posing in a push-up bra or wearing "fcuk" across their breasts?' Karen Ross and Sujata Moorti ask rhetorically of postfeminists.[46] Thus, postfeminism is rather one aspect of a larger postmodern sensibility that Ravenhill tends to grasp, and critique, in his drama as determined by the commodification of everything.

There are both continuities and substantial differences in emphasis between *Queer as Folk* and Ravenhill's work that may be highlighted by the symbolic significance each invests in a sexual practice associated especially with gay men: rimming. In *Queer as Folk*, this is presented as a revelation and liberation for Nathan in his initial one-night stand with Stuart. Depicting this was clearly calculated to test the limits of audiences' adventurousness by confronting them with something that is both intensely pleasurable and liable to be found disgusting. Indeed, the disciplinary familial propriety that determines such visceral responses is graphically

---

45  James Patrick Herman, *New York Entertainment*, 26 January 1998, http://nymag.com/nymetro/arts/features/2160/ (accessed 20 January 2009).
46  Karen Ross and Sujata Moorti, 'Editors' Introduction', *Feminist Media Studies*, 3(1), 2003, p. 99.

highlighted by Nathan's father at one point. Alluding to Nathan's sister, he insists 'as far as Helen is concerned, the anus is for shit'.

In Ravenhill's *Shopping and Fucking*, by contrast, the central figure of Mark attempts to cure himself of various addictions, but can only conceive of independence in terms indebted to counselling-speak. At an early point in the play, in a scene that helped establish Ravenhill's 'in-yer-face' credentials, he expresses his doomed bid for autonomy by rimming a rent boy, Gary. Here, the act suggests non-reciprocity, but also ironizes Mark's attempts to overcome his neediness, suggesting rather his continuing abjection. Ravenhill characteristically intensifies the potential of the scene to disturb by having Mark emerge with his mouth covered in blood. This, we discover, is from the unhealed wounds that have been inflicted on Gary during an earlier enactment of his violent fantasy of being abused by a father figure. Mark himself later participates in that fantasy as the culmination of the constantly evolving and inverting, financially mediated relations of dependency between the two that form a significant part of the play's focus. Ultimately, Mark stabs Gary with a fork.

Both writers, then, exploit the taboo of rimming, but to different effects. In Davies' case, the emphasis is on pleasure and the moral-corporeal re-education of Nathan: 'No one told you about that, did they?' remarks Stuart. In Ravenhill's play, the implication is quite the reverse. If Nathan's initiation into anal pleasures suggests that his uprightness is being undone, in *Shopping and Fucking* Mark and Gary are infantilized in a purely negative sense, and turned into a powerful visual symbol for the characters' more general helplessness.

This is wholly typical of Ravenhill's plays up to and including *Mother Clap's Molly House* (2001), which I focus on here: gay male life is consistently presented as exemplifying postmodern purposelessness and entrapment. The title of *Mother Clap* is taken from Rictor Norton's study, in which he interprets the eighteenth-century molly houses as precursors of modern gay life, but Ravenhill's play reworks Norton's text in ways that Norton himself found unacceptable, claiming in *Gay Times* that the play failed to acknowledge its indebtedness, but also managed to be inaccurate. Ultimately, Norton condemned it for being 'dominated by themes of perversion, abnormality, unnaturalness, shame and self-hatred', and for deforming historical persons by deploying 'homophobic stereotypes'.[47]

Still, Ravenhill, like Norton, sees the molly tradition as pre-figurative of the contemporary scene, less because he wishes to recover some authentically gay tradition and the history of its repression, than out of a desire to establish and imaginatively chart the specifically commercial origins and development of the scene. This is perhaps a further, unstated reason for Norton's disquiet, since he has also written polemically against queer theory's supposedly Marxist conviction that homosexuality is a modern phenomenon: according to him, homosexuals form a permanent, and recognizable, minority in all societies.[48] The play is certainly influenced by Marxism. Indeed, it is Ravenhill's most obviously – one might even say conventionally – Brechtian work, and he quotes a version of Marx's base-superstructure formulation in the preface to the published version. But it is this emphasis that actually distinguishes the play's perspective from the discursive determinism more characteristic of queer theory, because its focus is on the economic conditions in which the molly houses

---

47   Rictor Norton in 'The Mother Clap Trap', *Gay Times* 276, 2001, p. 34.
48   See Rictor Norton, *The Myth of the Modern Homosexual: Queer History and the Search for Cultural Unity*, London: Cassell, 1997.

developed, rather than the emergence of the homosexual as a 'species' in the late nineteenth century.

The eighteenth-century context Ravenhill presents is one in which commerce is understood as divinely sanctioned: 'Enterprise shall make you human', declares the figure of God as part of the scene-setting opening Chorus, establishing the paradox the play will explore: a dynamic principle is supposedly the basis of identity. Enterprise is not merely about the discipline of the work ethic either; it also entails consumption. Desire and morality are experienced as irreconcilable by Stephen Tull, who trades in women's dresses to the female prostitutes he longs for. The tensions this precipitates in him give him a heart attack early on, resulting in his wife's transgressive takeover of the business.

This, though, is only the start of the play's focus on conflicts between commerce and the morality rooted in traditional familial roles. One of the prostitutes, Amy, is recently arrived from the country and has carelessly become pregnant, a fact that threatens her market value. The need for her to have an abortion is met with horror by the childless Mrs Tull, who still sees motherhood as the natural and desirable condition of woman. The leader of the prostitutes seizes her chance, arguing that, if the baby is not to be aborted, Tull must lower her prices. Such contradictions between commerce and sex – between the work ethic and lust, profit and the threat of childbearing, and God and the figure of Eros in the play's Choruses – are only resolved when Tull finally decides to suppress her objections and hire her clothes to the mollies in the house that she establishes in 'a marriage of purse, and arse and heart'.[49] The molly house, then, represents a rejection of both

---

49  Mark Ravenhill, *Mother Clap's Molly House*, London: Methuen, 2001, p. 56.

puritanism and the 'natural' order that places constraints on the profitability of sex.

However, the commercial resolution to Tull's problem sets in train a history that culminates in the contemporary scenes of the play depicting a sex party, the preparations for which open Act II. Gays are still good for business, as the coke dealer, Charlie, now recognizes:

> Not like before is it? Now it's your poofs know how to enjoy themselves, it's your poofs with the money nowadays. Poofs running the country now, in't there? Do all my business with the poofs. Well, you don't get the hassle, do you? (*To* Tina) Poofs pay for your piercings.[50]

'Poofs' continue to constitute a distinct category, partly because they are identified with success and even political influence for this presumably underclass (because 'dysfunctional') entrepreneur. The ironic aside to his girlfriend, Tina, constitutes a reproof for the homophobia she persistently voices, but also establishes a parallel between the experimentation of the poofs and her own 'unnatural' obsession with piercings.

The character of Tina exemplifies a persistent feature of the representation of women in the play. She establishes visual parallels with the first act through the profuse vaginal bleeding from her pierced labia that at one point threatens her life, since this recalls both the reported desire of Amy's client to take her hymen in the earlier scenes, and the subsequent unstaunchable bleeding after her abortion. If Amy must abort her child in order to stay profitable, Tina is alienated from the very possibility of

---

50  Ibid., p. 60.

giving birth. Charlie calls her the 'Iron Lady' and argues that any child 'would have to fight through half a ton of ironwork just to get out of her' (p. 58). The Thatcher reference consolidates the play's suggestion that capitalism erodes desirable maternal instincts.

The nature/culture dialectic in the play is complex, though. If there is a tendency throughout for urban women to be represented as having rejected their biological potential to have children, the disposition towards cultural experimentation on the part of the mollies, by contrast, is driven by the fact that they needn't worry about reproduction (they play at 'birthings' using dolls, for instance, an authentic molly house practice highlighted in Norton's account[51]). However, this propensity for experimentation in gay men is also apparently determined by crude biological impulses, according to the former prostitute, Amelia, who takes over the molly house at the end: 'Oh yes, Lord spoke. And he said to me: It's a bugger's world. And he said: Your man don't really like your woman. And he said: All your man wants to do is find a hole and work away and he said: Arse will always triumph over cunt.'[52]

Amelia is rationalizing a business decision by appeal to the Lord, as other characters do in the play, but her perspective is given some justification by the figure of the pig farmer, Lawrence. He goes to the molly house for a fuck when he comes to town because his 'wife's insides got messed about with all that carrying and birthing, so ... wife in't been worth fucking in years'.[53] His need simply for a 'hole' is reinforced in the scene where he instructs Martin to pretend to be a sow while being penetrated. This insistence on an overwhelming, hydraulic male sex drive represents an alternative

---

51   Rictor Norton, *Mother Clap's Molly House: The Gay Subculture in England 1700–1830*, London: Gay Men's Press, pp. 97–100.
52   Ravenhill, *Mother Clap's Molly House*, p. 106.
53   Ibid., p. 88.

to the play's critique of desire as bound up with the market's imperatives, and generates problems for any coherent perspective expressed in it, as we shall see.

Ravenhill has said that he sees past and present as comparable in terms of their 'problems and possibilities', but continues:

> I think that the eighteenth century characters are sort of freer, as they have no label or box. They are much readier to role play, ready to put on a dress, give birth, have a gang-bang, and there's this sense of naiveté and excitement that doesn't occur with the twenty-first century characters. The modern types are locked into the world of *gay*. The world of Calvin Klein and the gym. But saying that, both sets of characters are trying to explore and trying to cope with a world in which a whole new set of possibilities is being offered.[54]

There is a parallel here with Hollinghurst's work, as it suggests a paradoxical diminution in freedom in the period following the decriminalization of male homosexuality and the expansion of the scene. The degeneracy of the present is communicated through Ravenhill's familiar hallmarks: sex as an interaction governed by the mediating, intensifying, yet alienating influences of drugs, sex toys and video.

The young, newly out figure of Tom is key to the ways in which the audience's attitudes towards all this are conditioned, and he further accentuates the play's overt concerns with history. Arriving at the party already on drugs in order to overcome his inhibitions, he is nonetheless always keen to take more. In having come out, left his judgemental family and arrived in London, he is self-

---

54   Ravenhill in 'The Mother Clap Trap', p. 35.

conscious about his own modernity, imagining that his trajectory mimics that of the play: 'Two months and I've travelled hundreds of years into the future. Only the future's like now. I mean, look at me. Clubs. E. Shagging all sorts of blokes. It's great. And now this.'[55] The dramatic action, however, generates the irony that undercuts Tom's confidence, culminating in the scene in which he is forced to suck off another character who is disenchanted with such parties, but keen to maintain the appearance of being up for it. Tom pushes him off:

> I was really looking forward to this evening. This is all I ever wanted. All them years stuck at home listening to me dad: Fucking poofs this, fucking queers that. And I thought: You're history, you. ... That's history. And I'm the future. This is the future. People doing what they want to do. People being who they want to be. So why ...? Why do you have to make it wrong?[56]

The autonomy and freedom that Tom asserts as integral parts of his newly claimed identity are presented here rather as the rhetoric by which joyless compulsion and dependency are rationalized. On arriving in London, he is catapulted into a future that consists in the kind of mechanical repetition represented synecdochically on stage by the various gadgetry of the party. As Adorno might say, what they want is forced upon them again.

The problem with Ravenhill's representation of male desire as governed by the market, though, is that the male sex drive is elsewhere presented as compatible with such repetition; indeed, as governing it. From this other perspective, it is difficult to see

---

55  Ravenhill, *Mother Clap's Molly House*, p. 64.
56  Ibid., pp. 86–87.

why these scenes should be regarded in terms of alienation rather than fulfilment. The representation of women further confirms the play's contradictory impulses: they are victims of capitalism through the price it places on their sexuality, but are also subject to men's innately rapacious demands. These represent contrasting feminist explanations of women's subordination. Moreover, the play encourages a misogynistic disgust at women's sexuality and corporeality through its visual insistence on vaginal bleeding in one form or another. Menstruation is being hinted at, though the bleeding is more specifically bound up with women's refusal of motherhood, such that the latter appears vindicated as nature's destiny for them. This, in turn, contrasts with the *in*consequential playfulness men are able to enjoy together. But while they are thereby 'liberated' from biological constraints, their desires are stimulated by a powerful repressive incitement.

Thus, the critique in this play is overdetermined by contradictory accounts of male sexual desire and women's subordination to it in ways that seem designed above all to intensify the bleak sense of compulsion (there is much humour in it, but little joy). Ravenhill has spoken of his desire for audiences to learn from his plays in a way that is not wholly authentic to the spirit of Brecht:

> I've always written against moral relativism. I want audiences to make moral choices: to decide moment by moment – intellectually and emotionally – whether what the characters are doing and the choices they are making are right or wrong. I find this dramatic. It makes good theatre ... To write against our ironic, easygoing times, where any hierarchy of values has melted away, to stage something that makes an audience say, 'That is wrong' – that is definitely something I've delighted in doing ...

... The permission to say, 'This is wrong' – without qualification
– takes us a step closer to 'This is right.' And to change.[57]

Morals for Brecht are part of the problem, of course. Mostly they
are for Ravenhill, in spite of what he says here, since his characters
appear trapped (Tom's options in *Molly House* of submitting either
to familial repression or a mechanized 'freedom' are typical). And
yet, morality does intrude on them, because the very helplessness
of his characters appears to cry out for the restoration of some
form of autonomy as a corrective to their various modes of
infantile dependency. The plays end up appearing judgemental of
the characters at least as much as their situations.

Perhaps, then, what is needed is the restoration of those relations
that have traditionally enabled people to *grow up*. 'Nobody in these
plays is fully adult,' Ravenhill has written. 'They are all needy,
greedy, wounded, only fleetingly able to connect with the world
around them. Consumerism, late capitalism – whatever we call
it – has created an environment of the infant "me", where it is
difficult to grow into the adult "us".' The shift of pronouns here
connects maturity to collectivity in a way that perhaps reminds us of
Christopher Lasch's desired corrective to the culture of narcissism:
the restoration of the traditional family.[58] 'There is a father-figure
in each of these plays', points out Ravenhill. 'But none of these
fathers offers much in the way of positive guidance.'[59] Mothers are
equally inept – and for similar reasons, if we think of another play,

---

57   Quoted in Aleks Sierz, *In-Yer-Face Theatre: British Drama Today*,
London: Faber, 2001, p. 129.
58   Christopher Lasch, *The Culture of Narcissism: American Life in an Age of
Diminishing Expectations*, New York: W. W. Norton, 1979.
59   Mark Ravenhill, 'A Tear in the Fabric: The James Bulger Murder and
New Theatre Writing in the Nineties', *New Theatre Quarterly*, 20(4), 2004,
pp. 311–312.

*Handbag* – but, in presenting them as such, they are also seen to fall short of an ideal that is thereby reinstated. In *Molly House*, families are repressive and homophobic, but the alternatives are female mutilation and self-mutilation, on the one hand, and a male experimentation that culminates in sexual compulsion, on the other.

All of this leads me to consider the reception of Ravenhill's work as a means of thinking about its potential for the kind of subcultural reflection Sinfield encourages. The plays are often compared to those of other playwrights prominent at the time of his own spectacular appearance on the grounds that their work is shocking. This strikes me as a further instance of the marketization of 'controversy', even though the tone of it is significantly different from that evident in *Queer as Folk*. That point has been registered by others, but worrying implications attend their articulation of the case in ways I think it important to register.

Vera Gottlieb has been critical of this group of playwrights, claiming that they seemed 'very much in touch with the malaise amongst their generation, all too aware of consumerism, but in effect the plays end up as "products": the "themes" of consumerism, drug culture and sexuality paralyze the plays'.[60] For Gottlieb, Ravenhill's work was tainted by association with the cultural marketing typical of the 'cool climate' of Blair's Britain. Ken Urban acknowledges in part the validity of Gottlieb's point, indicating that the Royal Court under Stephen Daldry set out to attract 'youth', and that 'the 'nineties were all about peddling the provocative'.[61] Nonetheless, via Nietzsche, Heidegger, Artaud and

---

60 Vera Gottlieb, 'Lukewarm Britannia' in Gottlieb and Colin Chambers, eds, *Theatre in a Cool Climate*, Oxford: Amber Lane Press, 1999, p. 212.
61 Ken Urban, 'Towards a Theory of Cruel Britannia: Coolness, Cruelty and the Nineties', *New Theatre Quarterly*, 20(4), 2004, p. 357.

Bataille, he finds in the cruelty of such theatre a form of immanent critique that makes ethical change possible in consequence of the suffering the spectator is made to undergo. But it is surely problematic to take for granted drama's potential in this respect: the tendency is to reify 'the audience', rather than try to understand particular audiences' cultural ways of making sense of things. Most people have surely become accustomed, even inured, to viewing cruelty in more or less spectacular forms.

What Gottlieb and Urban have in common, however, is their tendency to regard Ravenhill as in some sense culturally central because part of the mainstream British theatrical tradition. Indeed, this is how Ravenhill thinks of himself: he once suggested, for instance, that 'the sense that our writing counts' is what distinguishes British from US playwrights.[62] Whether this is the perspective he set out with, or one he has developed as a consequence of being taken up by certain companies and institutions – including Max Stafford Clark's *Out of Joint* company, the Royal Court and the Royal National Theatres – it is clear that the address of his plays is not specifically, and certainly not exclusively, subcultural. Alan Sinfield considers this question of 'address' crucial: it indicates 'whose knowledge, experience, beliefs and feelings are being appealed to, and, more importantly, taken for granted'[63] in the writing and performance of a play. But, if this is the case, it is clear that Ravenhill's drama draws on powerful ideological formations that are not specifically queer, and that these also substantially condition his sense of being 'postgay'.

As Urban suggests, the institutions that have promoted

---

62  Mark Ravenhill, 'Me, My iBook, and Writing in America', *Contemporary Theatre Review*, 16(1), 2006, p. 138.

63  Alan Sinfield, *Out on Stage: Lesbian and Gay Theatre in the Twentieth Century*, New Haven: Yale University Press, 1999, p. 343.

Ravenhill's work have no doubt done so out of a market-led desire to proclaim their own modernity for reasons in part critically explored by Ravenhill himself in the plays. The parallels with Channel Four's sponsorship of Russell T. Davies are again obvious. The 'controversial' qualities of Ravenhill's work, then, are bound up with his willingness to be explicit linguistically, in depictions of the violence he associates with contemporary capitalism, and in representations of sexuality that emphasize its depravity. Indeed, the term so often used about his work, 'in-yer-face', suggests a tendency to see each of these elements as part and parcel of a more generally shocking whole.

This raises a significant problem. If Ravenhill's work impresses on us the idea that gay men have been taken over by their identities, consumed by them in the process of commercially consuming them, and that they have become in that highly specific sense the system's most representative subjects, this important point is likely to be congenial to a liberal-left theatregoing audience whose prejudices it will most likely confirm. Indeed, that very confirmation may ironically determine certain negative evaluations of the plays. I discern this in Gottlieb's comments – what, after all, is the difference between a theme and a 'theme'? – but it is more strikingly evident in Patrice Pavis's suggestion that, when badly performed, Ravenhill's earlier play, *Some Explicit Polaroids*, is 'full of superficial, provocative effects, going for entertainment based on primary sado-anal needs, played at speed so as to prevent reflection, and with a profusion of visual gags'.[64] In fact, there are no specifically anal, let alone 'sado-anal', references in that play, and even if Pavis is confusing *Polaroids* with *Shopping and Fucking*

---

64   Patrice Pavis, 'Ravenhill and Durringer, or the *Entente Cordiale* Misunderstood', *Contemporary Theatre Review*, 14(2), 2004, p. 15.

the claim appears to be that these works need to be redeemed of any explicit preoccupation with sex between men.

It may sound as if I am now complaining with Norton that, in these early plays, Ravenhill is dealing in stereotypes for the consumption of straight audiences, so let me qualify the point. First, the discourse of stereotyping is problematic insofar as it makes appeal to the host of unique individuals being misrepresented, as if groups do not possess certain common traits. It also stigmatizes those, especially effeminate men, said to conform to the stereotype.[65] Second, Ravenhill's work brought gay audiences – and not only those normally interested in the arts – into the theatre, and so *was* serving subcultural purposes. Third, I acknowledge strong common ground between his work and the project of this book, but equally I aim to be sensitive to the ideological tendency to uphold and critique gay men specifically as dupes/representatives of the system to which other spheres, and especially the family, offer humane alternatives. Alternatives have to be created, and not just by queers, and there is plenty of evidence in work other than Ravenhill's of a reserve, at the very least, about the commodification of sexuality. And fourth, given that the manifest dependence on the market is one consequence of queer marginalization historically, the implicit appeal to the theatre's more complacent humanist traditions as those by which the scene might adequately be judged seems to promote audiences' smugness. The humanism I advocate in this book, by contrast, is a critical one that resides in the belief that we hold the potential to transform our world and ourselves on the basis of our critical grasp of our condition.

---

65   David M. Halperin considers this tendency as it emerged out of gay liberation in *How to Be Gay*, Cambridge, Mass.: Belknap Press, 2014, pp. 33–66.

## The meanings of postgay

Together, the work of Russell T. Davies and Mark Ravenhill suggests the parameters of the postgay as this term has circulated. While both register persistent social hostility to gay men, they nonetheless demonstrate forms of integration that may be celebrated or despised, depending ultimately on one's relation to the system to which they are being assimilated. In Ravenhill's case, the category of gay has come to epitomize one-dimensionality in a world of relentless repressive incitement. But even Davies's more celebratory, generically comic work registers something of this in its hankering after a human depth and intersubjectivity.

There is now a fairly considerable literature of supersession, all of it seemingly directed at gay male identity.[66] Daniel Harris, in one of the first such treatises, *The Rise and Fall of Gay Culture* (1997), acknowledges assimilation as the consequence of marketization. He insists that this process is one that has been welcomed and pursued by gay people themselves, rather than imposed on them by business CEOs, as some (like me, no doubt) articulating a 'simplistic Marxist fairy tale' tend to suggest.[67] Nonetheless, he

---

66 Other work includes: Mark Simpson, ed., *Anti-Gay*, London: Cassell, 1996, a collection of essays with diverse agendas; Bert Archer, *The End of Gay (and the Death of Heterosexuality)*, London: Fusion Press, 2002, which is focused largely on the sexual indeterminacy of film, television and celebrity; and Dennis Altman's typically more thoughtful, but inconclusive, *The End of the Homosexual?* Queensland: University of Queensland Press, 2013. Altman's title, however, ironically echoes the more revolutionary thoughts contained in the final chapter of *Homosexual: Oppression and Liberation*, London: Allen Lane, 1974, in which he anticipated 'the creation of a new human for whom such distinctions [as homosexual and heterosexual] are no longer necessary for the establishment of identity' (p. 238).

67 Daniel Harris, *The Fall and Rise of Gay Culture*, New York: Ballantine Books, 1997, p. 6.

views the fall of gay culture ambivalently: as inevitable and desirable, given that it is predicated on the end of overt oppression, but also as a form of cultural impoverishment, since 'we recoil from the sight of the extreme homogenization of American culture, of a monolithically uniform melting pot gobbling up its minorities'.[68] In fact, it is Harris's own crude anti-leftism and reduction of complex processes to the stark alternatives of autonomous choice or the imposition of power that generate this merely nostalgic, and quickly repudiated, regret in the face of a progress that is taken to be inevitable. Harris can only conceive of the refusal of others to follow his lead as stubbornness or delusion: he ends up being a cheerleader for one-dimensionality.

A similar thing might be said of the former editor of *Out* and *Attitude* magazines, James Collard, whose promotion of a postgay lifestyle was critiqued some time ago by Michael Warner for its privileged rejection of struggle and 'separatism', and embrace of domesticating affluence.[69] Collard subsequently expressed some ambivalence about this agenda in a way that alerts us to the circumscribed nature of the diversified dominant. In an article for *The Times on Sunday* in 2007, he took London Pride as the pretext for elaborating his position: 'all those rainbow flags, that tired "identity politics", the queue for Portaloos ... No thanks.' Nonetheless, he recognizes that his is the perspective of someone who lives in 'a liberal, largely gay-friendly country where many of our battles are won', and goes on to note the contrast between London's Pride march and those taking place in the former Eastern bloc, expressing admiration for those westerners who have participated in them out of a sense of solidarity. While in Russia, he reflects, liberty looks

---

68   Ibid., p. 271.
69   Michael Warner, *The Trouble with Normal: Sex, Politics and the Ethics of Queer Life*, New York: Free Press, 1999, pp. 61–71.

'more and more like a lost cause', things might be different among the newest members of the European Union. Collard claims that nationalism and the churches played a positive role in resisting Soviet oppression, but that a huge cultural leap was now required of the populations in those countries to overcome the prejudices instilled in them through these same attachments.

> Europe is a package deal: lock, stock and liberal barrel. And if they're under the illusion that membership simply means access to our markets or subsidies for their infrastructures? Well – and I don't know how to say this in Latvian – they can shove it. Shove it where the sun don't shine.[70]

The thing that stirs in Collard here is not really any vestigial militancy, but rather an *amour-propre* wounded by barbarians from afar. Too sophisticated for the apparent indignities of Pride, he nonetheless wishes it on Eastern Europe through a neoliberal narrative that sees religion and nationalism as having played merely instrumental roles in the overthrow of an oppressive 'communism', rather than having actively determined profoundly reactionary, even fascistic, political ideologies that retain their potency in response to the insecurities generated by the very order he advocates. He conceives of cultural change in equally instrumental terms, after the fashion of a corporation that peremptorily demands it of 'flexible' workers. Collard is not interested in challenging authority, but rather identifies with it and its capacity to compel others to come to terms with the cosmopolitanism that has treated him so generously, and made

---

70  James Collard, 'If you're Part of the Club, you get the Rainbow Flags', *The Times on Sunday*, 30 May 2007, http://www.timesonline.co.uk/tol/comment/columnists/guest_contributors/article1857132.ece (accessed 20 March 2012).

him feel so special. This is truly a narcissistic projection of power. Meanwhile, collective life is beneath him (the Portaloo is an apt synecdoche for his elitist disgust), and others are left to do the hard work of campaigning.

More pervasive than either Harris's or Collard's polemical positions, though, is a generally more relaxed sense of being a part of, rather than at odds with, a society that is itself more liberal in many respects, and in which fun and repressive incitement have acted as solvents of morality. An insistence on being gay in the expectation that such assertiveness will be necessary on a daily basis is for many simply not part of their experience, at least in much of the west, even though hostility and violence from some quarters persist. Consequently, a feeling that stridency is no longer necessary is to be found everywhere, and often justified as a matter of style. In Britain, *Gay Times* discreetly became *GT* in March 2007, presumably all the better to *in*differentiate it from the titles of other magazines, such as *GQ* and *FHM*, and thereby to consolidate continuities within the male homosocial spectrum.

If 'gay' is an obsolete identity for Collard, and less polemically so for others too, it is not only for Mark Ravenhill that it functions as the very sign of the lifestyle he wishes to subject to radical critique. Protest in this respect has been various, but relatively marginal. In London, the alternative club and cabaret night, Duckie, has promoted an annual 'Gay Shame and Lesbian Weakness' event since 1996 to coincide with London Pride. In 2004, the theme was 'spend your pink pounds at the consumerist (f)unfair'. The 2005 event, it claims, 'put gay rights back by 50 years and featured quite a lot of staged suicides'.[71] The dominant

---

71  http://duckie.co.uk/generic.php?id=34&submenu=shame and http://duckie.co.uk/generic.php?id=59&submenu=shame (both accessed 20 July 2011).

mode is parody, and the emphasis is determinedly anti-PC. Nonetheless, the humour would fall flat were it not for the fact that such things as suicides feature less prominently now than in the past. The mode of address is clearly subcultural, but aimed at a self-consciously critical crowd. The Duckie collective claim to be 'purveyors of progressive working class entertainment', a line in which every word – even, and perhaps especially, 'progressive' – suggests an ironic, 'retro' sensibility that distances itself temporally and stylistically from the uncritical contemporaneity of Pride itself. It nonetheless looks ironically to the past, not the future.

One thing that does distinguish Duckie is the Arts Council funding it has received since 2008. This has not discernibly affected the content of events, but such official recognition signals that, like more mainstream theatre and performance, Duckie plays to those who know broadly what to expect and are prepared to pay for it. It is therefore distinct from the theatricality of Gay Shame in San Francisco that for a time took confrontation on to the streets, attacking gentrification and the 'cleaning up' of queer neighbourhoods, depoliticization, 'body fascism' and other aspects of assimilation. Its politics were anarchist, and its website invokes a familiar, if in this context (intentionally?) provocative, metaphor to describe itself as 'a virus in the system'.[72]

Gay Shame claims to welcome everyone, but is also avant-gardist in a way that appears designed to put some off. One of its vegan socials proclaims itself 'a drug-free radical queer/trans political space for those who can't figure out why there aren't more drug-free radical queer/trans political space [sic] in

---

72  http://gayshamesf.org/ (accessed 20 July 2011).

fucking san francisco'.[73] This perhaps raises questions about the relationship between the group and the disenfranchised it claims at times to represent. Its campaign against the 'pro-gentrification attack squad', Lower Polk Neighbors Association, for instance, objected to the way the latter 'works with the police to rid neighborhood streets of "undesirables", i.e. hookers, hustlers, drug addicts, homeless people, trannies, needle exchange services, working class queers and other social deviants'.[74] Social cleansing is clearly objectionable, but there may be a risk here of romanticizing as queer forms of 'deviance' that are diverse and not in the main chosen as such (the problem I noted with Halberstam's comments in the previous chapter). Besides, how many of these figures would feel welcome at a drug-free, radical, queer/trans, vegan social?

Gay Shame activists attended a conference of the same name at the University of Michigan in 2003, and got angry with participants over their apparent academic appropriation and neutralization of authentic radicalism. One of the activists, Mattilda Bernstein Sycamore, accused the conference of 'trickle-down academia, by which academics appropriate anything that they can get their hands on – mostly other people's lived struggles, activism, and identities – and claim to have invented them'.[75] This is an odd reinflection of 'trickle-down', and also assumes a neat separation between academics and activists that results in haranguing academics themselves for the divisions of labour that exist in

---

73   http://gayshamesf.org/thesocialevery4saturday.html (accessed 20 July 2011).
74   http://gayshamesf.org/lpn.html (accessed 20 July 2011).
75   Mattilda Bernstein Sycamore, 'Gay Shame: From Queer Autonomy to Direct Action Extravaganza', in Sycamore, ed., *That's Revolting: Queer Strategies for Resisting Assimilation*, Brooklyn: Soft Skull Press, 2008, p. 285.

our societies, not to mention the increasing corporatization and neoliberalization of their institutions that many of them try to resist. For these Gay Shame activists, wedded to a sense of academia as ivory tower, what goes on there is not part of any transformation of the 'real world'. Gay Shame highlights real injustices, and brings much-needed critique to the subculture, but it also risks alienating those with whom it might establish productive alliances.

This prompts me to query whether the various postgay critiques of gay pride – either the events or the sentiment – can be regarded as subcultural, or to what extent they entail a rejection of subcultural identification, as is sometimes suggested. Duckie's Gay Shame is clearly subcultural and mostly takes place in the institutions of the scene. Even the work of activist Gay Shame might be seen as subcultural if we take into account Sinfield's argument that the subculture need not be seen as cosy or without divisions: Gay Shame activism evinces a profound sense of betrayal directed specifically *at* lesbian, gay and queer constituencies, some of whom it presumably hopes to influence. The sense is of a movement that has been hijacked. Nonetheless, the pressures exerted by such groups on a subculture that must be predicated on at least some degree of integrity and solidarity are considerable. Similarly, assimilationist individuals may be disdainful of explicit subcultural identifications and see themselves as having achieved as much equality and freedom as they individually want or need without being in any sense deluded. The accusation of homonormativity may wrongly imply that these people should feel *more* guilty about their privileged lives than others simply because they're not straight, but that doesn't follow if sexuality is no longer any barrier to class integration, and may even, in some circumstances, facilitate it. Richard Florida has notoriously highlighted gay people as an important constituency in what he calls the 'creative class' that brings 'wealth generation' (and greater inequality) to cities, and further epitomizes coolness.[76]

Let us consider the dynamics of one apparently trivial, though actually rather complex, cultural phenomenon as a symptom of broader shifts indicative of the erosion of subcultural integrity: the figure of Daffyd Thomas in the BBC sketch show, *Little Britain*. He is absurd because of his insistence, despite all the evidence to the contrary, that he is 'the only gay in the village'. The fetish gear he wears to differentiate himself from the rest of the village also holds him up to the ridicule of the viewer: it takes us back to an earlier moment, perhaps, when people still wore Lycra at Pride. Daffyd's attachment to his identity results from a self-righteous investment in the notion that he is oppressed. The sketch may also express a metropolitan disdain for the backwardness of small-town life, even as it suggests that such life is itself far more modern and progressive than Daffyd wants to believe. Daffyd's Welshness plays a role in this, defining his 'radicalism' as actually now provincial, while those around him appear effortlessly modern. The actor who plays Daffyd, Matt Lucas, is himself known to be gay, thereby conferring 'legitimacy' on the humour of it all, though the repeated suggestion of the sketch that same-sex passion is actually pervasive is one that has been consistently important to lesbian, gay and queer convictions (Sedgwick's 'universalizing' impulse). Daffyd's often proclaimed isolation, though, is linked to his exceptional

---

76   See Richard Florida, *The Rise of the Creative Class: And How its Transforming Work, Community and Everyday Life*, New York: Basic Books, 2003, especially pp. 255–258 on the so-called Gay Index as an indicator of openness, tolerance and creativity. Jim McGuigan discusses Florida, but not the prominence given to sexuality in his work, in *Cool Capitalism*, London: Verso, 2009, pp. 162–165.

failure ever to have had sex, such that his militancy is made to seem like a rationalization of the fear of it. 'Politics', then, is a form of prudery rather than liberation; it isn't fun, though it is funny, ridiculous. The ultimately repetitive satire of the sketch is therefore directed at the supposed paranoia of the militant stuck in the past and delusionally hostile to a society that no longer has any problem accommodating his desires.

The way in which this sketch is understood will no doubt vary according to the dispositions of its viewers (straight, gay, metro-politan, rural, liberal, conservative, and so on). It is conceivable that it may serve to reinforce straightforward hostility to gay people as absurd, even disgusting, figures – Daffyd, squeezed into his clothing, is intentionally grotesque, if simultaneously childlike and petulant – but its more likely tendency is to demonstrate to diverse audiences that gay men can poke fun at themselves and their past, and therefore no longer threaten anyone. It may be significant in this context that Matt Lucas was one of the first gay celebrities in Britain to have a high-profile civil partnership.

As with so much carnivalesque humour, *Little Britain* more generally expresses a form of conservatism and even cruelty that is at its most pernicious in other sketches from the show, in their entirely unironic, merely derisive representations of the feckless poor or malingering disabled. Such reactionary messages only appear to be in tension with the liberalism required of the viewer by the series' self-consciously surreal and 'outrageous' style: an aesthetic tolerance thereby masks the intolerance necessary to approve its vicious contempt for 'recognizable' social types. Hence, it is difficult to make sense of Daffyd as addressing a specifically subcultural audience. He is surely rather one instance of a larger process of a *cultural* assimilation in which the distinctiveness of gay traditions is both registered and integrated into a more general, if far from uniform, set of perceptions and values. After all, the title of the series is suggestive of its satiric scope, and it was broadcast by a national, public institution, the BBC, that must justify its politically contested, distinctive funding through a licence fee everyone with a television must pay. Its address must therefore be inclusive, but this now means recognizing diversity of all sorts – national, regional, communal. The opening and closing voiceovers in the posh voice of the actor, Tom Baker, even signal self-consciousness of this, alluding to the BBC's formerly quaint, but elitist, public service commitments and tendency to portray Britain as an organic community.

In different ways, *Queer as Folk* and Daffyd in *Little Britain* recognize and celebrate assimilation, while using sensation to appear to challenge 'conservative' sensibilities, among which are now numbered those of radical activists of the past. 'The only gay in the village' is a catchphrase that is no doubt multiaccentual, available for use by gay men themselves in whatever context, but also by right-wing journalists intent on undermining the human rights campaigns of Peter Tatchell.[77] Nonetheless, its effect is unavoidably to undermine the legitimacy of protest or complaint. It is anti-PC in both style and content: leftists, it says, are simply killjoys. Daffyd, then, has become familiar to the point of having given form and definition to otherwise diffuse perceptions and values, and having consolidated what was at the time a certain structure of feeling, but has now become more sinisterly evident.

Let us take another, more recent instance. In 2009, the straight comedian, Sacha Baron Cohen, who also specializes in sensation,

---

77  Johann Harri notes this in his sharply critical discussion of the series, 'Why I Hate *Little Britain*', *The Independent*, 22 November, 2005, http://www.independent.co.uk/opinion/commentators/johann-hari/johann-hari-why-i-hate-little-britain-516388.html (accessed 18 July 2011).

and has consistently courted accusations of stereotyping, released the film, *Bruno*. Focusing on the career of a gay Austrian fashion model, it records others' 'real life' responses to his naïve, yet hyperbolic, vanity. Debate around the film inevitably focused on whether or not it was homophobic.[78] Universal Studios and defenders of Baron Cohen claimed it was designed to point up homophobia in others, though he went to the greatest possible lengths to provoke their reactions by playing a figure fully deserving of anyone's contempt. Part of the point, perhaps, is that his victims found Bruno plausible at all: the character confirms their most lurid imaginings. He was nonetheless dreamt up by Baron Cohen, and the film's satire relies on Bruno being recognizable to audiences, however much of a parody he is.

The error in many of the discussions of the film is therefore to look for coherence and a singular message, when actually the film is provocative to no particular end other than to confirm the specific liberalism of Baron Cohen himself in relation, first, to the narcissism and vacuity of the celebrity industry (figured as connotatively 'gay'), and, second, to the vulgar, non-metropolitan cultural particularisms of a range of 'homophobic' others, including nationalist Palestinians, orthodox Israeli Jews (for the sake of balance, no doubt), and US rednecks, all lumped indiscriminately together in their reactions. That the world is full of freaks and it is often difficult to distinguish in this respect between fact and fiction is probably the only consistent 'message' the film intends.

---

78   See, for instance, the generally positive review in *The Guardian*, 10 July 2009, http://www.theguardian.com/film/2009/jul/10/film-review-bruno. The Gay & Lesbian Alliance Against Discrimination (GLAAD) condemned the film: 'US Campaigning Group not GLAAD with Bruno', *The Guardian*, 13 July 2009, http://www.theguardian.com/film/2009/jul/13/glaad-comes-out-against-bruno (both accessed 14 December 2013).

Its radicalism lies in the lengths Baron Cohen goes to in order to embarrass his audience into laughter, though he was always going to be safer from the phobic responses he provoked among the various groups he sought to shame than those everyday queers who have to find accommodation with such groups on a daily basis.

Such seriousness of comedic purpose as there is in Baron Cohen's films is comparable with that of reality TV and its combination of the artificial and the spontaneous to effect wholly uninstructive conflict. Like reality TV, *Bruno* is clearly both related to, and to be differentiated from, the documentary tradition whose supersession was bound up with the increasing budgetary constraints and competition imposed on TV production in the 1990s, resulting in work that was both highly contrived yet not strictly predictable, contained yet sensational. It sought to produce affects in participants and audiences that were rooted in, yet abstracted from, actual social dynamics, and manipulated for the purposes of entertainment. Jonathan Bignell suggests that, whereas the documentary had a 'modernist' seriousness of purpose that lay in highlighting social problems and pressing for remedies, reality TV and films like *Bruno* are postmodern not only in their pseudo-reality, but also their orientation towards consumer affect divorced from any discernible sense of purpose.[79] Moreover, just as one advantage of the reality format is that it is marketable and transportable in a way that documentaries may not be, *Bruno* is cosmopolitan in its simultaneous autocritique of celebrity excess and disdain for the non-cosmopolitan.

Both *Little Britain* and *Bruno* are therefore symptomatic of the

79 Jonathan Bignell, *Big Brother: Reality TV in the Twenty-First Century*, Houndmills: Palgrave Macmillan, 2005, p. 27.

extent to which *critical* representation of gay men has entered the mainstream. They have become familiar in the form of out celebrities, from Graham Norton to Elton John, through television such as *Queer Eye for the Straight Guy*, and Hollywood comedies such as *I Love You Phillip Morris* (Glenn Ficarra/Far Shariat, 2009). The preponderance of camp humour as an identifying and differentiating trait is instructive. There are exceptions, of course. In Britain, these might include Ian Gallagher and Mickey Maguire in the Channel Four series, *Shameless* (Channel Four, 2004–2013); then there are the central characters of *Brokeback Mountain* (Lee, 2005). However, their exceptionality is determined by the incompatibility of camp with various modes of non-cosmopolitan existence that are presumed to be intolerant of it, as well as with generic requirements: in *Shameless*, a highly stylized 'grittiness' largely precludes it, and in the case of *Brokeback Mountain* the dignity necessary for *genuine* tragedy, rather than melodrama, demands masculine seriousness. Even here, assumptions may be confirmed, though. In one episode of *Shameless* in which Mickey Gallagher is identified as gay at a James Bond fancy dress party by a black man in drag everyone else takes to be a woman, it is because he knows all the words to 'Diamonds are Forever': he cannot suppress his true sensibility, the one that the show's audience will also recognize as such.

It is necessary to be clear, therefore, about the pressure on the subculture that is exerted by this kind of mainstreaming. Just as the scene itself has witnessed greater investment from both gay entrepreneurs and mainstream business, so representation has either focused on that burgeoning reality or deployed modes that are effectively an extension of it. Thus, 'gay culture' is recognized and validated as part of the embrace of diversity now self-consciously pursued by business as proof of its modernity. This acknowledges that the kind of 'talent' and 'creativity' that generates profits is likely to come from various sources, some of which may have a particular reputation for these traits, but it also relies on a specific sense that gay life is characteristically, pioneeringly modern, and perhaps in an entirely uncritical 'post-' kind of way that is exceptionally good for markets. Between them these pressures have the effect of undermining the relative autonomy of subculture, even as they define and render a thing called 'gay life' more substantial, visible, domesticated and open to 'critique' from all sorts of positions.

# Postscripts

## New sensations

As I finish writing this book, Channel Four has been screening Russell T. Davies's latest series, *Cucumber*. Like *Queer as Folk*, it clearly aspires to capture the way we live now, and not merely in a subcultural sense, though that is the primary one. As a result, and not least through its focus on generational shifts, the series contains reflections on sensibilities that are being superseded and refashioned. In its own ways, it is preoccupied with many of the things I have focused on in this book: sensation and repressive incitement, technology and (de)privatization, the appeal of sacramental love in the face of its supposedly progressive erosion, and the postgay breakdown of that formerly abrupt division in the male homosocial spectrum governed by homophobia. It is for these reasons that this postscript opens with discussion of the series, not so much in order to provide an interpretation of it, but rather in order to expand on some of its concerns. It is good to think with.

First, *Cucumber* is stylistically very similar to *Queer as Folk* for reasons that again have to do with the needs of Channel Four: it is sensationally preoccupied with sensation, designed to attract notice. In publicity for it, Channel Four boasted both that it would be so explicit it could not be broadcast in the US, and that it would confirm their mission to 'lightly outrage' *The Daily Mail*.[1] Gay men remain handy as a means of asserting distinction through institutional symbolic capital.

The series itself focuses on the intensified repressive incitement of daily life through its relentless encroachments on, and reconfigurations of, privacy. The kinds of virtual technology I focused on in chapter two are prominent. As with *Queer as Folk*, there is acknowledgement of the marketization of desire: most episodes begin with the main protagonist, Henry, pushing a trolley round a supermarket, mulling over a particular problem about sex and relationships while subtly cruising other customers. But the series is also complicit with all that it objectifies potentially in the form of critique. The significance of the title – an article from Henry's supermarket trolley perhaps – is clarified at the outset: it really is, as we have been challenged to *dis*believe, an allusion to the firmest of all hard-ons.[2]

Though *Cucumber* is focused on gay men, it is not exclusively so, but that is partly because subcultural life itself is less concentrated on particular spaces than it used to be. Technology is assisting in making Manchester's gay village on Canal Street more or less redundant, though heterosexual tourism is cited by characters as an irritation. The scene is more porous now, but the correlative

---

1   Ian Burrell, 'Channel Four Plots to Shock with its New Gay Drama *Cucumber*', *The Independent*, 24 August 2014, http://www.independent. co.uk/arts-entertainment/tv/news/channel-4-plots-to-shock-with-its-new-gay-drama-cucumber-9687845.html (accessed 4 March 2015).
2   Other titles, *Banana* and *Tofu*, in the 'multi-platform' group of programmes associated with *Cucumber* refer to different states of male arousal, which functions as the yardstick, as it were, of all desire represented or discussed in them.

to this is that gay men also feel less of a need to frequent it. In Manchester, the mixed area known as the Northern Quarter is increasingly popular.

The two central characters of *Cucumber*, Henry and Lance, break up because they no longer have sex – though Henry is, in any case, averse to the fucking that others feel defines both sex and themselves through the roles they adopt within it (the top/bottom distinction). In episode one, after trying to revive their romance on a date, each goes to his room to masturbate to pornography, the promise of something better that is both permanently available and out of reach. In one of the scenes in which they fail to get back together, Henry has a speech about looking for that 'one last cock' he imagines waiting for him out there. Even the way he pronounces the word cock conveys all his absurd, transgressively 'anti-bourgeois' hope, and the phallic fulfilment he implausibly anticipates from it: cock is something someone/no one else possesses.

The complex breakup leads to Henry moving in with two young men he used to work with (he has also been suspended from his job because of false allegations against him of racism). He is sexually obsessed with one of them, Freddie, who is bisexual. Freddie's sexuality appears to have less to do with positive preferences than a narcissistic indifference to his partners that renders their sex unimportant. The problem is that they are not indifferent to him. In one scene, he imagines all the hassle he will get (calls, texts) if he has a relationship with the woman he is at that moment having sex with; men are less demanding. She doesn't appear again.

I don't want to discuss the whole series in detail, but am struck by episode four in particular. Its opening scene presents a sequence of metaphors: the growth of civilization is depicted through the expansion, multiplication and intersection of paths and roads that generate the temptation to leave them altogether and head off into the wilderness. Paths represent fixed directions, routes mapped out for us, constraints, Haussmann-style city planning, but also the confusing monotony of mazes – all alienating, impersonal and highly structured. The wilderness, however, leads to disorientation and panic; freedom is disconcerting. Henry begins telling people that, in breaking up with Lance, he got lost.

These familiar metaphors, though, represent a betrayal of the series' principal insight. Of course, work requires routine, and settled life is a part of this, attended by the comfort, security and humanity we crave; but confusion is systemically driven, not the product of some natural urge to burst forth. As Lukács pointed out, capitalism combines rationality, through its need to overcome obstacles to accumulation, with irrationality, through the systemic unpredictability of competition.[3] Subjective experience is also governed by this contradiction and its determinations of work and leisure: we may feel utterly controlled and unfree, yet simultaneously out of control and in need of restraint. Neither feels remotely satisfying. This is perfectly normal, and we must get used to it; self-management of one sort or another is one way, but that maybe sounds as if we are incorporating too much of the impersonal aspect of the system into our personal lives, thereby limiting our freedom. (Of course, pretty much all these terms – impersonal, personal, freedom and so on – should now be understood as carrying quotation marks to register their incoherence.)

Age difference in *Cucumber* is registered in terms of sensation. The actor, Vincent Franklin, plays Henry as an edgy sort of character, but the teenagers of the series, like Freddie, are cool.

---

3   Georg Lukács, 'Reification and the Consciousness of the Proletariat', in *History and Class Consciousness*, trans. Rodney Livingstone, London: Merlin Press, 1983, pp. 102–103.

They have been brought up with heightened levels of repressive incitement and lack the nervousness of the older generation around erotic stimulation. And 'nervous' is a game that Henry persuades his nephew, Adam, to play with Adam's friends for the purposes of producing YouTube videos to make money. These are playfully homoerotic, though not pornographic, and feature straight lads. 'Nervous' is a game Henry used to play when young, and consisted in a boy placing his hand higher and higher up a girl's leg and asking, 'are you nervous?' Here, though, the gambit is that it tests straight lads' tolerance with each other. All but one of the lads, however, fail to get the point: why would they be nervous of being touched by another guy? One of them is, though; his videos prove popular with viewers.

But what appears to be innocent fun with boys turns out to have more troubling consequences. As in *Queer as Folk*, moral limits are reasserted by a woman. Henry's sister, Cleo – his nephew's mother – finds out about the videos, but only because of the role they play in the humiliation of her twelve-year-old daughter, who has confessed to plucking her newly pubescent vagina, and circulating pictures of this to prove to boys she remains desirably hairless. One of her tales is of a boy approaching her at school, putting his hand directly into her knickers, and asking, 'are you nervous?' Sexual guilt returns to trouble both Henry and the audience, which has perhaps found the YouTube scene humorous. We remember the innocence we ideally predicate of childhood, and the persistent, yet reconfigured, power differentials between men and women.

The lads' lack of inhibition in *Cucumber* testifies to the greater integrity these days of the male homosocial continuum. Certainly, many straight young men appear not only unfazed, but actually excited, by performing for gay audiences. Two popular porn websites, fityoungmen.com and englishlads.com, feature (mostly) straight, well-groomed, obviously middle-class, even privately educated, athletic men who have regular jobs. They are not desperate, and don't need to do this for money, though no doubt it is handy from time to time, and maybe provides an alibi for their transgressions. Often they progress from the first site (photographs involving nudity, erections, perhaps masturbation) to the second (photographs and film, always involving a cumshot, possibly sex toys, possibly mutual masturbation with others, possibly fucking). In each case, then, there is a 'narrative' of limits being tested and overcome – or maybe the model will prove relatively unadventurous, a bit too nervous, in which case the punters' feedback and ratings, which have helped promote him from one site to the next, get more negative, and the model won't be invited back. There is a wealth of similar sites, each in competition with the rest.

Nonetheless, this dissolving boundary between gay and straight can still promote anxiety and panic. In one episode of *Cucumber*, this has spectacular consequences (when first screened, the Channel Four announcer enticingly cautioned audiences it would be 'explosive'). Lance is ultimately murdered by an avowedly straight man, Daniel, who has been flirting with him. The two tentatively start having sex. Daniel enjoys stimulation – indeed, the quality of his desire thrives on the limits with which he is playing, stepping just over the line only to retreat, then advancing once more – up to the point at which he comes, and masculine control reasserts itself over narcissistic bravado at Lance's expense. 'Look what you've done to me now,' Daniel cries after he has struck Lance with a golf club. For gay men, receiving a beating from another man *after* he's orgasmed is not an unfamiliar script.[4] However, *Cucumber*

---

4  See Jonathan Dollimore, *Sexual Dissidence: Augustine to Wilde, Freud to Foucault*, Oxford: Clarendon Press, 1991, pp. 242–248.

suggests that the potential gay-basher no longer needs to frequent obscure cruising grounds; he can parade his faux, laddish tolerance in public spaces. Subsequently, others persistently attempt to make Henry feel guilt for Lance's death, as if his 'irresponsibility' were the cause of it. In failing to settle down, and choosing rather to prolong his adolescence, he has rejected sacramentalism.

There are other storylines of boundaries being crossed, including one about a former teacher of Freddie's, Gregory, who used to have sex with him at school. When they randomly bump into each other again the now mature, experienced and normally affectless Freddie is discomfited, but asserts his power, first, by proposing to fuck Gregory, and then, when refused, texting a naked picture of the teacher to Gregory's wife's cousin. The flip side of incitement and exhibitionism is surveillance and revenge through humiliation. Hierarchies – here of age and vocation – are technologically democratized in ways that facilitate private forms of 'justice'. Similar uses of other anti-social media are prevalent everywhere. A peculiarly vicious moralism is pervasive amid all the supposed openness and fun. Politicians, who have been busy deregulating markets and encouraging innovation, feel the need to step in to clamp down on 'individual' behaviour; 'revenge porn' has necessitated specific legislative action.[5]

The episode with Gregory is instructive in other ways. Some gay liberation movements were once at least prepared to countenance alliances with paedophile groups, but such possibilities now appear remote, as does Gayle Rubin's anticipation back in 1984 that 'in twenty years or so … it will be much easier to show that

5  'Revenge Porn Could Lead to 14-year Sentence New Guidelines Clarify', *The Guardian*, 7 October 2014, http://www.theguardian.com/law/2014/oct/07/revenge-porn-14-year-sentence-cps-guidelines (accessed 16 March 2015).

[boy-lovers] have been the victims of a savage and undeserved witchhunt'.[6] Rubin clearly did not have violent abusers in mind when she wrote that, but the conflation is persistent.[7] Revelations in the UK about the sexual abuse of institutionalized or otherwise vulnerable children on a hitherto unimagined scale, stories about the extensive grooming of children on the internet, investigations into and prosecutions of older celebrities – all these things that dominate the news in the UK repeatedly as I finish writing this book are clearly contributing to a renewed anxiety about the need to protect childhood innocence all the more earnestly amid the intensified adult incitement. The widespread abuse of girls by British Asian men in Rotherham and Oxford is latched on to by the neofascist British National Party and English Defence League as a means of advancing their agendas, while media coverage of these crimes is not matched by that given to abuse by white men.[8] Some complain that the abuse of Asian girls and women is being overlooked in all of this.[9]

The point could be endlessly reinforced with more or less serious instances. Newspapers profit from the exposure of celebrity 'love

---

6  Gayle Rubin, 'Thinking Sex: Notes for a Radical Theory of the Politics of Sexuality', in Carole S. Vance, ed., *Pleasure and Danger: Exploring Female Sexuality*, London: Routledge & Kegan Paul, 1984, p. 273.

7  Rubin has commented on the increasing hysteria around child protection, the naivety of some of her own remarks and the misinterpretation of them in 'Blood Under the Bridge: Reflections on "Thinking Sex"', *GLQ*, 17(1), 2011, pp. 37–39.

8  'Nazir Afzal: "There is No Religious Basis for the Abuse in Rotherham', *The Guardian*, 3 September 2014, http://www.theguardian.com/society/2014/sep/03/nazir-afzal-there-is-no-religious-basis-for-the-abuse-in-rotherham (accessed 16 March 2015).

9  Iman Amrani, 'Beyond Rotherham: Muslims are Also Silent Victims of Sexual Abuse', 2 September 2014, http://www.theguardian.com/commentisfree/2014/sep/02/rotherham-muslims-victims-sexual-abuse-vulnerable-girls-muslim-communities (accessed 16 March 2015).

rats', while the *Jeremy Kyle Show* holds up poor people's messy lives and relationships to ridicule, highlighting the roles played by the kinds of social media, such as Facebook, that are effectively protagonists in fermenting hostilities. The show's pretence, giving credence to Kyle's persona of moral paragon, is that it is helping people (counselling is 'responsibly' on offer). Actually, though, the more desperate the situation, the greater the conflict, the 'better' the TV, and everyone knows this. The show appears to promote a return to older moral and familial norms through Kyle's faux incredulity and anger at participants' behaviour, but it thrives on their breakdown: audiences find gratification in it, evidence of their own superiority and of the apparent need for greater discipline for those who are 'dysfunctional'. A US version of the show was short-lived, apparently because it featured disproportionate numbers of poor, black participants.[10] In Britain, however, it tends rather to consolidate perceptions of the supposedly feckless 'white working class' and the chav,[11] the 'legitimately' despised figure. His aggressive and untamed image is nonetheless harnessed by those strands of the gay porn industry not directed at narcissistic affirmation amid the physically toned and groomed in order to fuel profitable fantasies that sex can still be dangerously masculine.[12]

If the sexual liberation movements believed that more sex would mean less guilt, that is not how things have turned out. Amid contemporary levels of incitement, guilt is no longer self-

---

10   Ian Burrell, 'Jeremy Kyle: Judge, Jury and Exploiter?' *The Independent*, 5 April 2013, http://www.independent.co.uk/news/people/profiles/jeremy-kyle-judge-jury-and-exploiter-8562459.html (accessed 10 March 2015).
11   Owen Jones explores popular cultural hostility to chavs, and the reasons for it, in *Chavs: The Demonization of the Working Class*, London: Verso, 2012.
12   Triga films feature porn actors as chavs in track suits, skinheads, football players, and so on. The sex is aggressively *filthy*, of course. See http://www.trigafilms.com (accessed 18 March 2015).

recrimination, the private suffering of the individual; it is rather the public accusation thrown around or projected on to others as part of the general breakdown of social solidarity or reaffirmation of existing enmities. Sex has become another weapon in the war of all against all, provoking the worry that we may all have got lost.

## We're not going shopping?

All of this, and a great deal more, is a symptom of the freedom we are said to enjoy, which resides almost exclusively in freedom of choice in the marketplace. It is the freedom that turns 'object choice' into consumer choice and legitimates it as a lifestyle (and that includes the family lifestyle and the diversification of it under 'equalmarriage'), but it is also the freedom governed by the compulsion of repressive incitement. It is the freedom that is bound ineluctably to exploitative production, the freedom that carries ecologically catastrophic implications in the abundance it is promised, and the freedom that transforms all value into the singular norm of exchange value. It is the freedom that is aggressively no one else's business, the freedom that exists unequally in a world of dramatic and rising inequality, the freedom indeed that generates such inequality, and the freedom that repudiates 'dependency' as the abject condition of those on welfare. It is the freedom of the contemporary performance principle. Is it irresistible?

Before attempting some response to this, I pursue further a point I have had reason to emphasize throughout relating to the ideological 'conspicuousness' of gay life. This remains a political problem, because through this process gay sexuality has become a – maybe even *the* – privileged sign of the diversified dominant. Russell T. Davies' celebrity, for instance, is not achieved in spite of being gay, or as if that were a matter for indifference, but because he represents gayness on the spectacular scale that appears to be its appropriate medium. One consequence of this conspicuousness is that it retains the potential to mobilize once again the old accusations of bourgeois perversion, albeit in recalibrated forms. Moreover, crisis conditions such as the world is apparently incapable of escaping from generate the search for scapegoats. The hopes on the left that were for a time raised by the election of Syriza in Greece in January 2015 were also qualified by its alliance in government with the anti-semitic, anti-immigrant, homophobic nationalist party, ANEL, in consequence of their common opposition to austerity.

I therefore feel ambivalent about some of the recent Marxist work on sexuality that is dismissive of its import for politics. Rosemary Hennessy draws on the early work of Kevin Floyd to argue in conventional Lukácsian terms that sexuality represents a form of reification that assists in obscuring our grasp of totality. She advocates a form of disidentification that 'does not mean a simple renunciation of identities – gay, straight, man, woman – but a critical working on them to make visible their historical and material conditions of possibility'.[13] What she has in mind is only sketchily outlined, but it sounds voluntaristic, with the potential result that, if it is taken up by anyone, it is most likely to be by those already critically conscious of sexuality as such. The risk, in spite of Hennessy's best intentions, is that heterosexuality would be reconfirmed as natural by default in the continuing absence of any persistent critique of that view.

More recently, James Penney has advanced a Lacanian Marxist case against what he perceives as the separatism promoted by

---

13   Rosemary Hennessy, *Profit and Pleasure: Sexual Identities in Late Capitalism*, New York: Routledge, 2000, p. 230.

queer theory. We must rather re-engage with universals. I am sympathetic to that case, and, to that extent, would differentiate my position from Sinfield's. But I am disturbed by the emphasis I perceive in his book's haste to convict 'queerness' of a privileged relation with consumption, and an apparent exoneration of the family whose norms he proposes at one point we might 'subversively' adopt as an alternative.[14] Following Mario Mieli's claim that those queers who identify their pleasures with the system represent 'homocops', Penney suggests that we must 'align most of mainstream queer theory with these homocops'.[15] His case strikingly neglects, however, the critique of homonormativity and the pervasive critical engagement with neoliberalism in that theory in recent years.

At one point, Penney suggests that the 'proper conclusion' of the anti-identitarian logic of queer theory should lead it to argue that the queer object of homophobic loathing is a fantasy. 'Never,' he goes on to suggest, 'does queer theory entertain the corollary that both the idea of a "gay/queer community", and the "compulsory heterosexuality" that forms its negative ground, might in fact exacerbate, rather than attenuate, homophobic passion.'[16] The point is, on an abstract level, irrefutable, but its lack of nuance at least rivals that of the theory he complains of. The presumption of heterosexuality remains powerful, and subculture provides

---

14   He entertains the idea that 'the more gay cultures are mainstreamed – not in the sense of the emergence of gay "markets" in global capitalism ... but rather with respect to the increasing resemblance of many gay couples and families to their heterosexual counterparts across the socioeconomic strata – the more the most foundational assumptions about the cultural intelligibility of sexual identities are called into question' (James Penney, *After Queer Theory: The Limits of Sexual Politics*, London: Pluto, 2014, pp. 57–58).
15   Ibid., p. 103.
16   Ibid., p. 14.

a context in which it does not hold. Its historical necessity has not been superseded entirely. Indeed, the conviction that sexual identity is irrelevant may itself be a sign of privilege: a recent tendency among the young to disdain such labels is self-consciously cosmopolitan.[17]

Significantly, Penney is reluctant to grant legitimacy to Kevin Floyd's recent argument that reification may have multiple positive consequences because of its capacity to generate perspectives from which social totality may be critiqued. Floyd suggests that this is one way of grasping queer theory's purposes.[18] Penney peremptorily insists in response that, for classical Marxism, it is the perspective of the proletariat that is fundamental, and that the openness to others is a form of relativizing postmarxism. This appears to presume both that the proletariat is an unproblematic category, and that it has no interest in these other perspectives.

This may not be surprising in the context of his argument, since he persistently reminds us that homosexuality is associated with privilege, historically through its 'cultural visibility' among the aristocracy and upper bourgeoisie, and contemporaneously in the global north. Queers in the south, he says, are likely to be westernized.[19] Peter Drucker, by contrast, is more careful on this point: he argues that sexual repression in the third world (the term he uses) has been allied to the strengthening of the state, a belief in the importance of promoting the nuclear family as itself a necessary aspect of modernization, and a more or less expedient

---

17    Rebecca Nicholson, '"I'm a Bisexual Homoromantic": Why Young Brits are Rejecting Old Labels', *The Guardian*, 18 August 2015, http://www. theguardian.com/society/2015/aug/18/bisexual-british-adults-define-gay-straight-heterosexual (accessed 18 August 2015).
18    Kevin Floyd, *The Reification of Desire: Toward a Queer Marxism*, Minneapolis: University of Minnesota Press, 2009, chapter one.
19    Penney, *After Queer Theory*, p. 87.

need for scapegoats during times of economic and political crisis.[20] Penney does not indicate whether he thinks those in the global south who identify with western categories are deserving of political consideration.

The argument for the supersession of queer theory in Penney's book seems ultimately to demand a similar degree of voluntarism to the project outlined by Hennessy, though here it resides in a commitment to the complexly articulated, because distinct, universalisms promoted by Lacan and Badiou that take us beyond the mundane realms of everyday values and identities to a 'special realm' to which access 'requires no specific qualities of status, personhood or subjectivity'.[21] I may have misunderstood Penney's argument, but this appears to entail not only detaching ourselves from queerness, but also the abandonment of the perspective of the proletariat, even if that perspective is still presumed straightforwardly to represent the universal.

There is, of course, a kind of warrant in Marx for Floyd's argument about the progressive possibilities of reification: under industrial capitalism, work became reified through its transformation into a distinct place of activity and a quantifiable input. But it also generated a new, and distinctive, form of agency. The reason the working class holds such a privileged place in Marxist theory is because of its dehumanization and lack of objective privilege in the world that it produces, as well as its capacity to transform the system owing to the structurally necessary function it serves. But the legitimate socialist project has always been about establishing a desirable existence for all, not one of extending and perpetuating

---

20  Peter Drucker, '"In the Tropics There is no Sin": Sexuality and Gay-Lesbian Movements in the Third World', *New Left Review* I, 218, July–August 1996, pp. 91–92.
21  Penney, *After Queer Theory*, p. 195.

the hardship that characterized that class's conditions of existence and its own attachment to the work ethic as source of moral legitimacy. The contribution of the sexual liberation movements to such a future lay in their insistence that bodily pleasure might be enjoyed as an end in itself, but they were never wholly divorced from the market determinations that have subsequently overtaken their impulses so powerfully. The problem may be registered in theory in all sorts of ways, but it will only be resolved through forms of social praxis that have appeared remote for some time, but may be coming into focus as neoliberal capitalism's contradictions intensify.

In the present, subculture may still play a role in diverse ways. Even in the existing, often problematic, forms I have been discussing, it holds the capacity to generate critical consciousness with which we might productively engage. The organizations and institutions through which subculture operates might become the object of a greater scrutiny designed to repudiate the logic of the diversified dominant in order to promote the kind of solidarity queer movements at their best have sought to develop. Subcultures exist in the here and now; they offer resources.

Even in *Cucumber*, there are hints at this: an oddly utopian queer 'collective' is proposed by Henry as a way of overcoming the general anarchy into which people's lives have descended as a result of marketized anarchy (a landlord scam originating in New York has rendered Henry, Freddie and Dean homeless). If this ultimately founders on various contradictions – the first of which is gay men's attitudes towards lesbians – it nonetheless testifies to the persistence of an ideal of autonomy not predicated on the traditional division between private and public.

One subcultural imperative in keeping with the emphases of this book would be to develop and expand welcoming, non-judgemental organizations, institutions and spaces that are at least not hyper-commercialized (there being no better options available). Through them it may be possible to encourage anti- or non-consumerist sensibilities. There is still potential for this in independent cinemas, universities and theatres, as well as certain kinds of bar or club. Duckie, in London, is a collective, an important fact. Lisa Henderson has explored subcultural milieux and modes of cultural production that detach queerness from its popular media associations with privilege.[22]

Moreover, alternative Prides are more or less established in different cities, just as Prides themselves have proliferated. Glasgow's strikes an appealing note:

> We don't want to compete nor are we dissing what Pride has always stood for ... we just want people to be able to have a great time, make new friends in a friendly environment and listen to good old live Rock and Roll.[23]

What could be more normal? So normal, indeed – so low-key and unassuming – that it appears genuinely radical. One problem with some self-consciously alternative spaces is that they have tended to cultivate an exclusive spirit through a cultural-political avant-gardism that aspires to marginality as a legacy of its countercultural roots, and to that extent has failed to learn from them.

The attraction of anti-consumerism is that it seems eminently plausible in conditions where other forms of resistance are problematic. Were it to spread the result would be quite as destabilizing to capital as any withdrawal of labour, and easier in current

---

22  Lisa Henderson, *Love and Money: Queers, Class and Cultural Production*, New York: New York University Press, 2013.

23  http://alternativepride.com/ (accessed 16 March 2015).

circumstances to achieve, given the relative weakness of the labour movement. Anti-consumerism meets an overwhelmingly true need that overrides all the false ones: it is objectively progressive, most immediately so for ecological reasons, and it should be argued for as such against pervasive relativism.

In persistent contemporary conditions of instability and crisis, however, the official political spectrum appears united in its belief that growth needs to be restored; the only question is how to achieve it. The left's contemporary weakness is nowhere more evident than in its almost wholesale colonization by Keynesianism, as if the return to countercyclical spending were the only plausible response to austerity. Even Keynes, though, envisioned a postgrowth society by around 2030 in which the working week would be limited to around fifteen hours, because through that everyone's needs might be satisfied.[24] Clearly, he had too much confidence in the rationality capitalism would permit.

Keynes's focus on the working week, however, instructively highlights that anti-consumerism as an ethic can never be sufficient in itself, but must rather be connected with a mode of political economic thought that seeks to reduce labour time while not threatening the destitution of individuals in consequence. The subsequent release from work this facilitated might be experienced as a form of subjective enrichment that would also qualitatively transform free time because of the reduction in the imperative to experience it as release, distraction and endless compulsory fun. If it is to be more than mere self-righteousness or personal asceticism, anti-consumerism must form part of a programmatically socialist politics whose object would be to transform the reality principle

---

24  Edward and Robert Skidelsky take this as the basis of their reflections in *How Much is Enough?: The Love of Money and the Good Life*, London: Allen Lane, 2012.

away from the performance principle. This is the kind of utopian imaginary that we might re-establish as a guide to the progress *the left* demands.

However, subcultures of whatever sort are unlikely either to be substantially transformed in the absence of more general social change, or to play decisive roles in that transformation. The suggestions I am advancing here are modest; they reflect current circumstances.

## Refusals great and small

James Penney has a point, nonetheless: the danger of much queer theory is that it can make us excessively defensive, because too acutely conscious of marginalization and stigma. To put this in terms that address Sinfield's agenda, subcultural work is no longer as urgent as it appeared to be in the beleaguered years of Thatcherism and its aftermath. Postgay sensibilities are related to shifts in the reality principle, and they are evident in a variety of contexts. These include the emergent protest movements of recent years that have challenged the shock doctrinal response to economic crisis pursued by neoliberal governments. I shall end with an image drawn from personal experience.

In November 2010, I went on a march in London to oppose the proposed rise in university tuition fees and the abolition of the Educational Maintenance Allowance by the Coalition government of that time. On the train there, I expected the usual drearily dutiful trudge past Whitehall by a contingent unconvinced of its potential to be effective, but on arriving at the assembly point it rapidly became clear to me that this time things would be different. Perhaps it was optimism of the will, but the mood was exuberant, defiant and humorous; people were having purposeful fun without making money for anyone else. This in itself felt liberating, a fusion of means and ends. One of the things that surprised me was the recycling of chants I'd not heard since the eighties about education being a right not a privilege; an alternative collective memory was in evidence, partly owing, no doubt, to the presence of activists and organizations that had been around for some time. At the end, thousands of marchers bypassed the official rally and moved on to Millbank, where the Conservative Party headquarters were situated, and continued the protest there. Several hundred broke into and occupied the building, thereby transgressing the limits set by repressive tolerance. Afterwards, politicians intent on ushering into law policies no one had voted for, and many had specifically voted against in giving their support to some of those actually in government,[25] ritualistically condemned the offence against democracy this represented. As Raymond Williams once commented, 'if people cannot have official democracy, they will have unofficial democracy, in any of its possible forms'.[26]

The atmosphere on that march was uncanny, not only because I could no longer claim to be one of the young, but because there were also subtle differences in the mood by comparison with those of several decades earlier. Higher education had dramatically expanded, for one thing, and was now socially less exclusive. Indeed, the proposed changes were obviously linked to that fact: higher education is being transformed into another domain of

---

25 Liberal Democrats, then part of the Coalition government with the Conservatives, had pledged to abolish tuition fees in the general election campaign of 2010.

26 Raymond Williams, *Culture and Society, 1780–1950*, London: Chatto and Windus, 1958, p. 303. Sinfield suggests this principle governs 'the persistent, though incoherent, strain of disaffection and aggression in postwar British society' (*Literature, Politics and Culture in Postwar Britain*, third edition, London: Continuum, 2004, p. 319).

employment training, the costs of which are to be borne by those who 'benefit' from it in this narrow sense, rather than by employers or taxpayers. But that very expansion carries with it the potential for students no longer to be stigmatized as privileged and out of touch; once again, quantity passes over into quality.

Various images from that day have stuck in my mind, but one registered with a force that is relevant to this book: that of two young men, arms around each other's shoulders, jumping up and down on top of a bus shelter while chanting along with the rest of the crowd, one wearing an 'I ♥ Justin Bieber' t-shirt. Postmodern protest? That hardly seems plausible – not if it implies recuperation – given that any ironies discernible in that gesture were caught up in the genuine spontaneity evident all around, and the way this sponsored manifold 'irresponsibilities'. The whole environment was suffused with oppositional intention of the sort that might be encouraged by theory and expanded through practice. There are no guarantees that smaller refusals of the sort evident in this event will cumulatively amount to a great one – this will require organization and conscious effort – but it is pure dogma dressed up as its opposite that rules out the possibility in principle.

# Index

# Index

authenticity, 195, 226, 228
authoritarian personality, 175
autobiographical approach, 2
autoeroticism, 200
automation, 69, 77
autonomy, 97, 108, 115, 125, 178, 179, 180, 296; of modes of power, 85; sexual, 109

Badiou, Alain, 295
Baker, James Robert, *Tim and Pete*, 181, 183–99
Baker, Tom, 277
bareback sex, 142
Baron Cohen, Sacha, 277–9
Barrett, Michèle, 107, 119
Beamish, Sally, 200
Bech, Henning, 110–11, 120, 131, 181
Bennington, Geoffrey, 10
Berlant, Lauren, 60–1, 95, 101
Berman, William C., 158
Bernstein, Jay, 73
Best, Steven, 47
Bieber, Justin, 301
Bignell, Jonathan, 279
Birmingham School of Cultural Studies, 226
birthing, 259
bisexuality, 284
Black Power, 170, 177
Black Pride, 170
Blake, William, 165; 'Jerusalem', 163–4
blood, 255, 258; vaginal, 262

Bobbitt, Philip, 88–9
bodily pleasure, as an end in itself, 296
Bohemianism, 172
Bourdieu, Pierre, 18
bourgeois, 182; use of term, 170–1
Branson, Richard, 16
brass bands, 5
Brecht, Bertolt, 169, 262–3
BRICS countries, 90
British Broadcasting Corporation (BBC), 275, 277
British National Party (BNP), 3, 289
*Brokeback Mountain*, 280
Brown, Norman O., 220
Brown, Wendy, 24, 53–4, 135–6
Browne, Lord, 22
*Bruno*, 278–9
brutality, 139
Buckley, William F., 173
Burnley (Lancashire), 3–5, 27
Butler, Judith, 227
Bystryn, Marcia H., 122

Callinicos, Alex, 60, 155
Cameron, David, 103
campness, 113, 126, 128, 211, 280
Canal Street, Manchester, 242, 244–5, 246–7, 249, 283
capitalism, 161, 297, 298; combination of rational and irrational, 285; contradictions of, 96; cultural aspects of,

# Index

Index

# Index

socialism, 94, 104, 107, 109, 112, 134, 169, 176, 295, 298; municipal, 252
society, denied, 102
sodomy, 106
solidarity, 205–6, 207, 222, 291
Soper, Kate, 19, 150
Stafford Clark, Max, 265
state: provision by, 104; repressive, 22
Stedman Jones, Daniel, 49
stereotyping, 267
Stone, Lawrence, 102
Stonewall riots, 31–2, 127, 178, 223, 241
structuralism, 46
Student Nonviolent Co-ordinating Committee (SNCC), 161, 177, 178
students, 163; experience of, 154, 159
Students for a Democratic Society (SDS), 155, 169, 173; 'one man one soul', 167; *Port Huron Statement*, 160, 167–9
subculture, 145, 224–81, 282, 296–7, 299; class implications of, 226; rejection of, 274; use of term, 2
subcultures: as sites of division, 232; theorization of, 32; urban renewal of, 237–53
subjectification, 17, 19, 23, 182
subjective formation, complexity of, 5

subjectivity, new forms of, 11
submissiveness, 218
suicides, 271–2
Sullivan, Andrew, 103, 141–5
superimposition, 99
Sycamore, Mattilda Bernstein, 273
Symbolic order, 195, 196, 199
Syriza party (Greece), 292

taboos: breaking of, 111; of sexuality, 80
Taft-Hartley Act (1947) (USA), 156
Tatchell, Peter, 277
Taub, Anneli, 220
technocracy, use of term, 164–5
terrorism, 204
thanatos, 72
Thatcher, Margaret, 49, 61, 102, 234–5, 238, 242, 259
Thatcherism, 7–8, 54, 231, 299
Third World Gay Revolution group, 178, 179
time-space compression, 56, 89, 206
tolerance, principle of, 183
totality, category of, 44–5, 46, 55, 83
Toynbee, Polly, 69–70
trade unions, 156–7, 222, 238; attack on, 159
Tull, Stephen, 257
Turner, Mark W., 110
Tyler, Imogen, *Revolting Subjects*, 80
Tyler May, Elaine, 157–8